ALSO BY DAVID HEPWORTH

The Secret History of Entertainment

NEVER
A DULL
MOMENT

NEVER A DULL MOMENT

1971

THE YEAR THAT ROCK EXPLODED

DAVID HEPWORTH

HENRY HOLT AND COMPANY   NEW YORK

Henry Holt and Company, LLC
Publishers since 1866
175 Fifth Avenue
New York, New York 10010
www.henryholt.com

Library of Congress Cataloging-in-Publication Data

Names: Hepworth, David, 1950– author.
Title: Never a dull moment : 1971—the year that rock exploded / David Hepworth.
Description: New York : Henry Holt and Company, 2016. | Includes bibliographical
    references and index. | Description based on print version record and CIP data
    provided by publisher; resource not viewed.
Identifiers: LCCN 2015042610 (print) | LCCN 2015041066 (ebook) | ISBN
    9781627794008 (electronic book) | ISBN 9781627793995 (hardcover)
Subjects: LCSH: Rock music—1971–1980—History and criticism.
Classification: LCC ML3534 (print) | LCC ML3534 .H465 2016 (ebook) | DDC
    781.6609/047—dc23
LC record available at http://lccn.loc.gov/2015042610

Henry Holt books are available for special promotions and premiums.
For details contact: Director, Special Markets.

Published in the UK by Bantam Press

Designed by Meryl Sussman Levavi

Printed in the United States of America

10   9   8   7   6   5   4   3   2

For Alyson

CONTENTS

Foreword   1

1. January: Get Down and Get With It   5

2. February: I Feel the Earth Move   20

3. March: Rock and Roll   46

4. April: Inner City Blues   68

5. May: Brown Sugar   91

6. June: Won't Get Fooled Again   122

7. July: Every Picture Tells a Story   141

8. August: Wild Night   167

9. September: Family Affair   195

10. October: Will the Circle Be Unbroken   216

11. November: Hunky Dory   238

12. December: American Pie   263

    Epilogue   281

    Appendix: 1971 in 100 Albums   287

    Selected Bibliography   289

    Acknowledgments   293

    Illustration Credits   295

    Index   297

NEVER A DULL MOMENT

FOREWORD

On New Year's Eve 1970, Paul McCartney instructed his lawyers to issue a writ at the High Court in London to wind up the Beatles.

The sixties ended that day, which was a year late, strictly speaking. You might say this was the last day of the pop era.

The following day, which was a Friday, was 1971. You might say this was the first day of the rock era.

That year, 1971, would also turn out to be the busiest, most creative, most innovative, most interesting, and longest-resounding year of that era.

Nobody dreamed the rock era would last as long as it has done. In those days nobody expected any form of entertainment to last. Least of all rock music. In fact, people joined rock bands to get away from things that lasted. Many of those people who first achieved stardom in 1971—David Bowie, Rod Stewart, Pink Floyd, Led Zeppelin, Elton John, and Joni Mitchell—have since gone on to enjoy careers longer than their contemporaries who became novelists, politicians, captains of industry, and actors, let alone their old friends who remained at school when they hit the road with a guitar over their shoulder.

Similarly, nobody imagined 1971 would see the release of more influential albums than any year before or since. That influence hasn't been felt merely by later generations of musicians, most of whom weren't born in 1971. It's also been felt by the performers themselves. Many of them are still around and more popular than ever. They're still reaping massive rewards from the rock industry that began in 1971. They wish they could still write songs that are as good, make records that are as strong, and express themselves as unself-consciously as they did in 1971.

Many of them were twenty-five at the time, the age that nobody appreciates being. You never get to be twenty-five again. For those of us who were listening, it never got any better than 1971. During those twelve months, in a surge of creativity, playfulness, ambition, technological breakthrough, ego, and blissful ignorance, a huge proportion of the most memorable albums ever made were released.

I was born in 1950. For a music fan, that's the winning ticket in the lottery of life.

I grew up therefore in the '60s. At the time, we didn't know these were going to become the Sixties and follow us around forever.

I was thirteen on that Friday when JFK was shot. I felt a bat squeak of patriotism a few months later when the Beatles conquered America. I was fifteen when Bobby Gregg's snare shot announced Bob Dylan's "Like a Rolling Stone." Bruce Springsteen, who was just six months older, heard it while he was in the car with his mother. He later described it as "somebody kicking open the door to your mind."

I came of age in 1971, the same year rock did. I was at college in London and spending what little spare cash I had on records. Like many similarly inclined young men—and we were mainly men—all my consumer appetites were channeled through the record shop. Jerry Seinfeld says that for the first ten years of his life the only clear thought in his mind was "get candy." We were like that with records.

All the cash that came my way—the forty pounds I had each term for anything more than board, food, and tuition, the pay I got for vacation jobs, birthday gifts from distant relatives, record tokens, obviously—was instantly converted into albums. There was simply nothing else I wanted to spend money on. I spent every idle moment hanging around record shops, being in the presence of, learning the names of, combing the covers of, and sometimes even listening to those things I wanted that I could not have. It was a life spent in pursuit of gratification endlessly deferred.

At the time, 1971 didn't feel like a particularly exceptional year. Nobody talked about the Year in Rock back then. Nobody tried to take the temperature of the business. Nobody pontificated about where things were going or had been. The habit of looking back, which is now so much a part of the music media game, and of which this book is a part, hadn't been invented. It's only in retrospect, and only quite recently at that, since the great digital Niagara of music has made it possible to have all fifty years of recorded rock and roll at our fingertips, to shuffle it, sort it, and subject it to endless listification, that I've come to realize just what an exceptional year my twenty-first year was.

At this point, you raise a skeptical eyebrow and say that for you too the music of the year when you were twenty-one, or eighteen or sixteen or whenever you felt most alive, still speaks to you in a way that no other year does. That's natural. That's just growing up. We all have precious memories of one soft infested summer when we were young. For us too the soundtrack thereof will always be rock's annus mirabilis.

There's an important difference in the case of me and 1971.

The difference is this. I'm right.

This book is a journey through the past to discover what happened that year, in what order, why it did, how the changes on the surface were responding to huge seismic changes underground, how it shaped and was shaped by a few hundred people who were in their midtwenties at the time, and why the music of 1971 still rings so clearly almost fifty years later. It's also to a certain extent about the world out of which that music emerged. It's a book about sex, drugs, hair, hot pants, taxes, technology, class, race, gender, and foolishness as well as Grammy Awards, platinum albums, and reviews in *Rolling Stone*.

On our journey we shall shatter the cliché that the early '70s were a mere lull before the punk rock storm, rather than the most febrile and creative time in the entire history of popular music; puncture the pious pretense that the words "new" and "exciting" are always interchangeable; wonder at the working practices that brought forth this many masterpieces; reconstruct the real world background against which all this invention took place; look at the lives of the artists who shaped it and in turn were shaped by it. At the end of each chapter I've included a list of records—singles and albums—associated with that month. Some were hits at the time, others were beginning their long march to classic status by being unveiled onstage that month, and a few are there because they deserve to be heard, particularly now that even the previously obscure gems of 1971 are just a click away.

There are moments in all creative stories where the right sort of talent meets the right amount of opportunity with just enough money and technology (but not too much) and then lays it before an audience that is in the ideal state of readiness to ensure that things will happen in a way they have never happened before and will never ever happen again. The year 1971 was one of those moments.

JANUARY

Get Down and Get With It

January 1971. The United States is in recession. Unemployment in the inner cities is nearing 10 percent. New York City subway tokens have just gone up to thirty cents. Transport, like much of the city, is in crisis. The streets are full of potholes. The wind that blows down the avenues blinds pedestrians with grit and makes uncollected garbage gather round their ankles. Gasoline is thirty-six cents a gallon. OPEC is imposing a 50 percent tax on oil extraction. Ford is thinking about making smaller cars. A seventeen-year-old from Washington Heights who calls himself TAKI 183 is becoming famous for leaving his tag on subway cars.

People are leaving the city in the face of crime and filth. Property values are dropping. An apartment in one of Manhattan's smartest addresses is on the market for $225,000, half of what it cost in 1969. All the movies made in New York, such as the recent Jack Lemmon–Sandy Dennis hit *The Out-of-Towners*, depict it as a place only the foolhardy would choose to visit. The city's magazines all carry sardonic survival guides. A picture of the half-finished World Trade Center illustrates an article in the *New York Times* promoting the unfashionable view that the city might yet be a desirable place to live. Someone in the convention business timidly suggests reviving a musician's saying from the 1920s and christening the city the Big Apple.

Some 85 percent of New York's twenty-five thousand police patrolmen are on strike over a pay claim. A cop earns around $11,000 a year, just above the national average. According to a detective named Frank Serpico, giving evidence to an inquiry into corruption, many can earn an additional $600 a month in bribes from illegal gambling rackets. Serpico will eventually be played on-screen by Al Pacino. Already in early 1971 the real-life corner-cutting detective Eddie Egan is the model for the fictional Popeye Doyle in the upcoming movie *The French Connection*.

Consumer prices are beginning to rise too fast to make it worth printing prices on menus. McSorley's Old Ale House, which has just been compelled to admit women for the first time, has adjusted its draft ale from 50 to 60 cents. However, a McDonald's hamburger is 20 cents and a Coke can be as little as 10 cents. It's still possible to have dinner for four at a smart place like 21 for $130 including wine and tips. The new John Lennon solo album is $3.49 at King Karol while George Harrison's triple album *All Things Must Pass* is $6.98.

The Tonight Show on New Year's Day 1971 is the last episode to carry a commercial for cigarettes. It's for Virginia Slims, a brand aimed at women that uses the slogan "You've come a long way, baby." Walter Cronkite presents the seven o'clock news. Ed Sullivan still fronts his variety show on Sunday nights. He is beginning to lose his memory. Sullivan won't be renewed, nor will *The Beverly Hillbillies* or *Petticoat Junction*. There are no celebrity magazines. The foremost celebrity of the year is Tricia Nixon, who is engaged to be married. The big media organizations are terrified that they are losing touch with the young audience. *National Lampoon* satirizes their attempts to stay in touch, such as *Cosmopolitan*'s search for a nude male model. A *Life* magazine survey finds America's most admired names are Robert Kennedy and Bill Cosby. Least admired are Fidel Castro and Eldridge Cleaver. Jimmy Carter, newly sworn in as governor of Georgia, says the state may have finally accepted integration. In cities like Cleveland, integration is resulting in the flight of second-generation European immigrants to the suburbs and the consequent hollowing out of the centers.

Hot pants are everywhere. "They are the kind of fad that topples institutions," one fashion observer tells *Life*. Men's barbershops are closing. Every businessman is growing sideburns. Jane Fonda, thirty-three, her blond, curly hair transformed into a harsh shag, has just completed her role as the call girl Bree Daniels in *Klute*. She has driven alone from California to New York to play the part. Once on set in a studio in Harlem, she insists the director let her sleep the night in her character's apartment, the better to identify with her pain. The film glories in the squalor of the city. "After you've been in New York a month, you become tense and nervous and alienated," says Fonda. Returning to California, determined to put her privileged life behind her, she sells her possessions and moves with her daughter into a house in a cul-de-sac in the shadow of the freeway.

Fonda puts her energies into supporting the increasing number of soldiers' organizations opposing the continuation of the Vietnam War. The nation is riven with mistrust over the conflict, and its political poles seem entirely incapable of dialogue. Speaking for the older generation, Bob Hope, profiled in *Life*, says that 80 percent of the hippies on Sunset Strip "have a social disease." The voting age is in the process of being lowered from twenty-one to eighteen. Employees report that the baby boomers now entering the workforce in unprecedented numbers want faster advancement and less formal dress codes, and in some cases even have to have the profit motive explained to them. On January 12 the gap between the older and the younger generation is dramatized in a new TV series called *All in the Family*, which pits Glenn Miller–loving working stiff Archie Bunker against his long-haired liberal son-in-law. Within months, even Richard Nixon can be heard complaining about the son-in-law on the newly installed recording system in the Oval Office. But for most young people TV is an irrelevance, as are the movies. Music is where it's at.

* * *

In January 1971 Bruce Springsteen of Asbury Park, New Jersey, was twenty-one and still unknown beyond the immediate area, which was leaving fame perilously late. He had just returned from a visit to his parents at their new home in California, where he had time to reflect on the future of his band Steel Mill. They had endured a rather traumatic night on September 11, 1970, only four months after national guardsmen had opened fire on demonstrating students at Kent State University, killing four of them, when local police moved in with clubs swinging to enforce a curfew at an open-air show that Steel Mill were playing in the deceptively idyllic surroundings of the Clearwater Swim Club. Although they met the invasion with a certain amount of bravado, reconnecting the power after the police had cut it off, Danny Federici pushing a stack of speakers in the direction of some police who were trying to climb onto the stage, and Springsteen using his emerging stagecraft to keep the crowd on his side, the experience put Springsteen off any further "kick out the jams" rebel rhetoric.

Like bands the world over in 1971 who weren't known for their own material, Steel Mill played anything and everything they could. Springsteen's bands performed Iron Butterfly's "In-A-Gadda-Da-Vida," they knocked out an Allman Brothers tribute called "Goin' Back to Georgia," and sometimes they even played a thirty-minute rock opera called "Garden State Parkway Blues." When Steel Mill played shows in New Jersey, sometimes attracting as many as four thousand people despite never having been on the radio, there wouldn't have been a single soul over the age of thirty, and there probably wouldn't have been anyone under the age of eighteen. Audiences were uniformly young and unjaded; whatever they were hearing they felt as if they were hearing it for the first time.

During Springsteen's holiday in California, he had been listening to the local FM stations, and his imagination had been captured by the breezy sound of Van Morrison's *His Band and the Street Choir*, with its attendant hit record "Domino" and the soul revue force of

Joe Cocker's *Mad Dogs and Englishmen*. It was during this trip that he decided Steel Mill would be no more, the band was going to boast horns, line up more like Morrison's and Cocker's, and the name on the marquee would henceforth be Bruce Springsteen.

There are few moves that require as much self-belief as taking a band that has previously been, at least notionally, a democracy and naming it after yourself. It can occur only if the leader has the nerve to lead and the musicians involved recognize the strength of his claim to do so. At the time Springsteen was living in a ground-floor apartment in Asbury Park, which he shared with Steve Van Zandt, John Lyon, and Albee Tellone. Once a week they invited more musician friends round and played Monopoly. (Sandy Denny and Trevor Lucas would invite friends round to their Fulham flat to do the same thing, a good indication of how little was on the TV in 1971.) It was during those games, which involved all manner of rule bending, covert alliances, bribery, and skullduggery, that the twenty-one-year-old Springsteen took to referring to himself, with tongue barely an inch into his cheek, as "the Boss."

By the end of 1971 he would bestow similar honorifics on the rest of his growing crew—"Miami" Steve Van Zandt, "Southside" Johnny Lyon, Vinny "Mad Dog" Lopez, and Clarence "Big Man" Clemons—as he played night after night at the Student Prince in Asbury Park and farther afield, where the band's standard performance would consist of four forty-minute sets with breaks in between.

Recalling this time in later years, Springsteen said, "Sometimes you'd come home with five hundred dollars in your pocket, and you could live on that for months. For a local band, that was a big success. And in that area, we were big local stars."

You couldn't really be a local star in the UK. You had to travel. In January 1971 Neville "Noddy" Holder, born in 1946, raised in a council house with an outside lavatory, his only proper employment a short period buying and selling auto parts, was the leader of a group called Slade. In his twenty-five years Noddy had already packed in a lifetime of experience of playing live: in his native Black Country, in German dance halls where the waiters carried guns, up and down the United Kingdom, and on a two-month residency entertaining holiday makers in the Bahamas.

On New Year's Day 1971 Slade played Wolverhampton Civic Hall, which was right in the middle of their industrial heartland. This was the first of no less than 150 shows they were to play in the next twelve months. Through that year Noddy Holder, Jim Lea, Dave Hill, and Don Powell toured the United Kingdom with an intensity that hasn't been equaled since.

One of the reasons it hasn't been equaled since is that the venues they played that year either no longer exist or for various reasons no longer host amplified popular music. Because Slade hadn't had a hit, they couldn't do the big dance halls where the hit acts played and could play only what was known as the rock club circuit. However, that circuit was extensive. Among the 150 shows were such venues as the Queen Mary Ballroom at Dudley Zoo, the St. Giles Youth Club in Willenhall, the curiously named Farx in Potters Bar, and the misleadingly genteel-sounding Ballerina Ballroom in Nairn. Slade performed amid the art deco splendor of the Floral Hall in Southport and the provisional prefabrications of Blades in Bexley. They rolled up and rocked in venues whose names still reverberate down the years, like the Marquee in Soho's Wardour Street. They played no less energetically at scores of places whose names no longer reverberate down the years yet still hint at a vision of a future that never entirely materialized in the way the namers might have wished. Places like the Teenage Centre in Fareham, the Showboat in Mumbles, and the Cosmos Youth Centre in Fife.

Slade didn't turn up their noses at any of this. They actively sought out people to play to. Sometimes they seemed to be almost harrying them. At the end of July, they played no less than three consecutive nights for Scottish holiday makers on the Isle of Arran. This was such a success that they returned to do a further show in late September.

Because Slade were not what anyone would call a headline name, they didn't only play in their own right. They also opened for others who were slightly better known. They supported Argent at the Lyceum in London, Yes at the Marquee, Atomic Rooster at the Kinetic Cinema in Birmingham, and the Alan Bown in Exeter.

Slade had no fear of distances. On September 4 they played the Kilmardinny Stadium in Glasgow; the following night they were at a schizophrenia benefit in London. In the days when the motorway system was not fully networked, this was a journey that would have consumed an entire cheerless, tedious, smoke-wreathed, bone-rattling day.

Slade's 1971 act was a crowd pleaser all the way. They began with their version of Ten Years After's "Hear Me Calling" (borrowed from the Woodstock sensation's recent album *Stonedhenge*), finished with Steppenwolf's "Born to Be Wild," had room to "slow things down a bit" with John Sebastian's "Darling Be Home Soon" and the Moody Blues' "Nights in White Satin," which featured the group's proper musician Jim Lea on violin and climaxed with their bravura, speaker-shredding version of Little Richard's "Get Down and Get With It." Through it all, they kept up a stream of patter, exhortation, and private jokery. Nobody could come away from a Slade show without feeling that they had been entertained by a band who didn't look down on them. "We wanted to have fun with our audience," recalled Noddy many years later.

Scores of other British groups would have followed a similar trail in 1971, rattling around in the backs of ill-maintained Ford Transits, sleeping with the wheel arch as their pillow, relieving themselves in milk bottles, doing the *NME* crossword with a blunt guesthouse pencil, dreaming of a cold Wimpy and chips, probing for each other's personal weak spots and exploiting them without mercy, and often risking life and limb by putting themselves in the hands of a driver who had taken a few drinks and didn't wear a seat belt. (The British folk-rock group Fairport Convention had been involved in an accident in May 1969 when returning to London from a gig at

Mothers in Birmingham. The driver was not feeling well and the other band members were asleep when the van came off the road and two passengers, their nineteen-year-old drummer Martin Lamble and a friend, Jeannie Franklyn, were both killed.)

The difference is that for Slade it somehow miraculously worked. It worked in a way that allowed all concerned to look back and claim they'd planned it that way. In late October they went into Command Studios in Piccadilly in London and recorded this by now road-hardened set for the record that became *Slade Alive!* By then they had already had a hit with "Get Down and Get With It," which was almost comically shrill but perfectly suited to the fine art of wardrobe-mirror miming, a sport in which Britain led and still leads the world.

The next step was to take the live energy into the studio and bake it into bite-sized biscuits. Like Brian Epstein bullying Lennon and McCartney into forming a partnership and Andrew Oldham locking Jagger and Richards in a room with instructions to compose, Chas Chandler insisted Holder and Lea write their own follow-up. Lea took him at his word and turned up—with his violin—at the Walsall council house where Noddy lived with his parents. Within half an hour they had written "Coz I Luv You," the first of their deliberately misspelled money spinners. They thought it was a joke. Chas Chandler thought it was number one. Chas would turn out to be right.

The year that had begun with them at Wolverhampton Civic Hall ended with them at number one. They got the good news while they were playing the Melody Rooms in Norwich. The cover versions were slowly dropped from the set. They soon had quite enough hits of their own, a string of hits that would eventually make them Britain's most popular band since the Beatles. Unlike the Beatles, the more records they sold, the more shows they played. They began all over again on New Year's Day 1972 at the Cambridge Corn Exchange. This time they played more than 150 shows. Having hit records was all very well, but the heart of the music business and, at the beginning of 1971, the money were in playing live.

* * *

At the same time as Slade were starting out on their 150 dates, the rising progressive group Yes were also trying to make their way via an apparently different route. They had recently finished recording their third album, *The Yes Album*. This record would be released in March, by which time they would have been playing the songs from it onstage for fully six months.

Yes were one of the first rock groups to build their career on the virtues of practice. Their growing live reputation was rooted in the fact that they didn't record anything that they couldn't play and, more impressively, sing onstage, without any help from technology. Yes were big favorites of BBC radio producers because they could be relied on to turn up, set up, and record three tunes in three hours, which is what a session with the Corporation, still one of the key routes to wider exposure, demanded.

Although the record company Atlantic Records had not concerned themselves with its making, *The Yes Album* was the record that had to pay back in order to ensure that their deal with the company was renewed. Yes were one of a number of long-haired groups who had been picked up in a sweep conducted by Atlantic's Ahmet Ertegun when he recognized that the future was likely to be both album shaped and white in color. Ertegun had used his roots music calling card to sign Crosby, Stills & Nash; Iron Butterfly; Cream; and many other groups he didn't really pretend to understand. He was a businessman who was smart enough to conceal what he didn't know.

The repertoire of Yes, who had come together in London in 1968, had begun with what they would have called "cover versions" of songs like "Something's Coming" from *West Side Story* and the Beatles' "Every Little Thing." Then they had moved to their own compositions, which all involved a bewildering amount of notes. Where Slade aspired to simplicity, Yes craved complexity. Their records were full of alarming stops and starts, unaccompanied choral pieces that would lurch without warning into breakneck instrumental gallops, subsections indicated by Roman numerals that begged to be compared to Tchaikovsky, and lyrics that had to be celestial poetry because they clearly made no sense on this earth.

The only way Yes's music could be quarried from their seething imaginations and brought into the open air was by rehearsing and recording it in short sections, often as brief as thirty seconds. These would then be edited together with the next section, a labor of almost monkish dedication given the rudimentary technology available at the time. When a track was finally razored and spliced into place, the five musicians would take a deep breath and learn to play it from the finished record. This was a complete reversal of the way that things had been done since the invention of recorded sound. Even the bleakest bebop and the most avant-garde classical music had not gone to the same trouble as the practitioners of this new progressive rock.

In January 1971 Yes joined a European package tour called the Age of Atlantic, which was an indication of how keen Ertegun was to brand his company as the home of the new rock. Bottom of the bill were a jazz-rock band called Dada (who would later become Vinegar Joe); top of the bill were the American heavy act Iron Butterfly. Yes came in between and stole the show with their epic unpacking of Paul Simon's "America."

Iron Butterfly were on their last legs by then and decided to break up at the end of the tour. This meant they were looking for a buyer for their PA system, which had dazzled the members of Yes by employing such undreamed-of refinements as monitors, which enabled the band to hear for the first time what they were playing. Since they now had management, via the film company Hemdale, they could afford to make the investment, and as a result, their reputation for polished performances continued to grow. Their new personal manager was Brian Lane, who was conversant with the dark arts of record plugging. When *The Yes Album* appeared in early February, it sold respectably in most places and healthily in the head shops. Because there was a postal strike for the first two months of the year, the record shops couldn't make their traditional returns, and so the Virgin chart, which briefly had Yes at number one, thanks to the preferences of shop staff and the promptings of Lane, got more profile than usual. To their chagrin, it wasn't enough to get them on the "album spot" that the BBC's weekly chart show *Top of the Pops* was proffering to the burgeoning market for long players.

Even for nationally known names, January 1971 was primarily about keeping a packed date book. Pink Floyd went into Abbey Road at the beginning of January to begin recording *Meddle* but still ventured out at weekends to play universities. They would load up their equipment at Abbey Road and then head out to play the Student Union Bar at Farnborough, the Theatre at St. Mary's College in Strawberry Hill, or Lecture Block 6 and 7 at the University of Essex.

In 1971, despite the massive publicity given to festivals at Woodstock or the Isle of Wight, live rock concerts were still a minority taste, accessible mainly to those who knew where to look for them. Music business veteran Andy Murray lived at the time in the northern town of Carlisle, which had a population of seventy thousand, and remembers, "If you went to see a rock band in that area in those days, you would see the other fifty people who were also interested in seeing rock bands. You'd even nod to them after a while. If you went to see Greenslade one week and then Jethro Tull the next, it would be the same fifty people. They were mainly blokes, and they were mainly wearing army surplus greatcoats."

They would also be readers of the weekly music press, which was about to enter its golden age. The leading UK title was the *Melody Maker*, which had traded its traditional support of jazz musicians for a similarly workmanlike focus on rock. Its lifeblood was its live news and listings pages, which were just about the only way a rock fan in Carlisle would have any idea that Rory Gallagher was likely to play in town. Local papers didn't bother with this kind of news, and local radio didn't exist. If you sat across a railway carriage from somebody else reading the music press, you would know that you were both members of a secret society with devices and secrets that the straight world simply couldn't begin to decipher.

Universities were an increasingly popular place to play, not least because they had halls big enough to be able to cater to the demand. The most prestigious of them, Leeds, had the advantage over the local Victorian town hall of being able to accommodate two thousand people in its refectory. Students wishing to see the Who, Led Zeppelin, or the Rolling Stones, all of whom played that refectory in 1971, had to do their drinking in the bar downstairs before joining the audience upstairs. The pubs would be shut at 10:30, which was long before the show finished. Most of that audience was sitting cross-legged, often feeling the chill imprint of the university's parquet floor through the thin seat of their cheap mail-order loon pants, an item of clothing so snug it made no allowance whatsoever for the gender of its wearer. Outside the charmed circle of the bohemian enclaves of London and the alternative press, drugs were available only to those who had the budget to be able to afford them and the contacts through which to secure them. Hence, audiences were overwhelmingly sober.

Student audiences were also obedient. Despite the ferment that had been taking place at Berkeley, the Sorbonne, and Hornsey College of Art, the students were still inclined to accept authority, possibly in the knowledge that they would soon be wielding it themselves. They transferred their habit of deference to rock musicians, who were accorded unquestioning respect to the extent that the audience's interest in them seemed to start and finish when they walked on and off the stage. Stage invasions were entirely unknown, and in most cases it wasn't considered necessary to post a guard backstage to keep "fans," which is not the word they would have used, from getting backstage and pressing themselves on the performers, for either a photograph, which they would have had no means to take, or an autograph, which they would have had no merchandise to add to.

Smoky, odiferous, uncomfortable, usually cold, unleavened by mood enhancements, and often ended by a walk home after the last bus, as an evening of entertainment live rock had little to recommend it beyond the music. It was, however, the place rock happened. Material was developed and polished on the road in front of audiences. Pink Floyd had entered Abbey Road in January with no material. It was only when they got in front of student audiences that spring that they began to whip new tunes like "Echoes" into shape.

The calendar wasn't divided between "writing" and "touring." It was all done at the same time. Neil Young, who had peeled off from Crosby, Stills, Nash & Young after their tour of the previous year, was on a solo tour of the United States and Canada, during which he played a set of songs that would become famous once he'd recorded them for *Harvest*. Elton John, who was being acclaimed as a big star in the United States, still played the last night of Mothers, a club above a furniture shop in Birmingham, and the Winter Gardens in Cleethorpes. The Who played a series of shows at the Young Vic, which were recorded for "Lifehouse," which was supposed to be Townshend's next grand project after *Tommy*. The road was how you paid the rent. Royalties weren't yet the main revenue stream of the music business.

This was something that even the former members of the Beatles were coming to realize in January 1971. Although Paul McCartney had issued his writ to dissolve the group's partnership in London, the center of activity for the members of the group was New York. John Lennon had made himself scarce by going to Tokyo, ostensibly because Yoko was trying to get access to her daughter, Kyoko, but also because he knew it would be best to be out of the way before January 21, when his interview with *Rolling Stone*'s Jann Wenner was published.

The main thrust of the interview, which was itself the culmination of primal scream therapy with Arthur Janov, was threefold: his new album, *Plastic Ono Band*, was the best thing he'd ever done, Yoko Ono was the only true artist and everything else, and the Beatles, in particular, was "bullshit."

When the interview appeared, Paul McCartney was in New York, recording at Columbia Studios, ostensibly with his wife, but the session musicians hired were in no doubt that only one person was in charge. George Harrison was also in town, avoiding Lennon, who was making unkind remarks about *All Things Must Pass*, which was at the top of the US charts, unlike John's album.

What the former Beatles were discovering, and the court case that got under way in London that month would bring into sharper focus, was that none of them could simply walk away from the group. They were connected by a partnership agreement they entered into just before Brian Epstein's death, locked into a management agreement with Allen Klein, who derived his power from the fact that he represented them as an entity, and by the fact that all their individual album releases, which to some ears appeared to be intended as darts aimed at each other, came out on their label Apple, a label they owned jointly. It was a pretty mess, and wholly without precedent.

Furthermore, they didn't have as much money as they expected to have. When their music publisher Dick James had sold his company in 1969, they were unable to afford to bid. The record business that the Beatles had dominated during the sixties had been tiny compared to what it was about to become. Teenagers were growing into young adults and taking their teenage enthusiasms with them. Singles sales were turning into album sales. Cents were becoming dollars. The kind of deal that Brian Epstein had done ten years earlier seemed like chicken feed next to what Peter Grant was negotiating on behalf of Led Zeppelin. The plates were shifting.

Although Klein had built his reputation on his ability to get back royalties out of reluctant record companies on behalf of his illustrious clients, the big money was in advances, and that had to mean looking forward, not back. Which is why when McCartney met Harrison in New York in January and said, "Look, George, I want to get off the Apple label," Harrison shot back with a line that perfectly encapsulates the sadness and venom that had brought the greatest group of all to an end: "You'll stay on the fucking label. Hare Krishna."

* * *

At the same time as the former Beatles were fighting over the spoils of the previous decade in New York, long-playing records were being completed elsewhere whose sales in the new decade would dwarf the ones the Beatles managed, in the process creating a whole new industry with a whole new way of doing things. One of them was being made in California by a woman the Beatles had long admired, a woman who had hardly ever appeared in public and whose music seemed as far as it was possible to get from the tortured virtuosity of Yes, the deeply thought-out self-mythologizing of Bruce Springsteen, the holiday camp jollity of Slade, and the volume of all of them.

That woman didn't particularly mean to, but she invented the album business.

JANUARY

Slade: "Get Down and Get With It"

Van Morrison: "Domino"

Yes: "America"

Elton John: "Your Song"

John Lennon: "Working Class Hero"

Dave Edmunds: "I Hear You Knocking"

Status Quo: "In My Chair"

Badfinger: "No Matter What"

T. Rex: "Ride a White Swan"

FEBRUARY

I Feel the Earth Move

Jim McCrary was the house photographer for A&M Records in Hollywood, California, in 1971. It was a sweet gig. It wouldn't make a man rich, but no two days were the same. Any time A&M needed a picture of one of the company's artists, Jim would be sent along. A&M, which had been started in the previous decade by musician Herb Alpert and his business partner Jerry Moss, was a happening label at the time. McCrary had taken the famous pictures of the Flying Burrito Brothers in their Nudie suits that appeared on the cover of their first album. He had photographed Richard and Karen Carpenter on a sailboat on Lake Tahoe. He had captured the muscle-flexing pose of Joe Cocker in the picture that became the brand of *Mad Dogs and Englishmen*.

On January 27 Jim drove to Appian Way, a residential street in Laurel Canyon in the hills above Sunset Boulevard. McCrary's assignment that day was to photograph the woman who lived with her two young daughters at number 8815. She was one of the many New Yorkers who had moved to the West Coast around the turn of the decade to get away from a city that seemed grimy, crime-ridden, and in irreversible decline. Moving to California meant she and her daughters could enjoy some sunshine while working in a recording industry that was similarly stepping westward.

Carole King wasn't natural photographic material. Twenty-eight years old, snub-nosed, freckly, and frizzy-haired, she had prepared herself for McCrary's lens by putting on a sensible pullover and jeans, much as she would have done had she been weeding the garden. Although she had been in the music business for thirteen years by 1971, this had mostly been in a capacity that didn't have much call for having her picture taken. She had little interest in or flair for glamour. She was fond of remarking, even then, that she was at heart a middle-aged Jewish lady from Brooklyn. When McCrary called, she was working on a tapestry.

They tried various shots around the house until McCrary asked if he could move King's cat Telemachus into the frame. The cat was placed on a cushion on the window seat in front of King, who was holding her tapestry. It provided a nice domestic note. McCrary went back to the office fairly satisfied with his work but unaware he had shot a cover that would prove more famous, more popular, and more ubiquitous than everything else he had photographed put together. The presence of the cat helped the picture strike a note of calm, warmth, and domesticity, a note that chimed perfectly with the music on the record inside that cover. It was a record destined to sell in quantities nobody had previously thought it possible to sell.

Tapestry, the album that recalibrated the record business, was made the old-fashioned way, in just five three-hour sessions taking place in January 1971 and was in the shops in time for Valentine's Day. It was recorded in a building on Hollywood Boulevard that had once been the home of Charlie Chaplin Productions. There were three studios at A&M on the corner of Sunset and La Brea. They were all busy that month: Joni Mitchell was in the small one, recording the songs that would make up *Blue*; Richard and Karen Carpenter were in the biggest one, recording the songs that would comprise their best-selling third album, *Carpenters*; in the middle one was this refugee from New York's Tin Pan Alley, who had written plenty of hits for other people but had not had any major success on her own as a performer. There was no particular reason to suspect that what was going on in studio B would come to be seen as more significant than what was going on on either side.

Carole King's real name was Carol Klein. She had married her chemistry student boyfriend Gerry Goffin while still in her teens. That's what girls did in the early sixties upon finding themselves pregnant. She and her husband wrote hits together for a major song factory called Aldon Music. She'd subsequently divorced Goffin, who had taken acid with predictable consequences for his mental health, and relocated, with her two young daughters, to California.

King could afford a certain amount of independence because her credit was on songs such as "Will You Love Me Tomorrow?" "Up on the Roof," "The Loco-motion," "Pleasant Valley Sunday," "(You Make Me Feel Like) a Natural Woman," "Goin' Back," and "Wasn't Born to Follow." Of all the songwriters who had labored in the mills of Broadway's Brill Building, among whom were such fabled mechanics of the heart as Cynthia Weil and Barry Mann, Neil Sedaka, Neil Diamond, Howie Greenfield, and Paul Simon, none was more admired than this undemonstrative young woman.

Like the Beatles, King was a triple threat: she could write, arrange, and sing. Lou Adler knew how good she was. He was the producer at the board on those five days at A&M. Adler was a Chicago-born record businessman who had worked with Sam Cooke and guided the career of the Mamas and Papas. He had sold his record company Dunhill to ABC Records, and now he'd started another one called Ode, which he'd licensed to the larger independent A&M Records. Before growing his hair and promoting the Monterey Pop Festival in 1967, Adler had represented Aldon, the New York music publisher that employed Carole King. He had noticed how the record companies to whom he sent out King's demos tended to hang on to them to listen to for their own enjoyment. There was something about King's voice.

Adler wanted to make a record with that demo quality, a record that felt like a portrait of a woman at work. He wanted the listeners to visualize Carole King sitting at a piano singing just for them. James Taylor had sold a ton of copies of *Sweet Baby James* in 1970, and it wasn't merely because of the quality of the songs. There was also something about his steadfast, modest delivery that appealed to everyone, even soul singers like Marvin Gaye. Adler wanted *Tapestry* to have some of that feeling. The backing instruments were knocked back accordingly so that the finished impression had some of the integrity of a pencil outline. It was not a record that leapt out and collared you. It was a record, like Taylor's, that asked you to lean closer.

The engineer was Hank Cicalo, who had previously worked with Peggy Lee, Vic Damone, and the Monkees. Cicalo understood the importance of getting a singer into the right frame of mind. Manipulation of mood was second nature to Hollywood people. When Sinatra had recorded at Capitol Records on Hollywood Boulevard in the sixties, they placed him on a podium and invited all the secretaries down so that his sessions had the feeling of a club show in front of adoring fans. King, who had never performed live, needed something different. Cicalo turned down the lights, no matter what the time of day, and placed her in such a way that she could have eye contact with the band and conduct them with her head.

Cicalo had avoided the larger Studio A and installed her and drummer Russ Kunkel, guitarist Danny Kortchmar, and bassist Charles Larkey in B, which was more suitable for combos. The best piano was in the smaller studio C, which had been locked out by Henry Lewy for Joni Mitchell, who was unwilling to give it up. King was so keen to use its distinctive sound that she and the band dashed in there one morning and recorded three tunes, the opener, "I Feel the Earth Move," her own version of "(You Make Me Feel Like) a Natural Woman," and a new one called "You've Got a Friend." It took them three hours, which was the standard length of a session as laid down by the musicians union.

The five days of recording were followed by some doubling up of voices, using the "sel-sync" technology that allowed artists to overdub without adding layers of tape hiss, the sparing addition of strings, and then mixing and sequencing, something that Adler considered particularly important. Here he was inspired by *Something Cool*, an album made by jazz singer June Christy in 1954. The whole thing was finished in less than three weeks. It cost twenty-two thousand dollars.

Two weeks after McCrary had taken his picture, the record was in the stores. It came out in the same week that the Los Angeles area was shaken by the Sylmar earthquake, which killed more than sixty people; and Britain, which was preparing to join the European Economic Community, said good-bye to pounds, shillings, and pence and adopted decimal currency; and that third record, *The Yes Album*, Harry Nilsson's *The Point!*, Janis Joplin's *Pearl*, Elton John's *Tumbleweed Connection*, and the Faces' *Long Player* were all released.

On a break during the sessions, young Charlie Larkey, the bass player who was also King's partner, collared Adler in the corridor.

"What do you think of all this?" asked Larkey, a relative novice.

Adler, the old hand, looked at him and said with the certainty that senior partners are permitted, "I think it's going to be the *Love Story* of albums."

Erich Segal's *Love Story* had been the best-selling book of 1970, and the movie starring Ali McGraw and Ryan O'Neal was the top box office film in January 1971 as *Tapestry* was wrapped up. Larkey, like most longhairs of the time, shuddered at the parallel with a film that seemed to represent mainstream entertainment. He knew that, unlike *Love Story*, Carole King's album was in no way designed to be a blockbuster. The way it was made seemed to have little in common with a traditional Hollywood smash.

Tapestry entered the *Billboard* album chart at number seventy-nine on April 10, with the artist's name listed without the "e." Within two weeks it was at thirty-four, by which point her name was spelled correctly. They would never spell Carole King's name wrong again. *Tapestry* kept on rising until in the week ending June 19, 1971, it was the best-selling album in the United States. Being overhauled by a record by somebody who wasn't a name, who had never even headlined a show (she was still playing piano in her friend James Taylor's band at the time), must have cast a shadow over the day of the artists who suddenly found themselves below her in that top ten. They were the Rolling Stones; Paul McCartney; the Carpenters; Crosby, Stills, Nash & Young; Jethro Tull; Aretha Franklin; the Partridge Family; and the producers of the soundtrack of *Love Story*.

Tapestry had been carried there on the back of the popularity of its single "It's Too Late," which went to number one, and "You've Got a Friend," which was also included on *Mud Slide Slim and the Blue Horizon*, the new album by King's friend, touring companion, and celebrity patron James Taylor.

A small number of albums get to enter the charts, a tiny minority of those are best sellers, and an infinitesimal handful of the latter go on selling long after the hit singles, the tours, the word of mouth, and all the other promotional thermals are becalmed. In the previous decade the soundtrack of *The Sound of Music* had been one such. Simon & Garfunkel's *Bridge over Troubled Water*, released in 1970, was another. Carole King's *Tapestry* would eventually surpass both, and in the process it would redefine success in the record business for the new decade. It remained America's number one album for fifteen weeks through the summer of 1971. By the end of the year, it was still selling 150,000 copies a week in the United States alone. This was achieved without TV appearances, without headlining more than the occasional show, and without stories in the press. By the end of the year, this record, which had been quietly released back in February, had sold five million copies. It had burst the bounds of "singer-songwriters A–K" and any of the other subdivisions of the nascent rock retail industry and had gone right into the same mainstream as *Love Story*, much as Lou Adler had predicted it would.

Although he had every faith in King's talent, Adler had hedged his bets by making sure that she included two songs that would already be familiar to record buyers. These were "Will You Love Me Tomorrow," which in this version sounded less like the pleas for gentleness on the part of a trembling virgin and more like a mature woman requiring parity in a relationship. (The backing vocals on this put James Taylor in one channel and Joni Mitchell in the other. This was interesting casting since neither of them were bywords for fidelity, particularly in 1971. During the recording of the album, Taylor had an affair with King's cowriter, the glamorous Hollywood scenester Toni Stern, and then moved on to begin an intense affair with Mitchell.) The other song was "(You Make Me Feel Like) a Natural Woman," which she and Gerry Goffin had written in response to Jerry Wexler's request for a song of that name for Aretha Franklin to sing.

Unlike most of the singer-songwriters who came in the wake of James Taylor, King had never really written on her own, and the recruitment of the feisty Stern suggested that the producers felt she could use some sass. However, the key song, "You've Got a Friend," had none of that quality and was entirely King's own work. King said she had no idea where it came from, which is what songwriters generally say when they've come up with something exceptional. When these flashes of inspiration occur, the best thing a songwriter can do is stay out of the way and, as it were, take dictation. When she played the song for fellow songwriter Carole Bayer Sager, she was told it was too simple. When she played it for lyricist Cynthia Weil, she was told it was too long. When she played it for James Taylor, he recognized that the qualities of guilelessness and lack of edge were what made it perfect. He begged her to let him record it. Hence, the song of the year became ubiquitous because it was recorded in two separate versions, using essentially the same musicians, in studios a few hundred yards from each other within a few days of each other, going on to dominate the airwaves for the rest of the year and to attract cover versions by everyone from Barbra Streisand to Dusty Springfield to Aretha Franklin. But no matter how accomplished those versions might be, none would quite eclipse the modest conviction of King's original.

The 150,000 people who were picking up King's album every week in 1971 took it home and sung along to it as they finished their college projects, did their housework, or hovered nervously over their first Betty Crocker–inspired cheeseburger pie. It was easy for them to believe that the sound that came out of their mouths was the same as the one they were hearing from the record player. That voice's concerns seemed to be the same as theirs, its temper no more extreme than theirs, its expectations of the world no greater than theirs. It seemed to be broadcasting on the same frequency.

Songwriter Carole Bayer Sager described it as "a voice every woman thinks she could have." Certainly, nobody ever thought they could sing like Aretha Franklin or be like Joni Mitchell, but many of them felt Carole King was the sister they might have had.

As Lou Adler had noted, there had been very few best-selling albums fronted by women. Janis Joplin's *Pearl* had been the number one album for a while in February on the back of the publicity attending her death in October and her version of Kris Kristofferson's "Me and Bobby McGee," but that was the exception. Bobbie Gentry had briefly been in the number one slot in 1967, but the top spot had largely been monopolized by male acts like Simon & Garfunkel, the Beatles, and Led Zeppelin. That's because up to that point most of the people who bought albums had been men. *Tapestry* changed that and pointed to a future where in order to sell huge numbers of long-playing records, you had to sell them to women.

The first few reviews of *Tapestry* were lukewarm. The one that changed it was a lead review that appeared in *Rolling Stone* on April 29, where Jon Landau said, "The simplicity of the singing, composition and ultimate feeling achieved the kind of eloquence and beauty that I had forgotten rock is capable of." The core readership of *Rolling Stone* was male, hairy, leftish, and inclined to believe that music worth their time was always loud and edgy. Landau's review was a reminder of the virtues of the pre-Woodstock era and the songwriting baby that might have been thrown out with the bathwater during the move away from the narrow back garden of the hit single to the rolling prairies of the album age.

In 1971 that market for albums was still quite small. The technology you needed to play these new stereo records on was still quite forbidding. Long-playing records came in inner bags with messages warning of the dire consequences that could flow from playing a stereo record on a record player that was wired only for mono. There was a widespread feeling that the old portable record players were no longer the appropriate machines on which to play these new, self-important long players in their foldout covers. Stereo was acceptable only for hobbyists prepared to have their living space dominated by snaking leads.

This was beginning to change with the baby boomers, who were leaving college and setting up their own homes, often communally, in rented accommodation. In 1971 none of these people would have even considered having a TV. It was widely accepted that there was nothing on TV that a long-haired person with a college degree could have the remotest interest in watching. Instead of a TV, they bought a record player. Having bought it, they needed something to play on it. It was quite common to go to a friend's flat in those days and find a new cheap, Japanese-made "music center" with a smoked plastic cover over the deck, dark-brown wood-effect boxes for the speakers, black mesh covering tiny woofers and tweeters. Propped up alongside it would be no more than half a dozen records. As likely as not, there would be one by the Beatles, one by Simon & Garfunkel, one by Santana, and, as the year went on, it was increasingly likely the other one would be *Tapestry*.

The 150,000 people a week buying *Tapestry* in the United States were members of a new constituency. They didn't have *Easy Rider* posters on their walls, they didn't hang around hip record stores puzzling over the smoking paraphernalia, they didn't carry around Richard Brautigan books and go to late-night showings of Sam Peckinpah's *The Wild Bunch*. Most of those 150,000 were from a section of the population who would ultimately decide whether a pop singer is a flash in the pan or here to stay. They were young women.

Chris Darrow, a respected Hollywood musician, went to see King play at the Troubadour in the week of *Tapestry*'s release and was immediately struck by the emergence of this new constituency. "It was crowded and almost all the people in the room were women, mostly high school and college age. Almost all of them were with their mothers."

Something was happening that was so gradual and profound that nobody even thought of writing a song about it. In the month of *Tapestry*'s release *New York* magazine published a picture of ten women who worked for *Time* magazine. They were all white, casually dressed but well groomed, and they posed in the New York offices of their employer to mark the success of their efforts to force Time Inc., the massive publishing empire of *Time* magazine, *Life*, *Sports Illustrated*, *Fortune*, and various other huge-selling journals of record, to recognize the fact that they were writers and not researchers. In this, they were following in the footsteps of *Newsweek*'s women, who had forced that magazine's owners, the Washington Post company, to similarly allow women to be recognized as writers. Up to then, even star writers like Nora Ephron and Ellen Goodman had been forced to accept the lowly title of researcher because the magazine's culture simply couldn't be seen to admit that women could write about mainstream subjects. All this despite the fact that *Newsweek*'s parent company was owned by Katharine Graham. In order to make the changes happen, the women had to use legal instruments introduced in the wake of the civil rights struggles of the sixties.

The fact that these women, at both *Time* and *Newsweek*, were the cream of the female graduates from some of America's finest universities gives some indication of the extent to which in 1971 it was perfectly possible for women to be not so much overlooked as looked through. The fact that they had to threaten *Time* magazine, the citadel of sophisticated East Coast values, with this kind of action in order to get this most modest of changes underlines how far working life in 1971 was out of kilter with the blithe reassurances of the Virginia Slims "You've come a long way, baby" ads. Lynn Povich, who eventually became *Newsweek*'s first female editor, wrote a book about the events of 1970. She called it *The Good Girls Revolt* because it featured girls who were well brought up, well dressed, and well spoken and had been raised to expect the world to function in a certain way. As she wrote, "Until 1970 women represented 10% of students in medical school, 4 percent of law school students and only 3 per cent of business school students." As Nora Ephron recalled, "For every man there was an inferior woman, for every writer there was a checker. They were the artists and we were the drones."

The Good Girls Revolt was a turning point. Nowhere in the *New York* magazine article will you find the word "sexism." Nor will you find it in Jill Tweedie's report in the *Guardian* on London's first women's lib demo, which took place at the beginning of March 1971. Nor did anyone at the time draw a line between these events and the fact that three of the big films of the year, *Get Carter, Straw Dogs,* and *Play Misty for Me,* depicted women as sexually voracious and dangerously unhinged. Nobody made a connection between that and the women's movement, and few suggested the music made by single mother Carole King might be considered feminist.

In a film made at Vassar in 1971, female students describe their ideal careers as if they don't quite believe they will actually happen. "I want to be a music teacher," says one, "but I suppose I'll be married and have children." One wants to be a pediatrician; another wants to be a recording engineer, which in 1971 would probably have made her the first one, but there was an acceptance that other things would probably get in the way.

While their male counterparts might be worrying about the draft, the key issue in the world of young women in 1971 was the sudden availability of the pill. In Britain the Family Planning Association instructed its clinics to make it available to single as well as married women, a change that would have seemed seismic a couple of years earlier. This meant that the generation who went to college in the late '60s, who were not expected to settle down and get married quite as soon as the previous generation, suddenly had the major disincentive to sex taken out of the equation. This resulted in a short period of time when people living in close proximity to each other felt almost compelled to sleep together as if the act were merely a natural extension of familiarity. Now that they couldn't get "in trouble" any longer, girls who didn't choose to sleep with the first person to ask them were often asked in all seriousness, "Are you frigid?" King's record was made in the midst of a milieu that seemed intent on separating the physical act from its emotional consequences. By the fall of 1971, she had achieved such eminence that Hollywood's senior cocksman Warren Beatty offered to sleep with her, on the grounds that he was curious to know what it was like to have sex with a pregnant woman.

The good girls who bought *Tapestry* identified not only with its tunefulness but also with its themes of shelter, stability, and trust. Ever since her parents had broken up when she was a child, Carole King had been open about the fact that home was her dream. Carole King was never held up as a symbol of fearsome independence and self-determination. She was a mild-mannered, quite shy person who had to be brought to the front when she played in James Taylor's band. She didn't go round doing interviews advertising her lifestyle. Nonetheless, as Cynthia Weil said, listening to *Tapestry* "made you feel a friend was taking care of you."

When you look back at lists of the biggest-selling albums of all time, *Tapestry* is the earliest one to be included. Even when she followed it with *Music*, which was written, recorded, and released later in the same year, the public duly noted the new record but kept on buying the old one in a way that indicated that to them it would never be the old one. *Tapestry* was the first evergreen of the rock era. Its continued success would make the record business realize that it could extend the commercial life of certain albums for years by continuing to release the strongest tracks as singles. Fleetwood Mac's *Rumours*, Meat Loaf's *Bat Out of Hell*, the Eagles' *Hotel California*, and Blondie's *Parallel Lines* were all beneficiaries of this approach later in the decade. A select handful of albums, including Pink Floyd's *Dark Side of the Moon* and Led Zeppelin's *Led Zeppelin IV*, achieved evergreen status without apparent help from pop success, continuing to notch up sales on the basis that the few people who didn't have it felt they ought to have it.

Tapestry's success became so huge that none of the people involved with it have ever been able to follow it in the conventional sense. It's made a lot of reputations and bought quite a few homes. In 2013 King reunited with James Taylor to do a tour designed to recapture the spirit of that year. Whenever she goes onstage nowadays, she still plays the songs from *Tapestry*. She's had a film, *Grace of My Heart*, based on her story. *Beautiful*, the musical based on her songs, is running on Broadway and in London.

By 2015 *Tapestry* had sold twenty-five million copies worldwide. This would never have happened without the changes that took place in American radio in 1971.

Lee Abrams was a radio nerd from Chicago. He had grown up in the sixties when the airwaves were the domain of fast-talking, self-promoting, sponsor-boosting names like Murray the K. Unlike most kids with a transistor under their pillow, Abrams didn't just lose himself in the rhythm and chatter. He started to make a study of what he heard. He corresponded with the stations. He read trade papers. He turned up at industry conventions. He managed a covers band. Because he naturally wanted to know which songs the band should play, he did what nobody had done before in the entire history of the music business. He asked the audience.

Abrams would hand out questionnaires at gigs, personal appearances, record hops, and radio station events, carefully compiling the results into typewritten reports listing the songs that people liked and the songs that they were about to like. He started calling the radio stations and offering to share this information with them. He took out ads in the trades that he called "Better Ideas for Better Stations."

What he and the radio stations needed to do was get ahead of the charts. If you were a program director, there was no use waiting until a record was number one before your station started playing it. You needed to be playing it just as the affair between the public and the record was in the first flush of infatuation. That's the sweet spot that radio needs to be in, where people's love of the record being played merges with their love of the radio station and spills over into a little bit of love for its sponsors and advertisers. This is important information for any radio station. In the United States of the late '60s, where a record could be red hot in Chicago and mean very little in Miami, it was vital intelligence.

In 1971 radio in the United States was just emerging from its brief, heady experiment with free-form. Associated particularly with the whiskey-voiced hipster Tom Donahue at KMPX and then KSAN in San Francisco from the Summer of Love onward, free-form refers to stations that took barely any notice of what happened to be in the charts and instead took pride in serving up the most arcane and challenging music they could get their hands on. This was the time when you could turn on the radio and find somebody playing all twenty minutes of Canned Heat's "Parthenogenesis" and then welcoming you back to the studio with the silence that indicated approval and eventually the word "nice." In Britain audiences would sit listening to the endless ragas of Ravi Shankar on Radio 1 unaware that John Peel had put them on in order to give himself time to go and have sexual intercourse with one of his girlfriends. The audience might not always have found the music to their taste, but they approved of the very idea that it was long and proudly uncommercial.

But for every genius of free-form radio, for every jock who knew how to put together a show that could shift gears between the exotic and the familiar, there were twenty tin-eared snobs who were simply on the radio because they liked to be on the radio. Thus, there were two kinds of radio: programming on the old AM model, which seemed as if it belonged in the long-gone days of the Beach Boys and the Turtles, and free-form programming on the FM stations, which had quickly become a self-indulgent bore and a turn-off for those people who didn't spend their days wondering what Grace Slick and Paul Kantner were up to. As one radio programmer put it, "It was either too hip or too hype."

By then Lee Abrams was getting his first job in radio. He believed the future was in FM. It offered a better signal, a warmer, less shrill sound, and the stereo that people were increasingly used to hearing on their records at home. The problem was that the people who ran FM didn't program the music that the mass audience wanted to hear. Abrams's idea, which he put into practice first at WRIF in Detroit and then at WPTF in North Carolina, was to program the hip music in unhip ways. His motto, which has dominated all radio since, was "familiar music works." The idea was that you didn't simply play the hot new record the DJ felt like playing or the one the program director had been lunched to play. You polled the audience all the time, often by phone, and you asked them to name the acts they most liked. Then you programmed the most popular cuts by those artists. You might let a DJ choose in which order to play them, although in time even that latitude was denied them, but broadly you took the personality DJ out of the equation and replaced him with a strong format that felt as if it was being put together by somebody as windswept and interesting as Clint Eastwood's character in *Play Misty for Me* but in reality was being read off a script provided by Lee Abrams or one of his consulting partners. This was the format that moved the bulk of listening from AM to FM and laid the foundations of the massive sales achieved later in the decade by the Eagles, Fleetwood Mac, and Linda Ronstadt. In 1971 it was just getting into its stride, and one of the first beneficiaries of this new way of doing things was the tuneful, female-friendly, and easy-on-the-ear record made by Carole King, a woman who was as much a refugee from the AM dial as her listeners.

The artists who weren't on the playlist loathed it. The artists who were on the list thought it was just fine. By the mid-1970s more than three hundred stations across the United States were programmed according to Abrams's principles. Some called it AOR (album- or adult-oriented rock). It was certainly no longer underground. It was the new mainstream.

Television had only the haziest clue what was going on beyond its walls. On February 15, 1971, Johnny Carson, the king of late night, presented *The Tonight Show* as usual. In the show's early days, it was broadcast from New York. Among Carson's guests that night, returning for her second appearance because he liked her so much, was a sassy twenty-six-year-old singer of Jewish extraction who had grown up in, of all places, Hawaii. Carson liked Bette Midler because not only could she sing, she could also hold her own in the wise-cracking stakes and presented herself with a cheery brassiness you didn't find in most pop singers of the era. Bette Midler was what Carson and other members of the ring-a-ding-ding generation would have called a broad. She didn't have a record contract at the time, and in 1971 she was marking time by playing the Acid Queen onstage in the first production of Pete Townshend's *Tommy* at the Seattle Opera or entertaining closely packed houses of gay men clad only in towels in the Continental Baths in New York City. The bathhouse performances were not directly referred to during her TV appearances. In 1971 you still couldn't use the word "gay" on TV, certainly not in a light-entertainment context. Midler, saucy tongue sheathed in rouged cheek, would simply say it was full of "happy people." Her act at the baths, which earned her the name "Bathhouse Betty," was made up of sixties pop favorites, chin-up tunes from wartime, and tearful torch songs that she cooked up and arranged with her accompanist, the equally unknown Barry Manilow, who sometimes entered into the spirit of things by playing while wearing only a towel.

A favorite torch song was confusingly known as "Groupie (Super-star)." Neither the original name nor its parenthetical name featured in the lyrics. It had been the original idea of Rita Coolidge, a member of the teeming cast of Joe Cocker's *Mad Dogs and Englishmen*, and had been inspired by her observation of the way certain impressionable girls seemed to queue up to be misused by the famous men onstage. The ballad had been written by the tour's musical director, Leon Russell, along with Bonnie Bramlett, and Coolidge had sung it every night on the Mad Dogs tour. It was subsequently covered by Cher and Vikki Carr. Midler found that its theme of being used and abused by a man also resounded with her moist clientele at the Continental Baths.

Watching the Carson show that night in the new five-bedroom house that he and his sister, Karen, had recently moved into in the Los Angeles suburb of Downey was Richard Carpenter. The

Carpenters, who were originally from Connecticut, had put out their first album in late 1969, but Richard was already under pressure to come up with their third. They had spent the day in A&M's studio on La Brea recording tracks for their third album, and he knew he needed follow-ups to the huge hits of the previous year "For All We Know" and "We've Only Just Begun."

The success of the Carpenters, which was already considerable, had been achieved at the expense of some of Richard's pride. As the older sibling and an accomplished pianist and arranger, Richard might have expected to be in charge. Things hadn't worked out like that. Although he wrote his own songs, the Carpenters' hits tended to come from composers such as Paul Williams and Burt Bacharach. Richard did some singing, but his vocals were not as distinctive as those of his gawky kid sister, Karen. Richard had steeled himself for stardom only to find that its mantle had fallen instead on his sister, who seemed manifestly unready for it. Their parents, the original driving force behind their children's efforts, still saw Richard as the talent. The rest of the world didn't agree.

Karen Carpenter had been included as a package with her older brother ever since they were teenagers. Their gimmick was that she played the drums. The session musicians who played on the Carpenters' records, who came from that loose federation of brilliant pop instrumentalists known as the Wrecking Crew, knew that while average drummers were ten a penny, voices like Karen's happened along only rarely. Joe Osborn, the bass player in whose garage they first learned to record, said, "She got no credit for anything. Richard was the star as far as the family was concerned." Drummer Hal Blaine, who played along with her on some of the studio recordings, says, "That voice was just incredible. She was born with that. She didn't learn that."

Karen Carpenter's problem was that while the requirements of show business demanded that she come out front and be the band's lead singer, her self-consciousness about her appearance meant she preferred to stay behind the drum kit. "She was kind of a tomboy," said Sherwin Bash, who managed them, "and the drums were traditionally a male instrument. She wasn't sure she was slim enough, svelte enough, pretty enough, any of those things."

Richard and Karen Carpenter prospered greatly in 1971, but they were scorned by those who considered themselves hip. They popped up on old-fashioned TV shows fronted by stars terrified that they were losing their way in a country that appeared to have gone youth crazy. In any show hosted by a comedian in a tux, you could guarantee the Carpenters would be the musical guest. There wasn't the ghost of anything edgy about them. In a world where people were expected to flaunt their attitude, the Carpenters didn't appear to have any. They sounded like creamed rice.

The fact that the Carpenters made it big speaks volumes for the willingness of a few record companies to invest in unconventional talent. A&M had made a lot of its money with the easy listening sounds of Herb Alpert's Tijuana Brass and the Sandpipers, so the company knew how to promote an act like the Carpenters. They were one of the first acts to sell big on eight-track and cassette. Their buyers were the great bulk of the American and overseas public who just liked good tunes and also found something in Karen Carpenter's profound contralto that spoke to them about their lives every bit as much as the songs of Leonard Cohen or Neil Young did for their fans.

"Groupie (Superstar)" was an odd choice for a Carpenters song. Then again, "We've Only Just Begun" was originally a jingle for a bank. Richard had never heard the song Midler sang before, which is an indication of the direction to which his personal radio was tuned, but he guessed his sister could sing the song, as she could sing pretty much any ballad.

He was right. Karen was less convinced, but she did what she was told. They made one change to the lyrics, "to sleep with you again" becoming "to be with you again." She did a guide vocal for the musicians to play along with. Even with only half her mind on the job, she delivered a perfect performance. The guide vocal never needed to be replaced. That was the special quality of Karen Carpenter, a quality that became even more poignant following her anorexia-related death in 1983. When Bette Midler performed, half the impact was in the twinkle in her eye, her coquettish body language, the way she carried herself. With Karen Carpenter, it was in her voice and her voice alone.

Russ Solomon started selling records in his father's drugstore in Sacramento just after the war. He named his business after the building in which it was housed, the Tower Theater. He opened the first big store on Watt Avenue in Sacramento. In 1968 he opened a store at Columbus and Bay in San Francisco. In 1970 he bought a plot on Sunset Boulevard in Hollywood, within walking distance of the Whisky a Go Go. It had its own parking lot. At busy times it even had its own parking attendant directing traffic in that parking lot.

Tower advertised itself as "the largest record-tape store in the known world," a claim also made by the HMV shop in London's Oxford Street. Claims of that kind are impossible to measure, but the key feature of Tower was that all the stock was out on the floor rather than in the storeroom at the back, so it certainly felt like the largest. New releases would be literally piled on the floor near the door and advertised at discount prices, making it impossible to resist buying them. At the same time, the store carried a depth of catalog that would be unknown in your local record store. Tower could do this because its stores were sited in busy cities with growing populations of young people who would buy records.

Tower took some of the ambience of the hippie record shacks like Rather Ripped in Berkeley or Virgin in London—Solomon promoted the fact that he wouldn't allow his staff to wear ties—while behind the scenes his staff were playing hardball with distributors and using Tower's growing muscle to negotiate discounts the hippie shacks could never match. The Tower stores had handwritten price labels above the racks. They organized in-store gigs and personal appearances (War drove a tank into the parking lot to promote their album). The stores became outlets for the growing market for local listings magazines and turned into de facto social centers, encouraging people to spend all day in the shops so it would be impossible for customers to leave with just one record. They did all the things that the little hippie stores thought they were too cool to do and the old-fashioned mom-and-pop stores would never have thought to do, and they achieved the objective of the record companies by making new releases seem like the most important thing in the world.

By early 1971 Tower on Sunset already seemed like the capital of the worldwide record business. It was within walking distance of the studios where *Tapestry* and *Mud Slide Slim* had been made and the Troubadour, where all the happening acts played and where on Tuesday nights a line of hopefuls (including, that spring, young Thomas Waits from Pomona) would turn up for their chance at the big time. It was near enough to the new West Coast headquarters being set up by all the record companies as their newly wealthy executives fled New York in search of a more congenial lifestyle and because of a feeling that LA was now the center of a different kind of world. For people who weren't that excited about what was going on in the cinema, didn't own more than one set of clothes, and couldn't afford anything more than a beat-up twenty-year-old car, Tower on Sunset was a temple into which all consumer desire was channeled. The pulse quickened on entering it in the sure and certain knowledge that you would experience some shock of the new in the shape of a new record by either an old favorite or a new name you had only heard about, had never heard, and had certainly never seen. The new record shops were medium and message combined. Most of the people who bought Carole King's *Tapestry* would not have had an earthly clue what she looked like until they went into the record shop and picked up her album and turned it over in their hands. The new generation of record shops had a magic that replaced the radio. They were the place where you came into contact with the product. You didn't merely shop at a place like this. You parsed every last detail of your surroundings at the same time. You stood among the racks studying every new release, memorizing paragraphs of the sleeve notes, piecing together your knowledge square by square. It was the love of rock turned into its purest expression—shopping.

The recorded music business was beginning to diversify into new product ranges. In their 1971 models, American car manufacturers were beginning to offer cassette or eight-track decks as extras in their luxury cars, and Phillips was advertising the previously undreamed-of sensation of "stereo in your car" with its own in-car players. In 1971 Henry Kloss introduced the Advent 201, which featured Dolby B noise reduction and chromium dioxide tape for higher-quality sound. Cassette tape, a technology that had once been considered good enough only for dictation, was now a perfectly acceptable way to listen to music. For the first time, record companies could sell music in more than one format and could conceivably sell it more than once. For people looking to purchase music who were not hooked on the romance of the 12-inch album and preferred convenience above all things, the cassette was a good choice. By the end of the decade it would be the leading music carrier.

Those lucky people who were able to drive out of the parking lot of Tower on Sunset and insert a cassette of a freshly purchased new album by the hottest new artist into their new auto-reverse in-car player, which would bloom into stereo using the vehicle's cabin as a huge sounding box, felt they were having a hit of human pleasure, a pinch of ease, a brief transport of delight that nothing else in their daily life would ever be able to quite match. They weren't entirely wrong.

In 1971 even financially comfortable people didn't get to indulge their fantasies, to live, even temporarily, the luxury life. The United States and Europe were still a long way apart. Transatlantic travel was the exclusive preserve of the very wealthy, the business traveler, or people making once-in-a-lifetime trips to visit relatives who might have emigrated in the years after the war. Air travel for the masses hadn't yet arrived. The first jumbo jet full of ticket-buying passengers didn't land at Heathrow until 1970. There were very few airlines, and few of them were offering budget fares. In 1971 Southwest Airlines opened its commuter routes between Dallas, Houston, and San Antonio, selling tickets that at twenty dollars were marketed as being roughly comparable to the price of the fuel needed for the trip. The other key feature stressed in the advertising of Southwest Airlines was that its flight attendants wore bright-orange hot pants and go-go boots.

The routes across the Atlantic were dominated by the old carriers, and they didn't offer discount tickets. The United States was not a holiday destination for many Europeans. In London, people who had actually visited the United States were interrogated by friends hungry for the smallest detail of this far-off land of dreams. In 1971 the average twenty-four-year-old Londoner would entertain small hope of ever making the trip, which might be a source of mild sadness for many. For somebody so obsessed with America and its popular culture that he had changed his last name in honor of an American frontiersman, it was more painful than that.

On January 24, 1971, David Bowie took his first flight to the United States. It was the most important journey of his life. Bowie's career had stalled since the success of "Space Oddity" in 1969, but he had a deal with Mercury Records, which was putting out his record *The Man Who Sold the World* in the United States. He also had a new manager, a solicitor's clerk named Tony Defries, who had managed to persuade Mercury to fly Bowie out to do some promotion. In 1971 artists had to have an official exchange agreement with the American Federation of Musicians in order to be able to perform in the States. Since he had no permit, Bowie couldn't play any shows. However, he had a few enthusiastic supporters in the US media and on the staff of Mercury Records. One of these, the East Coast publicity boss Ron Oberman, met Bowie when he arrived at Washington's Dulles Airport. There was barely any budget for the visit, and therefore it was agreed that he would stay with Oberman, who at the time was living in his parents' home in Silver Spring, Maryland. For the Obermans, it was an adventure to go to the airport, and so Ron took his parents with him. Like most of the people in the terminal, they were taken aback by Bowie's appearance when he came through customs. He had been detained for forty-five minutes by officials unaccustomed to seeing young men in electric-blue fur coats with velvet trousers tucked into black motorcycle boots and hair swept into a style reminiscent of Veronica Lake. If they had looked in the traveler's bags, they would have seen that he had packed one of the men's dresses that he and his wife Angie had picked out from the London designer Michael Fish.

Angie didn't travel with him because there was no budget and also because she was six months pregnant with their first child. She remained at their home, a rambling mansion in Beckenham, Kent, called Haddon Hall. The people she was sharing it with had pretensions to be a commune but in fact were largely dedicated to trying to launch the career of David Bowie.

The three weeks that Bowie spent in the United States in January and February of that year, traveling to New York, Detroit, Minneapolis, Texas, and California, shaped his future. Like any young man coming from England in 1971, when that country had just one pop music radio station and a total of three TV channels, he was stupefied by America's plenty and intoxicated with the relative ease of life. Far from the responsibilities and well-trodden pavements of home, Bowie was free to make himself up, to say things he wouldn't have said back in the UK, describing his last LP as "reminiscences about my experiences as a shaven-headed transvestite" to a San Francisco DJ and delighting in his ability to stop the conversation in any restaurant by the simple act of walking in.

Those three weeks changed his view of music. He was played the Velvet Underground's *Loaded*, which included "Sweet Jane" and "Rock & Roll" and would not be released in the UK for a few months. He was sufficiently enthused to see them at the Electric Circus in New York and was so overcome that he talked his way backstage to shake the hand of the man he thought was Lou Reed. It was only later that he learned that Reed had left the band, and he'd been enthusing over the hastily elevated Doug Yule, further indication of how shrouded in mystery a cult band could be in 1971. In Manhattan he met the avant-garde street musician Moondog. In San Jose he heard the Stooges for the first time. Having failed to make a commercial breakthrough and seeking consolation in heroin, the band was at the point of breaking up. Bowie and Stooges vocalist Iggy Pop would meet for the first time later in the year. By the time Bowie arrived in Los Angeles on February 13, he told his new friend the radio plugger and scene maker Rodney Bingenheimer that he had an idea for a whole album based on a character called Ziggy Stardust.

In Hollywood he stayed with RCA executive Tom Ayres, who lived just off Sunset Boulevard in a home previously owned by the silent movie star Lillian Gish. He and Bingenheimer borrowed Ayres's convertible Cadillac to drive to radio interviews. This would have been a kick even for someone from suburban California. For a boy from Beckenham, it was unimaginably exciting. There was recording equipment in Ayres's house, which Gene Vincent was using at the time. Bowie took advantage of this to record a demo of a new song called "Hang On to Yourself," which he offered to Ayres for Vincent.

The week in Los Angeles passed like a dream. Wearing one of his Fish gowns, Bowie performed a few songs at a lawyers party in the Hollywood Hills, perched on a waterbed, the item of furniture all rich hippies favored at the time, and playing his acoustic guitar. He went to a party for Ultra Violet, one of Andy Warhol's superstars, and socialized with the handsome young film actor Don Johnson. Like all first-time visitors from Britain, he didn't quite get to grips with the lack of public transportation. On Valentine's Day he walked two miles down Sunset Boulevard to attend a rehearsal with Christopher Milk, the band led by *Rolling Stone* writer John Mendelsohn. This took place in the same studios where Carole King had just completed *Tapestry*. Together they played the Velvet Underground's "I'm Waiting for the Man," which would soon become a part of Bowie's act.

Like any musician on the make, Bowie focused in on somebody who might be able to help him—in this case, Ayres. Bowie's contract with Mercury was expiring, and his new manager was shopping for a new home. Ayres suggested his own employer, RCA, because the only big act it had was Elvis, and that wasn't going to last forever. It was thanks to the contact Bowie had made with Ayres that the *Ziggy Stardust* album, when it arrived, would be on RCA alongside those of the King, the singer with whom he shared a birthday. Ayres introduced him to Grelun Landon, the company's august head of publicity. Landon, who had worked closely with Elvis Presley, said of Bowie, "He's very bizarre, but I think he's going to be the Bob Dylan of the seventies."

When Bowie flew back to London on February 18, it was clear that he was infatuated with the United States. He babbled excitedly to friends and audiences about the freeways, the subways, and even the violence, in a way that seemed to be boasting as much as anything else. Rubbing shoulders with American music business people and hearing American music radio made him think outside the box of his suburban Arts Lab world. Seven years earlier, the collision between English sensibilities and the actual experience of visiting America had led the Beatles and the Rolling Stones to create their defining music. Now it was David Bowie's turn. By the end of the month, he had organized a session at Radio Luxembourg's studio in Mayfair to record "Hang On to Yourself" and "Moonage Daydream," another song that would eventually find its way on to his breakthrough album. He wasn't planning to sing it himself. He was going to be the puppet master for a cute young gay guy named Fred Burrett. He and Angie had taken to spending time at a London club called the Sombrero. There they had met the tiny handful of people in London happy to describe themselves as gay. His plan was to transform young Fred into Freddie Burretti and make him a star. David would be the one pulling the strings Simon Cowell style. It didn't work out quite the way he planned. It would be another year before Ziggy Stardust would be properly set before the public, and when it did, Bowie would find himself playing both puppet and puppet master. However, the seeds of his breakthrough idea had been sewn during his intoxicating trip to the New World, and although they probably wouldn't have believed it, Lou Reed and Iggy Pop were rescued from the obscurity that seemed to be beckoning before Bowie made that fateful trip.

FEBRUARY

Carole King: "It's Too Late"

James Taylor: "You've Got a Friend"

Joni Mitchell: "Little Green"

Janis Joplin: "Mercedes Benz"

Todd Rundgren: "We Gotta Get You a Woman"

Roy Budd: *Get Carter* soundtrack

David Bowie: "The Man Who Sold the World"

The Velvet Underground: "Sweet Jane"

Andrew Lloyd Webber and Tim Rice: *Jesus Christ Superstar* soundtrack

The Temptations: "Just My Imagination (Running Away with Me)"

MARCH

Rock and Roll

In the early years of the present century, I was taking a holiday in the highlands of Scotland. I stopped in a lay-by at the side of Loch Ness, one of the most desolate, beautiful parts of the country. Here it's possible to escape the crowds and feel pleasantly cut off from your fellow man. I took a few moments to contemplate the chilly depths of the loch and brood on the stillness of the surrounding mountains.

There was only one other vehicle in that car park. It was a small van, dispensing drinks to passing tourists. On this occasion, it was staffed by one young woman. She might have been a postgraduate university student, working her way through the vacation, or just a member of that vast army of polite young people with surprising flecks of color in their hair and runic tattoos on their ankles who nowadays can pop up anywhere in modern Europe, passing their time in a job far below their education and capabilities as they wait for life to provide them with a road map.

To pass the time between customers, she had a book and, oddly enough, a cassette player. From this old-fashioned machine arose a piece of music that reached back even further, all the way to the spring of 1971, its melancholy merging perfectly with the view of the loch. It also provided the perfect soundtrack for the dispensing of a cup of tea in a polystyrene cup, marrying sound and image in a way that made me unsure whether I was watching a commercial or actually in a commercial. The music was "At the Chime of a City Clock" by Nick Drake from his 1971 album *Bryter Layter*.

The patina around Drake's music has been steadily built up over the years through so many layers of hindsight that it's impossible to know whether that twentysomething alongside Loch Ness was responding to the actual music as was put on tape by engineer John Wood in Chelsea in November 1970 or to the identification between Drake's music and a certain quality of bruised soulfulness, an identification that has grown over recent years thanks to the music's frequent use on soundtracks. We have experienced it in movies such as *The Royal Tenenbaums*, the TV series *Parenthood*, or the VW commercial in which a bunch of educated young people born in the era of mobile phones and GPS choose to spend the evening driving around listening to Drake's music and looking at the moon rather than mixing with the beery oafs at a party. Drake's music lives in the mainstream as a signifier for "alternative."

Of all the records put out in 1971 none was more heedlessly passed over at the time than Drake's *Bryter Layter*, and none has been more warmly adopted by subsequent generations, most of whom weren't even born at the time he died. Some music from 1971 sounds more pertinent now than it did at the time it originally came out. This is certainly the case with Drake's. Linda Thompson, a fellow musical striver and girlfriend of Drake's back in the early '70s, heard his music in the twenty-first century over a supermarket loudspeaker in Los Angeles and, as she remarked, "couldn't believe how right it sounded. How did he know?" Drake's career, if we can call it that, since he was absent by reason of death throughout it, has been the slowest burn in rock.

At the time *Bryter Later* came out in March 1971, Joe Boyd, the talent scout who had first signed Drake to his Witchseason productions, had produced him, found him live shows, established him in a flat, and done all the other things that Drake showed no sign of doing for himself, was already on his way to a new job in his native United States. Hence Drake was without the patron, advocate, and twenty-four-hour irritant every artist needs to elbow the way into prominence. However, Island, the larger independent to which he was in fact signed, continued to pay him a twenty-pound-a-week retainer, comparable to the earnings of somebody who actually worked for a living. Later in 1971 he dropped in on John Wood, the engineer who had been at the board on his previous albums, and in two nights recorded the unadorned *Pink Moon*, which came out in 1972. That was the end of Drake's recording career. He died in 1974 at his parents' home in Tanworth-in-Arden, apparently after an overdose of antidepressants. He was twenty-six.

In the years that followed, Island kept his records in the catalog out of respect, but there was no groundswell of interest. It wasn't until 1992, when the country rock artist Lucinda Williams released a version of Drake's "Which Will," that his music began to exert a powerful fascination on the many artists who think of themselves as refugees from the established categories. His songs were covered by everyone from the rock band the Flaming Lips to the jazz artist Brad Mehldau. Robyn Hitchcock and Mogwai are just two of the acts to write songs named after him. Prominent people were eager to tell us how much they liked him. It seemed to advertise their sensitivity. Brad Pitt waived his fee to narrate a BBC radio documentary about Drake's life. The film actor Heath Ledger claimed to be obsessed with him and was eventually found dead in circumstances that echoed Drake's death. These days Drake's reputation is greater than the reputations of many people whose success he most envied in 1971. Nobody talks about Lindisfarne or Brewer & Shipley with the same reverence. Drake is a latter-day James Dean, revered as much for what he's seen to represent as for what he did.

The Pulitzer Prize–winning writer Louis Menand has written about what he called "the iron law of stardom." This law decrees that in show business you've got only three years. Three years is about as long as you can remain interesting and as long as an audience can maintain its interest in you. There are exceptions, but it's surprising how many rock careers are effectively about three stylistically linked albums made over a period of three years. Drake's brief career, which started with *Five Leaves Left* in 1970 and ended with *Pink Moon* in 1972, is a classic case. His death meant he never got the chance to let anyone down. He is the classic case of the artist who, in the words of Elvis Costello, didn't stick around to witness his own decline. Now that his life is safely defined by just three albums, he remains not just an artist who made some appealing music but a perfect emblem of misunderstood genius.

In 2013, forty-two years after *Bryter Layter*'s original release, Universal Music, the huge multinational entertainment company that swallowed up A&M, Motown, Island, and many of the most charismatic independent record labels of the '70s, announced the release of yet another reissue of Nick Drake's second album. This time it would be presented in a box set containing a record pressed on "180 gram virgin vinyl for the audiophile" and packaged inside a foldout cover that had been painstakingly and expensively aged to replicate the original textured cover of the 1971 LP. It would be accompanied by a replica shop poster and, especially for the collectors who were expected to file their copy away unplayed to make sure it retained its value, it came with a code enabling the buyer to download the music on a choice of formats, including high definition 24 bit and a version "dubbed from disc."

With its curious combination of antique trade fakery and digital sheen, the 2013 *Bryter Layter* project was the most elaborate example yet of the heritage rock industry's attempt to conjure the allegedly magical moment in early 1971 when that record was released. In truth there was no such moment, magical or otherwise, no feeling that something precious was happening or even that an opportunity had been missed. The concept of rock posterity hadn't yet been invented. Drake died unknown in 1974. Those few music fans who read the news item at the time knew Drake as the guy who made the quiet, watercolor music they might have heard on Island sampler albums like *Nice Enough to Eat*. Here his "Time Has Told Me" was sequenced immediately before King Crimson's bludgeoning "21st Century Schizoid Man," which seemed destined to obliterate all traces of anything that had come before.

In 1971 Nick Drake had no noticeable following. At the time, either you had made it or you were about to. Nobody had yet settled into that position of middling cultdom in which most of today's rock bands live, breathe, and have their being. The cult of the noble under-rated hadn't been invented. Fashionable people didn't drop Drake's name. He didn't stand for anything. Nobody had his picture on the wall. He was just another singer-songwriter making music, nothing like as celebrated as Al Stewart, let alone Leonard Cohen; more like Harvey Andrews or Amory Kane, a provider of the kind of music that was vaguely and approvingly described in the nasal argot of the day as "nice" but bought by absolutely nobody you knew.

The early weeks of March 1971 should have been the fullest of Nick Drake's life. He was twenty-two, comfortably off, devastatingly attractive to women, a guitarist that other players tried to copy but couldn't, and one of the handful of performers who had a sound and a style of their own. He had his second record just released on Island, which was Britain's hippest record company, and yet his day slipped by un-seized. He almost didn't have a day at all.

Bryter Layter's release had been penciled in for 1970, but it was held up by the British postal strike, which interrupted deliveries to shops. This action, which was in pursuit of a 15 percent pay rise (fairly standard at the time), began in January and lasted for seven weeks. It made the nation's switch to decimal currency, which took place in February, even more complex and meant that the post office was forced for the first time to license private firms to carry the mail. The strike ended on March 4, and *Bryter Layter* was released in the UK a week later. There was no single and barely any radio play. There was a half-page advert in the *Melody Maker* and a short inter-view in *Sounds* in which he talked to Jerry Gilbert about his dislike of live performance. It was the only interview he did in his life.

Other things were going on. Bigger things. *Bryter Layter* came out in the same week that Muhammad Ali fought Joe Frazier at Madison Square Garden for the heavyweight championship of the world. Ali had been stripped of his title because of his refusal to fight in Vietnam. This was his way back. It was billed as the Fight of the Century, and it lived up to that billing. It went to fifteen rounds. Frazier had Ali on his backside and eventually won on points. The only way Frank Sinatra could get a ringside seat was by serving as the accredited photographer of *Life* magazine.

Bryter Layter came out in the same week that three off-duty Scottish soldiers, one of them only just seventeen, were lured away from a pub in Belfast city center to a field on the outskirts of the city and shot in the back of the head by a Provisional IRA death squad. It was said that girls had done the luring, which made everyone shudder. The papers started to use the word "honeytrap" with a new familiarity. The soldiers' deaths indicated that the British army's presence in Northern Ireland, which had begun as a police operation to protect besieged Catholics, could turn out to be more difficult to end than it had been to begin.

It came out the same week Michael Caine's film *Get Carter* opened. Here he played a London gangster traveling to Newcastle to find out who killed his brother and mete out brutal treatment to anyone who got in his way, whether male or female. Things were grim whichever way you looked, and in such a climate a record as pallid and lyrical as *Bryter Layter* was blown away in a gust of grit.

This was not helped by Drake's reticence. Among the sons and daughters of the upper class, arrogance often masquerades as shyness. A further problem was that Drake wouldn't take any of the simple steps that are generally associated with achieving popularity. The curious contradiction of the singer-songwriter's trade is that while the music has to hint at a soul that does not easily yield its secrets, it needs to be accompanied by an iron-clad confidence that enables the artist to get up in a crowded room and demand the attention. It's a quality that peers Bob Dylan, Richard Thompson, John Martyn, and Joni Mitchell had, and Drake, in spite of his privileged upbringing, didn't.

His few efforts to play live onstage resulted in performances that didn't project much farther than the lip of the stage. During one show, he left halfway through a song. This was either the understandable retreat of a soul too sensitive to live or the gross dereliction of duty of a person who has set himself up as an entertainer. As Joe Boyd said years later, dismissing the idea that all the Hollywood interest in Nick Drake might ever result in a biographical film about him, "Nick didn't have a very interesting life. He spent most of his time alone in his room, smoking a joint."

Drake was an upper-class hippie. The members of Led Zeppelin may have had similarly long, apparently unkempt hair, and they may have had a lot of the same interests in arcane music, mysticism, and travel to the third world, but their approach to their music and the selling thereof could not have been more different. Whereas Drake believed that success was his due, the members of Led Zeppelin knew that it had to be fought for. Thanks to their manager, they were one of the first groups put together in order to achieve massive success and to make a great deal of money. Precisely how massive the success and how much money that would mean, they had very little idea.

If Nick Drake wouldn't stir from his room, there were many people who would. P. G. Wodehouse's advice to aspiring writers is "first apply the seat of the trousers to the surface of the chair." In 1971 a new generation of rock musicians were beginning to realize that if they wished to make their name and their fortune, they had to adopt the same kind of work ethic. There was a feeling that this could be a perfect time to do so. While the former members of the Beatles were arguing in court or plotting their own solo records, the Rolling Stones were trying to get themselves organized for relaunch, and Bob Dylan was moving back to New York and thinking about what to do next, their established positions in the hierarchy were being usurped by a band that was appealing to a generation that was too young to be wholly under the spell of those sixties acts. This band was reaching these people by going out and playing for them.

On March 5, 1971, on the same night that the Rolling Stones played two shows at the Free Trade Hall in Manchester and Aretha Franklin recorded in front of the love crowd at San Francisco's Fillmore, Led Zeppelin began their 1971 tour at the citadel of unionism, the Ulster Hall in Belfast. They were still putting the finishing touches to their new album, which wouldn't come out until the winter. The problems of Northern Ireland hadn't yet hardened into "the Troubles" and it was still just about possible for visiting bands to appear there. This wouldn't be the case for the next forty years.

This March tour entered the burgeoning lore of the band known familiarly to its young, hairy fan base as Zep as the Back to the Clubs tour. Announcing the plan to the *Record Mirror*, guitarist and group leader Jimmy Page explained, "The audiences were becoming bigger and bigger but moving further and further away." He said this tour was an attempt to say thank-you to the clubs that had helped the band in its early days and to enable them to play in cities that didn't have large venues. Tickets and fees would be pegged at the level they would have been in the past. Thus the tour took Led Zeppelin, who were at the time the biggest-grossing, most popular band in the world, to such venues as the Nottingham Boat Club, Newcastle's Mayfair Ballroom, and the Belfry in Sutton Coldfield.

Although it resulted in small venues being swamped by the demand and made no financial sense, the Back to the Clubs tour was interesting because it seemed to be trying to make amends for injuries the British audience had yet to sustain. Only the band knew what was coming down the road. Led Zeppelin had glimpsed the scale of the demand for their live shows in the United States in the previous year, and they knew that when they went there later in 1971 they would be playing for crowds five times the size of the biggest crowd in Britain. The Back to the Clubs tour was doubly curious because the club days that they were planning to get back to had been a mere three years earlier, in 1968. Since then they had released three albums, which had sold massively (although the third one had not done as well as the previous two), but even then the largest venue they had played in Britain, apart from the odd festival, was the Albert Hall. This was considered the largest venue any band could reasonably expect a British audience to tolerate. It seated around four thousand people. When Page talked about the audience appearing to be just specks on the horizon, he was clearly thinking about some of the venues in the United States, where Led Zeppelin were starting to play arenas.

Meanwhile back in the Ulster Hall, which had a capacity of less than two thousand, the *Melody Maker*'s Chris Welch reported that the MC who was working on behalf of the hall still addressed the audience as "boys and girls" and was asking them to leave when the band came back for an encore. This wasn't unusual. Nobody had yet worked out how they were supposed to behave at a big rock concert. Tickets were just over a dollar, less than a pound. Chris Welch, who had flown out to cover this big moment, spoke to one young fan who had previously thought Led Zeppelin were American and had laid eyes on them only once before in one picture she had on her wall. He also noted that among the new songs that the band played that night was one called "Stairway to Heaven." Because this was the *Melody Maker*, he felt duty-bound to tell his readers that on this tune Jimmy played his twin-necked guitar, giving him a six- and a twelve-string sound on the same instrument. "An excellent ballad, it displayed Robert's developing lyricism," he added, approvingly.

Recalling that night many years later, bassist John Paul Jones said that during "Stairway to Heaven" the audience were bored to tears waiting for something they knew. It certainly took a while for the song to be greeted with any apparent enthusiasm. At first it was received by audiences with polite puzzlement, its early passages seeming to belong on their previous record *Led Zeppelin III*. Nobody at the time suggested it owed anything to "Taurus," from the American band Spirit. After a while it started to get more reaction, and Peter Grant, doing what great managers always do, which is watch the audience during the show, realized that it was hitting home and therefore made one of the very few artistic suggestions he ever made to the band: When the song is finished and the last chords have died away, don't immediately start tuning up for the next one. Don't go out of character. Hold the moment. Milk the drama. Maintain the mood. Grant had spent some time as a wrestler. He knew about hokum, which at the time very few rock bands did.

In 1971 Peter Grant was thirty-six, more than ten years older than the youngest members of Led Zeppelin. Like many of the managers and fixers who were beginning to come to the fore in this new music business, he was a member of an older generation. Born in the 1930s, he'd known hardship that his band hadn't, which made him more inclined to value whatever success they were having. Grant was always happy to have people find out that he was a former professional wrestler, knowing that if you have a reputation for violence, it often saves you the trouble of resorting to it. In later years the band's preposterous success and his immersion in cocaine led him to behave in a way that he had previously only threatened to; in the early days he was as important a member of the band as any of the people who played the instruments. Like the besotted parent of a gifted child, he was dedicated to implementing the vision of his favorite member, Jimmy Page. The mere fact that Led Zeppelin had such a vision marked them out from all the bands that had come before them and meant that their legacy was, if anything, greater. The biggest bands usually have an influence that is anything but beneficial. The Beatles made bands think they had to write their own songs. The Stones made bands think they had to be rebellious. Led Zeppelin made bands think they had to be loud.

Grant's original business partner was Mickie Most, who managed and produced the Jeff Beck Group, the band that established the template for the four-piece group with lead singer, in many people's eyes the perfect division of rock labor and since emulated by U2, REM, the Killers, and hundreds more. But whereas Beck simply didn't have the patience for the long march, walking out on his own group in the middle of a US tour, Page had a little bit of money saved up, and in Grant he had someone who was prepared to go to the big record companies and demand an advance. Page and Jones banked their three-thousand-pound share of it. (It was almost two years' salary for the average British worker at the time.) Like many musicians, Plant had to think about sheltering the girlfriend he'd hurriedly married when she became pregnant, and he used his money to make a deposit on a house. John Bonham went out and bought a sports car, which was a clear indication of how he planned to deal with success.

When Led Zeppelin played the University of Kent in Canterbury on March 12, tickets were sixty pence (twelve shillings for those who hadn't yet adjusted to decimal), and they were sold out immediately to the people who queued up outside Eliot College on the appointed day. A few of them, reported the student paper, had actually been there since the night before. Although they had inherited the mantle of the Yardbirds, Led Zeppelin's success was built on a new generation of fans who had been born just slightly too late to experience the midsixties as teenagers and had come through their adolescence to the sound of Jimi Hendrix and Cream. This meant they were wired in a slightly different way and were inclined to regard rock as something that needed to be measured rather than enjoyed. Unlike Led Zeppelin's American fans, who were already inclined to whoop, the disciples in their home country thought that the best tribute they could pay to a group was to appreciate them, and they believed that this was something best done in silence and, given the restrictions of sight lines, from a cross-legged position.

The report in the student paper of that Canterbury show, which Zeppelin performed atop the kind of platform that might have been better suited to a cookery demonstration, suggests a certain awkwardness from both band and audience. During "Moby Dick," Plant had to actually chide the audience into standing up. This was on the eve of the release of their fourth album, the one that was to put them in a commercial category that neither the Beatles nor the Stones ever reached, and yet still their shows had more in common with classical recitals than pagan rites. At the end of the Back to the Clubs tour, they played at the Paris Theatre in Lower Regent Street for a John Peel recording. The Paris was a four-hundred-capacity seated venue where the BBC recorded many of its comedy programs. John Peel, who would in due course come to deny Led Zeppelin thrice, introduced them nervously, and the crowd received them as though they were a mayoral party come to open a fete. Even young, long-haired people tended to be restrained in public places in 1971, and people were easily intimidated by the sheer majesty of the BBC. When the band played "Rock and Roll"—a song that had been inspired during a recording session when Bonham started playing Earl Palmer's intro from Little Richard's 1957 hit "Keep A-Knockin' "—they were clearly summoning up the primal throb of the so-called jungle music that had shocked fifties America. Nonetheless the performance was received as if the quartet were tackling Beethoven's late quartets.

What impressed Led Zeppelin's audience, who were now at university and therefore even further advanced in their wrongheadedness than before, was that this music appeared difficult to play. That's why they were more inclined to appreciate the passages during which Page bowed his guitar on "Dazed and Confused," the periods of relief from the groove rather than the groove itself. Nobody at the time suspected that it was the groove that made Led Zeppelin remarkable. That certainly accounts for how sampled they are more than forty years later. It's the groove that escaped most of the hundreds of bands who set out to follow in their footsteps, in the mistaken belief that volume was the end rather than the means. Then there was the breadth of their musical hinterland. Led Zeppelin created their music from a diet of Bert Jansch, Memphis Minnie, John Fahey, Billy Fury, Phil Spector, Richard "Rabbit" Brown, Moby Grape, Manitas de Plata, and Om Kalsoum. Those who came afterward were content with a diet of Led Zeppelin, which is not the same thing at all.

Most sixties groups didn't tour as we would understand it today. Instead they played regularly, recording during the week and going out at weekends to play gigs that were within driving distance to make money. Led Zeppelin would change all that. Ever since they formed in 1968 around session guitarist Jimmy Page, Led Zeppelin had toured with a steely determination. In fact, they didn't appear to tour so much as campaign. Like politicians running for office, they appeared to have an objective in view. They were perfectly equipped for this, because they were built around Page and John Paul Jones, two musicians who had been around the music business long enough to realize that the people who made the money were the ones with the songwriting credits. They were formed at the behest of Peter Grant, a manager from an earlier generation who had learned that there was far more money to be made than promoters and agents would readily admit, because much of it would have to be gained at the direct expense of promoters and agents.

Grant, together with their American agent, Frank Barsalona, was reinventing the concert business in 1971. They started with the financials. The old promoters had paid a fee for a band's services and made their money out of the difference between that fee and the amount they could make from tickets. People like Bill Graham, who was famous for running the prestige hippie showcases the Fillmore in San Francisco and New York, became rich because he had a brand, and even the biggest bands, including Led Zeppelin, would play his venue for a flat fee.

Frank Barsalona put a stop to all that, which is one of the reasons Graham closed both Fillmores in 1971. He was tired of dealing with the agent's demands for more money and the musicians' demands for special treatment. In 1971 Barsalona was in his early thirties and dressed like an old-fashioned show business agent. He ran an agency called Premier Talent, which represented Led Zeppelin and the Who, loud bands with strong live reputations. Premier Talent was the first agency to specialize in representing rock acts, rather than renting them out alongside jugglers and light comedians. From this position of strength, Barsalona was able to flip the model, as Silicon Valley would subsequently say. Instead of letting the promoter dictate to the band how much of the ticket money they could have, he told the promoter how much of the band's money the promoter would be permitted. He knew Led Zeppelin didn't need any actual promoting, that they would sell out on the growing strength of their name, and therefore the promoters should consider themselves fortunate to be invited to have the honor of hiring a hall for them and providing them with fresh towels. What Barsalona and Grant realized was that live performance was no longer the music business's disreputable rodeo clown, as it had been in the days of package tours. It was now a massive business on its own. For acts like the Who and Led Zeppelin, the concert business was far more important than the record business.

Barsalona was starting to develop acts that could sell their presence even if they couldn't move product. In 1970 he signed two acts, one from London and the other from Boston, Massachusetts, that would prove his point. The first was Humble Pie, a band fronted by Steve Marriott and Peter Frampton, two refugees from teen pop groups whose whiskery prettiness seemed to suit the 1971 taste for fallen angels; the second was the J. Geils Band, an act from Boston that purveyed Chicago blues with the expeditious razzle-dazzle of a soul revue. With the best will in the world, neither of these groups had an original musical idea to their names, and they couldn't write songs to save their lives, but wherever they played they could be relied upon to tear it up.

Premier Talent was also the agent for Grand Funk Railroad, a young three-piece from Flint, Michigan, that openly advertised themselves as "heavy rock." Grand Funk were put together by an older hustler named Terry Knight, who could see that there was a market for music that was above all loud, particularly if it was purveyed by a bare-chested high school Adonis such as Mark Farner. In July 1971 Grand Funk sold out Shea Stadium and got a lot of coverage. This was the first time since the Beatles that a musical act had managed to do that. In the same week they played a free show in Hyde Park in London. At both concerts they were supported by Humble Pie. Whereas Led Zeppelin's chosen path had been to let their deeds speak for them, Knight believed that the media would take a band at its own estimation, so he talked Grand Funk Railroad up relentlessly. This got under the skins of a number of people, from critics at *Rolling Stone* magazine to bands like Led Zeppelin, who feared that fans couldn't discriminate between their rich textures and Grand Funk's callow riffing. When Jimmy Page spoke disparagingly in interviews about "other bands" that were not like Led Zeppelin, he was talking about Grand Funk. It's not surprising that he felt this way. Grand Funk were almost entirely without merit musically but were far advanced in showmanship. One of the highlights of their act was when the drummer Don Brewer played his kit with his head. This seemed an eloquent testimonial to the group's approach to life.

Both Humble Pie and the J. Geils Band were managed by Dee Anthony, a pugnacious character built along the lines of Benny the Ball from *Top Cat*, often to be glimpsed at the side of the stage at their shows. Like Peter Grant, Anthony was a carpetbagger when it came to rock. He was born in the 1920s and had worked with nightclub singers Jerry Vale and Tony Bennett. There was nothing peace and love about Dee Anthony. Dee had three mottos: get the money, don't forget to always get the money, and remember to not forget to always get the money.

Anthony also brought with him something that too many rock bands, then and now, prefer to think is optional: a stress on showmanship. It was Anthony who told the J. Geils Band that they should never ever go onstage without being introduced first. It was Anthony who instructed Humble Pie on how to move in front of an audience and ensured that their set was put together on the basis of its ability to please a crowd rather than the need to play a string of songs from the new album. It was Anthony who told the J. Geils Band's Peter Wolf to go out to the lip of the stage because, he argued, it worked for Al Jolson. This is something that's just basic professional practice in most areas of show business, but many rock-and-roll bands hadn't yet come to terms with the fact that they were in show business. Old soldiers like Dee Anthony never for a moment doubted it, and he knew that the bigger the venues, the greater the need to project, the bigger the gestures had to be, and the more the showmanship would matter.

Both Anthony's bands started out trying to make it on their original compositions. Both eventually gave in to Anthony's argument that they had to record live in order to bottle what it was that people liked about them. In April 1971 Humble Pie went into the Fillmore in New York and recorded a set that became almost as famous for its overplayed Cockney introductions ("We go 'ome on Monday, but it's been a gas this time") as for their crunching assaults on warhorses like "I Don't Need No Doctor." The album *Performance: Rockin' the Fillmore* was the making of them. It sustained their career for the next few years, providing them with a template as unchanging as the Harlem Globetrotters or the Glenn Miller Orchestra. It didn't matter if individual members moved on. The brand was fixed. By the time the live record was mastered, Peter Frampton had left the band to go solo, but he didn't leave Anthony. Dee oversaw Frampton's solo career, eventually persuading him to record all his best-liked numbers in front of an audience and put it out as *Frampton Comes Alive!* in 1976. It sold eleven million copies. The live album, which had started life as the souvenir of the live concert, became the item that made you want to go to the concert in the first place in order to taste in person the experience it had so artfully synthesized.

There never was a great deal about the rock concert experience that was actually spontaneous. It was always learned behavior. Most of the learning was done by listening to live recordings, which poured forth in unprecedented profusion in 1971, and watching films like *Woodstock*. *Woodstock* the film was a greater watershed than Woodstock the event. For all the people who actually endured three days in the mud and chaos of that field in Bethel in 1969, the festival was the standard mixed bag. The people whose heads were really turned were the millions who had the experience mediated through the dazzling split screens and Martin Scorsese's edits of the film and drank it all in in the warm and dry of their local cinema. For this younger generation *Woodstock* was a gateway to a new entertainment experience, one in which they were keen to play their part.

In the previous decade there had been two kinds of audience: teenage girls who came to scream and serious young men who came to nod their heads approvingly and applaud respectfully. In 1971 the audience was growing dramatically and bursting those old categories. As the crowds got bigger, they had to behave differently. Eventually they had to behave like the sporting crowds who normally occupied the places the bands were beginning to play. They were no longer there just to watch. They were there to become part of the spectacle.

In the Who's *Live at Leeds*, which had been recorded a year earlier, the crowd is just a distant presence, as distant as the traffic outside, because nobody has bothered to point a microphone at them. It's not changed much when the Rolling Stones played Leeds in March 1971. The recording is a faithful account of what the band played and nothing more. In subsequent live recordings the audience become a character in the drama, and the venue becomes a space that vibrates with accumulated associations.

One English band who were starting to get a reputation for being able to tear up the dance halls was Free. Their *Free Live!* album was recorded in two locations in England, Sunderland and Croydon, in 1970 and 1971. The producer Andy Johns could rescue only two songs from the Sunderland shows, but he used the crowd noise from the traditionally more demonstrative northeastern audience throughout the album. What producers like Andy Johns were starting to realize was that the sound of the crowd was a key element in rendering an impression of the live music experience. It was a matter of communicating the excitement of the live show and if necessary exaggerating it. Emerson, Lake & Palmer's first album had been released at the end of 1970, but it was with the release at a bargain price of the March 26 recording of their *Pictures at an Exhibition* at Newcastle City Hall, which was also in the Northeast, that they broke through. Here the audience noise has been promoted in the mix, to ensure that everybody gets the message that gigs are above all about excitement and the joy of abandon. Similarly, Crosby, Stills, Nash & Young's 1971 live album *4 Way Street* was designed as a sound experience, from the way it began with a song just coming to its end, to Graham Nash's introduction of Neil Young, to the pregnant silence that accompanies Young's intro to "Cowgirl in the Sand" and the explosion that greets the first line.

The album is short on music but long on drama. It's a band's rather inflated view of itself, made even grander by the audience's willingness to participate in the illusion. In March 1971 Richard Williams wrote about a Neil Young concert at London's Festival Hall. It was a favorable review, but he couldn't help taking issue with the way the audience still demanded encores long after Young had given his all. "They seemed more concerned with applauding themselves than acclaiming the musicians," he wrote. At the time few would have known what he was talking about. We do now.

The new generation of managers, agents, promoters, and fixers were bulkier, balder, and more brusque than the softly spoken PR men who had managed big acts in the sixties. They came from earlier generations and could remember World War II. There wasn't a hippie among them. The promoter Bill Graham's mother died in Auschwitz, Dee Anthony had been in submarines, and Peter Grant had been a wartime evacuee from London. Tom Dowd, who played a crucial role in the defining live album of 1971, was a cut above: he had worked on the project that perfected the first atomic bomb.

Dowd was the best recording engineer in the world. He'd been doing it for a long time. He had started off working on Eileen Barton's 1950 hit "If I Knew You Were Comin' I'd've Baked a Cake." He was the man who conjured the magic of Atlantic Records' sixties sides from studios improvised in offices or in radio stations. Born in 1925, Dowd was the epitome of old school. Nonetheless he had great admiration for the musicianship of lots of the hairy rock players that Atlantic increasingly paired him with. He had produced Eric Clapton's "Layla," which was beginning to climb the charts in an edited single version in 1971. He had recorded one album with the Allman Brothers Band, the southern group who were fast gaining a reputation as one of America's premier live bands.

On March 12 Dowd arrived at Kennedy Airport on the last leg of a long flight. A couple of days earlier he had been in Accra, Ghana, recording the live performances of Wilson Pickett and the Staple Singers, who had flown there as part of the "Soul to Soul" concert project, the first attempt to take contemporary African American music back to Africa. He had intended to have a few days relaxing in Europe but was disturbed by the fact that it was snowing, so he decided to go home. Arriving in New York, he called the Atlantic office and was told that the Allman Brothers were due to begin a three-night stint at the New York Fillmore in a few hours.

Dowd immediately took a cab down to the venue in time to catch the first shows from the recording truck. He was horrified to discover that the Allmans had decided to bring along an under-rehearsed horn section for such a date-with-vinyl destiny. After the Thursday shows, he went backstage, got the band together, and gave them the kind of dressing down that they would have accepted only from this gray-bearded father figure. "I was pissed," he recalled later, "and I gave them hell." Specifically, he instructed them to "get those horns out of my life. They are out of tune, and they don't know the songs."

Amazingly, the Allmans did as Dowd told them. They respected his genius for listening and his ability to get on with musicians. The group's Dicky Betts recalls that when Dowd started working with them in 1970 he would address them as if they were a 1940s big band. He called them "cats." He applauded their ability to solo and to play in mathematically demanding time signatures; he also admired the way they could sweetly return to the main theme. Their performances had ample room for improvisation, but it was always within the context of an arrangement, and that arrangement always served the tune. In that sense they were very much like a big band. Dowd recognized what neither the band, their fans, nor the legions of imitators that the band inspired recognized; the Allman Brothers Band swung.

The nights from Thursday, March 11, to Saturday, March 13, were billed as "an evening featuring Johnny Winter And [the name of the Texan guitarist's hard rock quartet] plus the Elvin Bishop Group" with the Allman Brothers Band as an "Extra Added Attraction." In 1971 people were relaxed about questions of billing, particularly at a Bill Graham show, which bands were generally invited to play by the promoter rather than being booked by the agent. The Allman Brothers were on last, starting their final Saturday show at two thirty in the morning and leaving the venue in time to mingle with early Sunday morning churchgoers.

The other brusque older man watching over the Allmans that night was Bill Graham, who was forty at the time. He was a German-born refugee from Nazism who had come up through the theater scene. Graham wasn't a rock-and-roll person. One of the things he tried to do was to expand the horizons of the people who came into his theaters, presenting Roland Kirk to the fans of Santana and putting Woody Herman on before Delaney & Bonnie and Led Zeppelin. Graham was a controversial figure. His standard card was to present himself as the hapless victim of selfish fans, arrogant musicians, and greedy managers and agents. He was an impresario, an egomaniac, and a snob, but he was all for trying things, and this seemed the ideal time to do just that. As he told me in the '80s, "What you have to remember about that time is we were out there with no compass." Graham came onstage himself to introduce the Allman Brothers Band's last performance. He said that they were one of the greatest bands the Fillmore had ever hosted, that what the people were going to hear was "the finest in contemporary music," a turn of phrase that was no doubt picked up on by some of the San Francisco bands Graham had come up promoting, the bands who fancied themselves as being the last word in looseness and improvisation. It seemed to him that the Allmans were on a different level. He was right.

The music the Allman Brothers played that weekend, the music that, thanks to Tom Dowd, is preserved on *At Fillmore East*, redefined what was possible on a rock stage. It was perfectly suited for the size of the venue. Like so many of the best halls for rock and roll, the Fillmore was anything but purpose built. It had started life as a Yiddish theater and seated two and a half thousand people, which would in today's terms make it ideal for an atmospheric showcase. What came out of that weekend turned the band into one of the biggest concert draws in the United States. It was musically extraordinary. From the insouciant "Statesboro Blues" through the jazz-flecked instrumental "In Memory of Elizabeth Reed" to the impassioned "Whipping Post," the two guitarists and two drummers of the Allmans played like a large truck that had found a way to handle like a Ferrari, in the process rendering all comparable attempts to record the rock jam as ragged and clumsy. The album was such a touchstone that even the strangled shout for "Whipping Post" that rose from the audience during a gap between songs was widely copied by wiseacres in the audiences at other bands' concerts. It happened so often through the rest of the decade that Frank Zappa eventually learned a version of "Whipping Post" and made it a part of his show.

At the beginning of that weekend in March 1971, the idea of rock improvisation was still somewhat unproven. By Monday it was arguably all over. Within six months, Duane Allman was dead in a motorcycle accident. He'd already played with the world's finest musicians, put his name on some of the signature records of the age, been widely acclaimed for the soulfulness and uncanny maturity of his playing, and on the weekend of March 13 had taken his band to the mountaintop and recorded there. He was twenty-four.

On the same weekend that the Allmans played the Fillmore, the Rolling Stones were appearing at the Roundhouse in London for the last night of their pre–tax exile tour, Led Zeppelin had moved on to play the Bath Pavilion, the more adventurous British record shops were taking delivery of their copies of the Velvet Underground's *Loaded*, David Crosby's *If I Could Only Remember My Name*, and John Lennon's "Power to the People," James Taylor and Carole King were playing Madison Square Garden, the *Doctor Who* episode was "The Claws of Axos" (starring Jon Pertwee), Elaine May's comic masterpiece *A New Leaf* was on release in US cinemas, and a venue called the Museum on Broadway was advertising a "Punk Mass at Midnight" featuring the avant-garde duo Suicide. War was brewing in East Pakistan, a region that the world, particularly the long-haired, music-loving bit of it, was soon to know by a different name. Bangladesh.

MARCH

Nick Drake: "Poor Boy"

Led Zeppelin: "Black Dog"

J. Geils Band: "Whammer Jammer"

Humble Pie: "I Don't Need No Doctor"

Allman Brothers Band: "Statesboro Blues"

Jethro Tull: "Aqualung"

Nancy Sinatra: "Hook and Ladder"

Judy Collins: "Amazing Grace"

Johnny Winter: "Rock and Roll, Hoochie Koo"

Freddie King: "Going Down"

4 APRIL

Inner City Blues

I n 1971 Berry Gordy Jr., the boss of Motown, was forty-two. He was the third man to bear that name and had already passed on the same one to his son. Berry ran his record company like a traditional family enterprise. It was founded in 1960 with a loan from his father. Two of his sisters were involved in the company in senior positions. He liked to think that the artists on his Motown label owed him the same fealty that he expected from family members. Wherever possible, he sought to secure those professional ties through marriage. His artist development specialist Harvey Fuqua married his sister Gwen Gordy. Marvin Gaye, the handsomest and most eligible artist on his label, married his sister Anna.

The latter was not the most obvious match. Anna was seventeen years older than her husband when they got married in 1963. Three years later, finding herself unable to conceive, she faked a pregnancy, at the culmination of which she produced Marvin III. Although nobody knew this at the time, the child had actually been born to Denise Gordy, a seventeen-year-old niece of Berry's. In later years Marvin confessed this to his biographer David Ritz, but it wasn't until Steve Turner's posthumous biography *Trouble Man* that the further assertion was made that he was also the father. Whatever the truth, life in the Gaye-Gordy clan required Shakespearean levels of duplicity. Gordy, the dapper, compact former amateur boxing champion, liked to feel he controlled everyone around him. When the success of his label meant he could move to Detroit's millionaire's row, he bequeathed his old house to Anna and Marvin. This was a reminder for the singer of where he stood in the value chain of Motown, a company that prided itself on being as much about process as those other great businesses that gave the Motor City its nickname.

All families have a secret. The secret is they're not like other families. This was even more the case in the family firm Motown. In April 1971 Gordy's personal favorite performer and Motown's biggest star, Diana Ross, was expecting her first child. The press naturally assumed the father must be Robert Silberstein, a presentable young white recording executive she had first met when she went into a men's fashion shop in Los Angeles to buy a gift for Berry. Ross and Silberstein had married in January 1971. "What you see is what she got!" announced one magazine aimed at black readers, the implication being that any black woman marrying a white man was clearly moving up in the world. The wedding in Las Vegas came as a surprise to everybody at Motown because as far as they knew the couple had never been associated before. Furthermore, some people in the company's inner circle also knew Diana and Berry had been sleeping together.

The marriage to Silberstein was accomplished so swiftly it even came as a surprise to the groom. Neither Berry Gordy nor the bride's mother knew about the wedding until the day after. Just two weeks later Diana, by then fully occupied in rehearsals for the ABC TV special that seemed the inevitable next step in her elevation into the pantheon of light entertainment, announced she was pregnant. Berry did his calculations and concluded the baby had to be his. He dealt with the shock by decamping on a short holiday in the sun with Chris Clark, the six-foot-tall California blonde he would repeatedly and unsuccessfully try to launch as America's Dusty Springfield. There was nothing Berry did that didn't have at least some element of social climbing about it.

Although it had been only seven years since the high noon of Motown's fame, in 1971 the stars of the company increasingly lived the kind of lives that previously existed only in the feverish imaginings of airport novelists. But then, as Cyndi Lauper was to observe many years later, money changes everything. Some even said, and some even believed, that mob money had always been behind Motown, and Gordy was being slowly eased out. Certainly, a greater proportion of the company's senior executives were now white than they had been five years earlier. What's also certain is that now that he had made his fortune Berry preferred to spend his time in climes warmer and more congenial than Detroit, a city where the signs of urban blight were apparent even to the people who remained on the wealthier side of town.

When Berry Gordy was born in 1929, Detroit was the fastest-growing city on earth. There were only thirty-two million cars in the world at the time, and 90 percent of them had been made in the United States, most of those in Detroit. Although he was later to claim that he had modeled his label on the production-line methods of the big three automobile manufacturers, Gordy was far too polished an individual to personally submit to life in the plant. Many of the people, black as well as white, who migrated from the southern states to work in those plants in the period between World War I and II came because it was one of the few places where lack of a formal education wouldn't be a handicap. The work certainly paid far more than a man could make on the land. Tens of thousands came north and duly prospered, notably during the war years, when the plants were turned over to making the machines with which the Allies would liberate Europe.

Berry Gordy's first hit record, "Money (That's What I Want)" by Barrett Strong, was released in 1959. The song was the most sincere and succinct mission statement made by a record label boss before or since. Motown was social mobility set to music. In the '60s Gordy's label put out some of the most aspirational pop music ever made. In sound and deed, through the cut of their cloth and the swish of their arm movements, the likes of the Four Tops, the Supremes, the Temptations, and Smokey Robinson and the Miracles may have been making "the sound of Young America" for the kids, but in Gordy's mind they were also looking to move uptown, to sashay their way into the supper club circuit, to overcome the de facto apartheid of American TV, and to stand toe to patent leather toe with the Sinatras and Streisands of the world.

This social climbing often meant Berry was badly out of step. His misfortune was to make it to the far side of the red rope in the year 1971, just as the glitterati decided the action was on the other side and began to dress in work wear. At the end of the sixties, when everyone else was growing their hair and carrying themselves in a countercultural way, Gordy was still showcasing his big acts via live albums recorded at Squaresville spots like the Copacabana in New York or the Talk of the Town in London, pressing them into musical shotgun marriages so that he could bill their new records as jazz-style summit meetings and obliging them to do tiresome Christmas albums. With all this in mind, and his growing passion for golf, Gordy was slowly moving his company to Los Angeles, which everyone but the artists and executives regarded as a betrayal.

Back in Detroit, the growing prosperity of the sixties had not proved to be the solvent of old racial divisions. In July 1967, at the climax of the summer of love, a raid by white police on an unlicensed Detroit bar patronized by blacks turned into a riot. This escalated so quickly that the governor called in the National Guard, and the president ordered in the army. Forty-three people, most of them black, were killed. It was the worst civil disturbance in the United States since the New York City draft riots during the Civil War. Few felt the same about Detroit after that. The population of the city, which had been 60 percent white, started to change as "white flight" to the suburbs was followed by a hollowing out of the inner city and a resulting growth in violence and crime.

By then, many of the Motown family had fallen by the wayside.

Liver problems forced Paul Williams to retire from the Temptations. Florence Ballard of the Supremes sued Motown over royalties and lost. Tammi Terrell, Marvin Gaye's dueting partner, was taken by a brain tumor. Among the living, there were jealousies. Anyone whose career didn't flourish would inevitably blame their plight on not enjoying the favor of Gordy, who was lavishing all his time and money on Diana. Even the Jackson 5, who were Motown's cash cow in 1971, had been presented to the public as Diana's discovery, when in truth she had nothing to do with finding them. On April 29 young Michael appeared on the cover of *Rolling Stone* with the line "Why does this eleven year old stay up past his bedtime?" Found in Gary, Indiana, the Jackson 5 did their recording in Los Angeles with the Corporation rather than the motor city's Funk Brothers. They weren't touched at all by the old machine, and even that old machine had a new master in the shape of Norman Whitfield, the producer who was behind such extended grooves as the Temptations' "Cloud Nine" and the Undisputed Truth's "Smiling Faces Sometimes," which were pointing the way that dance music would take in the '70s.

The acts that had made it at Motown were dealing with the financial consequences of success. The more artists earned from their hit singles, the more they stored up tax problems, and here they found the company's legendary paternalism didn't extend to helping out. Tax demands for the fat years inevitably arrived in the lean ones. For some of them at least, there were also problems with drink and drugs.

Thirty-two-year-old Marvin Gaye's career was certainly becalmed. The massive success of "I Heard It Through the Grapevine" in 1968 should have made him secure, but he couldn't claim to have authored it and resented the fact that he didn't have the kudos of a self-sustaining creative unit like Stevie Wonder or Smokey Robinson. He didn't like performing live and didn't care for the way he was positioned in Berry's firmament. He couldn't imagine himself in Vegas. Marvin Gaye was Berry's male sex symbol, and that's how Berry preferred him to remain. Consequently, he stayed at home, fought with Anna, who was known to occasionally set about him with the sharp end of a shoe, and got high. This last may explain why he also at this time entertained a delusion that he could make it as a professional athlete. Marvin was in reasonable condition—for an entertainer. Since this is far from the fitness level required of a professional athlete, the Detroit Lions, his team of choice, didn't even bother to give him a trial. Marvin made this decision easier for them since he had never played a game of football in his life. Throughout his life, much like Ronald Reagan, Marvin was apt to think that if he was photographed doing something, he could actually do it. Lover, golfer, thinker, athlete, sophisticate: if he could look the part, that was as good as actually fulfilling the role.

The album that Marvin Gaye released in 1971, *What's Going On*, has come to be seen as occupying a pivotal position in the story of pop music, to a certain extent because of the direction that music has taken in recent years. In some lists of all-time great albums, many of which are compiled by white rock critics with inevitable guilt complexes, it has been known to come out on top. Albums that figure in these lists generally have a backstory. The narrative behind *What's Going On* runs something like this: artist grows tired of obeying the suits at his record company, gets in touch with his inner feelings, and, moved by the plight of his brothers and sisters in the inner city, delivers searing personal statement, then fights the powers that be to get it released.

It wasn't quite as mythic as that. It rarely is. The song "What's Going On" began, like most things at Motown, with a wisp of melody rather than a big idea. That wisp occurred to Obie Benson, the bass singer in the Four Tops, who developed it with Motown songwriter Al Cleveland. Obie saw his song as a gentle exhortation to worldwide brotherhood, much like the Coke commercial "I'd Like to Teach the World to Sing," which came out in the same year, and claimed that he tried to plug it to Joan Baez during one appearance on *Top of the Pops*. Benson and Cleveland developed the idea over a few weeks and thought it might suit Marvin, the Motown artist who had a talent for the soft, jazzy style the song seemed to demand. They sang it to him. He wasn't impressed. They pressed him further for over a month without apparent success. Reluctant, as most artists are, to be caught following someone else's lead, Marvin eventually made some tweaks of his own and was apparently thinking of giving it to the Originals, a group he had been producing. Gaye was never brilliant at making up his mind and perhaps suspected, with some justification, that Berry would not want to see his label's great lover waving a placard.

Eventually, he went into the studio, in July 1970, to produce himself singing it. Here his lack of experience as a producer paid dividends. He brought a few football buddies in to make the party noises at the beginning. He was indebted to the saxophone player Eli Fontaine for improvising the opening solo while warming up over the track. Having thus invented one of the most distinctive intros of the era, Fontaine was sent home. The story goes that Gaye got bassist James Jamerson—by then so advanced in the drinking that would eventually kill him that he carried a bottle of Metaxa at all times— out of a bar and let him play the bass line while lying on the floor. The story, which has attached itself to the myth of "What's Going On," is denied by people who were there. Certainly the double-tracked vocal came about by accident when Gaye happened to hear both during a playback and decided he liked the effect. Like Paul McCartney and other artists suddenly enjoying the luxury of not having anyone to argue with in the studio, he preferred to turn yesterday's mistakes, the false starts and sounds stumbled upon, the smudges at the edge of the canvas, into today's marks of unique authorship.

There was still no certainty that the record would ever come out. At Motown, singles were supposed to pass a quality control panel before they were deemed worthy of release. The single of "What's Going On" eventually emerged in January 1971 and was a hit before the West Coast–based Berry Gordy could object. When asked about it, he loudly proclaimed that it was a disaster for Gaye and the label. He thought its jazzy feeling, "that Dizzy Gillespie shit," as he called it, was dangerously retrograde, and he was quoted as saying it was "the worst piece of crap I ever heard." He also worried that the record's sentiments would prevent it from getting on the radio. Conversations that Marvin had with his brother Frankie about the latter's experiences in Vietnam were as near as the singer had gotten to the nightmare being undergone by thousands of his contemporaries. Marvin's complaints about how much the government was spending on arms were indirectly connected to his reluctance to pay the back taxes he owed. However, radio took to "What's Going On" immediately, and within a week it sold a hundred thousand copies. As soon as the single was number one on the soul charts and number two in pop, the mogul in Berry Gordy took over. He forgot his previous objections and immediately demanded to know why they had no album to follow it with.

The accompanying album was recorded hurriedly in March and released in May. It was mixed once in Detroit in early April and then remixed by Marvin in Los Angeles. Considering that mixing had previously been a job thought too important to be left to the artists, this was a very bold thing to do. Gaye's Los Angeles mix, which is the one that came out in May, was like an ink wash version of the Detroit version. It reduced the crisp separation of the Motown sound and replaced it with the shimmer that became its winning characteristic. Here he worked with the engineer Larry Miles, who is quoted in Ben Edmonds's book *What's Going On: Marvin Gaye and the Last Days of the Motown Sound* as saying that "Marvin wanted to keep the rhythm going throughout like the heartbeat of a late night party." In that sense, it belonged in the tradition of Marvin Gaye, an artist more at home in the boudoir than at the barricades.

In the UK—where EMI packaged it as shoddily as it did most albums by black artists, and fans were looking for the kind of singles that filled dance floors and not much else—it passed without any great fanfare. In America, it changed people's expectations of a Motown album, which at the time rarely amounted to much more than a couple of recent hit singles, something by the Beatles, and a standard for the Vegas crowd. Even though Berry Gordy hadn't noticed, things had moved on. People were starting to expect long-playing records to be more than the sum of their parts. Critics were desperate to see them as statements, record companies were eager to position them as luxury items, and artists started to see each one as their bid for some sort of immortality.

The establishment critics were so keen to hail a long-form record by a black pop artist that they either went overboard with their hosannas for *What's Going On* or were so busy acclaiming it for having its heart in the right place that they missed the qualities that made it popular. Some writers in the broadsheets compared Gaye to Ellington. If so, it was the rather stiff, sanctimonious Ellington who was always trying to get into the concert hall rather than Ellington the genius of the dance hall.

No white artist would have dared serve up anything quite as stagy as a track like "Save the Children." Had they done so, they would have been ripped apart for their pains, probably by the same critics who hailed Gaye's song, as his official biographer and collaborator David Ritz later did, as "a socioreligious work of astounding originality." Vince Aletti, the man *Rolling Stone* used to call when the magazine wanted to cover soul, broadly approved, but even he said that the lyrics were "hardly brilliant" and pointed out that its continuity of mood, which was itself quite unusual, was in danger of being boring.

The myths around *What's Going On* cloud the truth, which is more interesting. The idea that it was an expression of what Marvin felt about the drift of American society masks the contribution of many people around him who were closer to that society. These people ranged from Obie Benson to James Nyx, the elderly lift operator in one of Motown's office buildings who contributed the title to "Inner City Blues." Because 1971 is seen as the moment when Gaye emerged from the factory years to the period of heroic individuality, it's forgotten how much he owed to the anonymous professionals like David Van De Pitte, who turned his stabbed piano notes into arrangements, and the players like Eli Fontaine, whose delicate touches are what keep the record alive fifty years on. *What's Going On* may not be a product of the Motown factory system, but it owed a huge amount to the people who labored there often in complete anonymity. There is nothing on it that Gaye could have done alone. Equally, there is nothing on it that would have been even half as special without him.

Ultimately, *What's Going On* is a beneficiary of the halo effect provided by a great opener and in "Inner City Blues" an even stronger closer. What nobody can refute is its influence. It made Marvin Gaye a force even for those white rock fans who tended to dismiss anyone who they patronizingly labeled as "singles artists," and it set him up for a golden period, which he was too fragile to take full advantage of. It was like a jazz record not merely because it had jazz manners and was slathered in strings and employed congas and triangle as its most prominent form of percussion. Gaye, a drummer by trade, was determined that the record would not have Motown drums, which was a major departure. But it's also jazz in the sense that nobody would put it on to listen to just one track. It plays like one long single. Although, like the overwhelming majority of records made at that time, it was done without benefit of automated percussion, it also anticipated a lot of contemporary music, where the sustaining of a mood is prized above all things. It originated a vibe, suspended somewhere between sensuality and foreboding, which is the room temperature of so much music made in the twenty-first century. It's for that vibe—the way its message dropped on the ear, rather than the message itself—that it's remembered. The ghostly samba of the music and the pained majesty of his voice live on, almost fifty years later.

Those looking for musicians who act out the promise of their songs in their own lives are usually disappointed. Marvin Gaye was more conflicted than most when it came to this. He preferred the lush life. He couldn't even bring himself to dress funky for the cover of *What's Going On*, looking instead like a man who had been caught in a sudden downpour while waiting for his limousine. His concern for the decaying inner city and its problems didn't keep him in Detroit. Within a year of making *What's Going On*, he was living in Hollywood and had left his wife, who was seventeen years older than him, for a girl who was seventeen years younger. The first thing he did after *What's Going On* was a violent grindhouse film called *Chrome and Hot Leather*. Such a move was every bit as much Marvin Gaye as *What's Going On*.

At the same time as *What's Going On* was enjoying its reign at number one, another Motown superstar, ten years younger than Marvin, left Detroit and relocated to New York with his new wife, Syreeta Wright. Stevie Wonder could finally afford this move because he was turning twenty-one in May 1971, and this meant he finally came into the large sum of money that Motown had been holding in trust for him. At the same time he was in a position to negotiate a new deal with the company that had been in charge of his life since he was ten years old. He threw a party in Detroit to celebrate his coming-of-age. Berry Gordy was a guest. Stevie didn't give him any inkling of what was coming. When Gordy returned to Los Angeles, he was faced with a letter from Wonder's attorney disavowing his Motown contract and announcing his intention to move elsewhere. To Gordy's mind, this was a betrayal.

Whatever Stevie did next, whether it was to remain on the same label or move to a different one, he was determined it would be outside the Motown studio system. Moving away from Detroit was an important step in this direction. Then there was a further, fateful accidental meeting. In New York he had a bass player named Ronnie Blanco, who engineered a meeting that would move Stevie Wonder to higher ground and change pop music at the same time.

Blanco had spent a lot of time at Media Sound, a studio housed in an old Baptist church on Fifty-Seventh Street. Here he'd made the acquaintance of the middle-aged British jazz musician Malcolm Cecil and his creative partner, a former filmmaker named Robert Margouleff. Cecil, who had played jazz with Tubby Hayes and blues with Cyril Davies, was working as Media Sound's night maintenance man, beavering away in the basement to keep the first generation of electronic equipment operating. Since Margouleff had been an early adopter of the Moog synthesizer, he was Media Sound's equipment expert. The two became friends and collaborators. When the studio was not in use, they busied themselves building a machine that would combine the music-making products of various manufacturers—Moog, Roland, Arp, Oberheim, and others—and building an interface that allowed these technologies to talk to each other. They called it The Original New Timbral Orchestra, TONTO for short.

TONTO looked more like the control room of a power station than a musical instrument and had to be operated by experts. Nevertheless, this first polyphonic synthesizer was the single most dramatic technological advance to hit pop music since the electric guitar. Because it had such a wide range of tone colors, the sounds that TONTO produced could not be matched by any conventional instrument or machine. Looking back at these events from the far shore of the great digital transmigration, it is almost impossible to recapture a time when the very idea that so many unusual noises and voices could be coaxed from something that looked like a telephone exchange merely by connecting the right leads and turning the appropriate knob seemed like witchcraft.

Cecil and Margouleff made an album called *Zero Time* by Tonto's Expanding Head Band to demonstrate their invention. It was released on a label run by jazz flautist Herbie Mann. *Zero Time* was the kind of record that only musicians and technophiles enthused over. This was the era when it was impossible to get involved with electronic keyboards unless you could read a circuit diagram and had your own soldering iron. Cecil and Margouleff were perfectly qualified in both respects. Ronnie Blanco played *Zero Time* for Stevie Wonder and told him that all these sounds he was hearing, all these slurring, slithering, spectral noises, were coming from one instrument. Stevie was impressed and asked Blanco to take him to, in his words, "see it."

The two of them turned up at Media Sound on the last Sunday in May 1971 and rang the bell. Cecil, busy at the time fixing Felix Pappalardi's Mellotron, looked out of the window and saw his unexpected visitors, one of them a young black man in shades wearing a pistachio jumpsuit. They brought Stevie into the studio, sat him down at TONTO's keyboards, and began putting the instrument through its paces. Cecil and Margouleff ran around making connections and turning switches while Stevie rejoiced in the unprecedented freedom of being able to actually make the music that he heard in his head without having to do it via instructions to other musicians. Margouleff and Cecil in turn enjoyed having the undivided attention of a name musician who would quite happily sit at the keyboard and play for hours. As they later recalled, "Stevie came and didn't leave for over a year. We worked weekends, birthdays, holidays, even Christmas Day." With Cecil playing the role of instrument technician, Margouleff engineering, and Wonder giving free rein to his musical imagination, which in its extraordinary fecundity was the diametric opposite of Marvin Gaye's, they recorded seventeen songs on that one weekend.

By the time he went into Media Sound, Stevie Wonder had already lost interest in the last album he had released on Motown. *Where I'm Coming From* came out April 12, 1971. It was a step forward from its predecessor, *Live at the Talk of the Town*, but the new music he was composing would make it seem every bit as stiff. *Where I'm Coming From* is a solemn declaration of independence, as exemplified by "I Wanna Talk to You," in which he takes on the role of a poor sharecropper asking his master to cut him a little slack. Although it features the same Hohner clavinet he would later use to great effect, it's employed in a rather stagy fashion as if it's always trying to quote from some more respectable kind of music. But it had a hit, "If You Really Love Me," written, like the rest of the songs, with Syreeta Wright. It sounded like the work of a man reluctantly working through other musicians.

In 1971 a handful of artists had already had a try at making a record single-handed, a record on which they would play all the parts themselves. *Runt*, the second album by Todd Rundgren, came out in March 1971. For this recording, Rundgren had played most of the instruments, taking advantage of the fact that he was the resident producer and engineer at Bearsville, the studios owned by Dylan's manager Albert Grossman, and could therefore use studio downtime without payment. Paul McCartney had done much the same the previous year with his first solo album, recording at home on a four-track tape recorder with no way of monitoring input levels. The resulting rawness was part of the charm, but the method didn't seem to have much of a future.

It would be difficult to imagine a way of working further removed from Motown's process-oriented system—which functioned like the big Hollywood studios, with committees for vetting material and an owner who thought of himself as the person most qualified to decide which artist would go best with which material—than the hands-on work Stevie Wonder started doing at Media Sound. Over the next two years, he moved his entire operation over to New York's Electric Lady before joining the inevitable trek westward to end up three hit albums later at the Record Plant in LA. Here he spent months in a room with three middle-aged white nerds, Margouleff, Cecil, and Johanan Vigoda, an eccentric lawyer Stevie had hired to sort out his business affairs. Vigoda looked like an unmade bed, which may have led Gordy to underestimate him. That underestimation cost his company $13 million, which was the eventual price of re-signing the former boy wonder. Vigoda's vision saw Stevie succeeding far beyond the narrow horizons of Motown. He was the first person to recognize that his client's future lay in the same album market as the big white acts. He was the one who had the idea of getting him a support slot on the Rolling Stones tour of 1972, an unprecedented move at the time.

Because he didn't have to explain to other musicians what he wanted or to get them on the same beam he was on, much of the music on *Music of My Mind*, which was made in 1971 and came out the following year, seems attractively rough edged and unfinished, full of odd turns, digressions, and fantastical spoken passages, all of which seem to come out of one imagination. Those sessions blurred into those for *Talking Book*, *Innervisions*, and *Fulfillingness' First Finale*. From then on, they were on what Cecil called "Stevie

Time," dictated by a man who really didn't want to do anything but play music and was delighted to be able to play it on an entirely new machine. This state of affairs couldn't last forever and inevitably didn't end happily. By the year's end, he had separated from his young wife, Syreeta. Margouleff and Cecil were so thrilled about the use to which their invention had been put that they carried on working for a day rate, in the hope that a royalty share would one day be sorted out. It wasn't. They stopped working with him after *Fulfillingness' First Finale* and sensed that one of the reasons they were no longer wanted was that by then Stevie's people didn't like him being beholden to two prickly white men.

The music that arose from the partnership initiated on that hot weekend in 1971, the records that eventually spawned "Superstition," "You Are the Sunshine of My Life," "Living for the City," and scores more were the purest expression of Stevie Wonder's genial cool. They also shaped the popular music made by everyone else just as surely as the Beatles had shaped it ten years before. This music came out of a room full of wires and plugs, a room reeking of solder and overheating machines, more a workshop than a conventional studio, a room where a visually handicapped young black man could work with three middle-aged white men, none of whom could in all honesty have been accused of knowing the first thing about funk. It was nonetheless the dawn of a new way of doing things.

Don Cornelius was a thirty-five-year-old black TV presenter working for a Chicago TV station when, in 1970, he persuaded his bosses to let him try launching a music show. To his amazement, they didn't insist he give up his rights to be the show's owner. Cornelius wanted his program to do for black music and black kids what Dick Clark's *American Bandstand* had done for white music and white kids since the fifties.

There were scarcely any black faces on television either side of the Atlantic, and black youth had more chance of appearing on-screen as threatening elements on news reports about urban strife than as talent. In April 1971, when *Ebony* magazine published its list of the one hundred most influential black Americans, there wasn't a single TV presenter on the list.

Initially, Cornelius put most of his effort into persuading acts to appear on *Soul Train*, leaning on locally based talent such as Curtis Mayfield and B. B. King. Like everyone who ever started a music TV show, he craved respectability most, but he found the excitement coming from an unexpected direction. As the show gained momentum and, thanks to a tie-in with America's biggest manufacturer of black hair products, was taken up by more stations, it became clear that the musicians were not as important to the TV audience as the young people who danced to the hits in the TV studio.

In 1971 Cornelius took *Soul Train* national and joined the exodus moving the rest of the music industry to Los Angeles. In California the show's vibe was immediately different. It was now shot in color, with the dancers recruited from the rich supply of exhibitionists who hung around the city's various arts initiatives, and suddenly Cornelius's show, which he hosted himself with the decidedly self-important air of a well-dressed young congressman, was America's first interesting music TV show.

The dancers, who were unpaid and were expected to sustain themselves through marathon taping sessions on a diet of soda and fried chicken, were what made it great television. The young men were snake-hipped and tall, with massive penumbras of natural hair treated with Afro Sheen. The girls were slender and dressed to ensure the maximum camera time. There was nothing vampish about their appearance, due partly to American TV's traditional prudery and partly to the atmosphere of the show, which was as much church social as discotheque. In their homemade jumpsuits and hot pants, the girls exuded the breeziness of *Sesame Street* rather than the stickiness of *Top of the Pops*. Cornelius was keen to make sure his people were shown in a good light. There was a regular feature in which the studio guests had to rearrange letters on a board to spell out the names of distinguished African Americans. To make sure nothing went wrong that might reflect badly on the people he was pledged to represent, this part of the show was fixed.

The sweet spot of *Soul Train* was the soul train line. Here the dancers formed a guard of honor down which couples took their turn to parade, showing off the moves that they had spent the week perfecting in the hope that all over the nation kids in the school yard would be attempting to imitate them over the following week. These dance moves, which took the generic frugs and twitches of pop dance and reclassified them into an entirely new terpsichorean taxonomy, swept the nation. They reached the black kids in the inner cities, giving their playground culture a national stage. They reached the suburban white kids, who for the first time saw a different and exciting way to move and to carry themselves.

Music is as much about body language as anything else. The *Soul Train* kids took the lead, and the music business began to follow. The musicians seemed to recede into the background. The cameras didn't go in for admiring low-angle shots. Instead they pulled back from the acts to show the dancers who were elbowing their way in front of each other as if their lives depended on it. For some of them, it did. *Soul Train* made the names of many people who didn't make records but instead danced to them. It made display a central part of popular music. In that sense it changed popular music even more than Stevie Wonder did.

While Marvin was remixing *What's Going On* in Hollywood, twenty-eight-year-old Sly Stone was down the road in Bel Air, living in a rented mansion that had formerly been the home of musical comedy star Jeanette MacDonald. It's unlikely that under the previous occupant the house had a safe full of drugs in a basement, as it did during Sly's eventful tenure. In it he kept, according to one of the many musicians who passed through and briefly lived at 783 Bel Air Road in that time, "pounds of cocaine."

Sly Stone was as big a musical star as you could find anywhere in the United States in 1971. A DJ, producer, and hustler from northern California, with his revue-style band the Family Stone, Sylvester Stewart had provided a string of hit singles such as "Dance to the Music" and "Everyday People," records that cleverly combined Aquarian Age sentiments with the demands of the discotheque, records that everyone related to from the bookers of TV shows to the editors of hip magazines; furthermore, he had beaten off all comers when it came to stealing the show as *Woodstock* hit the cinemas. For all his shrewdness, charisma, and talent, Sly was arguably the least reliable superstar in the history of popular music.

He was two years late delivering a new record, so late that Clive Davis, the boss of Epic and Columbia, was withholding his back royalties until he delivered it. The Black Panthers, rarely far from the door of any brother with access to cash and prominence, were leaning on him to get rid of the two white members of his band and his white, Jewish manager. Meanwhile, the manager was threatening that if his client didn't deliver the record he would set his own enforcers upon him. The many women in his life were giving him grief about the many women in his life. The people who sold him the drugs were keen to sell him more. On top of all this, he was experiencing the traditional musician's fear of actually delivering the record and the judgment that would inevitably follow.

A twelve-track console had been installed in the basement of the house in Bel Air, and here Sly worked, calling in members of the band to play occasional parts. Because he was less a musician than a conceptualist, Sly preferred to start with the Maestro Rhythm King-1 drum machine and build from there. This way nobody could ask him whether he had any idea what he was driving at, and he was free to just putter around until the music fell into an appealing pattern. The argument for working this way is that what's lost in abandoning the natural sound of a live band is made up for in control.

More in hope than anything else, the record company was promising that the album would be called *The Incredible and Unpredictable Sly & the Family Stone*. It was presumably expecting more of the buckskin-fringed happy-clappy music with which Sly had electrified

Woodstock just a year before. Sly was one of the few black performers who was a hot ticket with the rock crowd, and the record company wanted an album that would sell to them. The cover with the star-spangled banner on the front and the saturated color shot of Sly performing for a massive crowd of white people in the foldout seemed to be anticipating a certain kind of record. It was far from the one that turned up.

What Clive Davis would have heard that spring would not have filled him with confidence. Lots of it was downbeat. All of it was difficult to decipher. Sly had even taken his band's upbeat hit "Thank You (Falettinme Be Mice Elf Agin)," slowed it down to a stumble, and called it "Thank You for Talkin' to Me Africa," which seemed plain bloody-minded. The single "Family Affair" had been made acceptable only after engineering consultant Richard Tilles had come in, muted most of Sly's guitar parts, edited the rhythm box to make it sound like a heartbeat, and accentuated the electric piano. The piano was played by Billy Preston, fresh from providing the same sound on the Beatles' last single. What nobody could get rid of is the tape hiss accrued through Sly's endless overdubbing. It lay on the surface of the finished record like the glaze of ages on a Rembrandt.

Apart from "Family Affair," which is not only the perfectly realized pop single but also the kind of thing whose meaning people interpret for themselves and then take to heart, the bulk of *There's a Riot Goin' On* is opaque. When it was released in November 1971, it sounded like a collection of demos with placeholder vocal parts and riffs that often trailed off into incoherence. It remains the least pat, least tidy, least house-trained album that ever dominated the number one spot on the *Billboard* pop and soul charts for weeks on end. It's incomplete. It's unsettling. It's full of loose ends. The songs aren't so much sung as narrated or remarked upon. It's the sound you hear in your head when you've done lots of drugs and haven't had enough sleep. The groove is pushed to the front. The songs have to take their chances in the space remaining.

Amazingly, it would turn out to be the future for lots of music, although none of it would be made by Sly, who was wrung dry by the effort. Some of that music would be made by Miles Davis, who changed his style under Sly's influence. Miles, who was one of the people called in to talk sense to Sly during these years, at the time couldn't help observing that Sly took a lot of cocaine. Although Sly made and continues to make records, he never wrote anything significant again.

He didn't need to. *There's a Riot Goin' On* made all sorts of things possible. Forty years later, its fingerprint is discernible all over hip-hop. Sly didn't have to wait that long to see how influential it was. As Greil Marcus has written, the great records that came out in its wake, by Curtis Mayfield, the Staple Singers, the Temptations, War, and others, records it would be patronizing to call "conscious," were suddenly "all of one piece; one enormous answer record."

On the morning of April 12, 1971, a film crew was working on Mott Street in New York's Little Italy. In the scene they were filming, an elderly man in a shapeless suit and a voluminous greatcoat was buying fruit from a curbside vendor. As he turned away from the stall to make his way to the car waiting for him, two gunmen appeared and shot him repeatedly. He collapsed on the hood of the car. The gunmen got in their car, which screamed away.

The elderly man was being played by Marlon Brando, doing his first day's filming on the Paramount picture *The Godfather*. It had taken a lot of careful diplomatic work by Albert Ruddy, one of the film's producers, to win permission to film on the streets of New York, particularly in Little Italy. Mario Puzo's book of *The Godfather* had been a best seller when it was published in 1969. The people who were either in the Mafia or happy to have people think they were in the Mafia didn't know whether to feel flattered or traduced.

Ruddy had to present himself before a meeting of fifteen hundred members of the Italian American Civil Rights League and Joseph Colombo Sr., one of its senior figures and a head of one of the five families who controlled much of the illegal gain in New York. It was only when Ruddy persuaded them that the film was simply a study of corruption rather than an attempt to slander an entire community that the film's crews found they could get on with their work free from petty obstructions and the unwanted intrusions of bureaucracy. By the time the film wrapped in the summer and made ready for its launch on Christmas Day 1971 (it was later delayed until March 1972), Paramount was feeling bullish enough about its prospects to be thinking about another one to be called *Son of Godfather*.

In 1971 the major movie studios were floundering. The big stars were still cowboys like John Wayne and Clint Eastwood. Their key projects were adaptations of Broadway smashes such as *Fiddler on the Roof* or best sellers like *Love Story*. They had few franchises. On April 23 a movie called *Sweet Sweetback's Baadasssss Song* premiered in New York. It was almost entirely the work of Melvin Van Peebles, an African American writer who had taught himself how to make a film. He had even composed the music himself and had hired the then unsigned Chicago band Earth, Wind & Fire to play it. "I had a tiny little chance," he recalled later. "But for a colored man that was a big chance." Realizing he needed to use any means possible to promote his film, he took the music to the Memphis-based independent record label Stax and persuaded the company to release it.

Van Peebles's film did well. It appealed to an African American audience, understandably pleased to see their own on-screen and every bit as keen on sex and violence as the audience in the white suburbs. There was also the undercurrent of a long-overdue evening of the score. The characters in *Sweet Sweetback*, twenty feet high, said what had previously been considered unsayable. For instance, as the boss of the ghetto gambling joint says, "Every dollar we make, the guineas get twenty, the police get forty, and Goldberg gets fifty. Anybody can tell you that don't add up to a dollar."

In the week of *Sweet Sweetback*'s release, Gil Scott-Heron, who was hailed as "a new black poet," went into RCA Studios in New York and recorded his second album, *Pieces of a Man*. It began with the proto-rap "The Revolution Will Not Be Televised." This was not without precedent. *This Is Madness*, the second album by the Last Poets, was between Bobby Womack and Wilson Pickett on the soul album charts, even though, as their record company pointed out, there was nothing on it that you could play on the radio. Sometimes black consciousness took the form of political action. More often, it expressed itself in consumerism. The entertainment companies were beginning to notice this.

MGM was already looking to make the move into what later became known as "blaxploitation" with a movie by fashion photographer Gordon Parks. This was to star Richard Roundtree as John Shaft, a handsome black private detective having trouble with the Mafia. Isaac Hayes was tapped to come up with the music, which was thought to be a vital part of the package. Hayes, along with David Porter, had written and produced some of Stax's biggest hits of the '60s. In 1970 he had emerged as a solo act. He specialized in bookending well-known standards like "Walk On By" and "By the Time I Get to Phoenix" with lubricious spoken passages wherein he would list the many varieties of sweet love he would make at the end of his journey. These went well with his shaven-head love god persona. Since he always copyrighted his raps, he also made as much out of his reading of "By the Time I Get to Phoenix" as Jimmy Webb, the man who wrote the actual song.

While *Shaft* was being shot and edited in Hollywood, Hayes and his band, who were heavily based on the Stax house band, the Bar-Kays, spent the weekend playing lucrative gigs on the East Coast and then flew to Hollywood for the week to add their music to the film's scenes. They did this entirely in their heads, confounding the soundtrack specialists with their ability to start and finish on cue. The "Theme from *Shaft*," the lyrics of which Isaac had composed after hearing some backing singers cooing about Roundtree, won him the Oscar for Best Original Song of 1971, where he triumphed over Henry Mancini and Marvin Hamlisch.

It's doubtful that the latter pair would have recognized how the theme from *Shaft* came to be composed. The drummer was told to play at the same tempo as the actors were walking on the screen. The guitarist was just testing his wah-wah pedal when Hayes told him to repeat what he'd just been doing. It was one of the first number one records that was narrated as much as it was sung. Hayes put a vocal on it in the end only in order to be able to enter it for Best Song at the Oscars. The signature line "Shut your mouth" was performed by Telma Hopkins. At the time she was also a member of Tony Orlando and Dawn, whose "Knock Three Times" had been a huge international hit in January. Thus, she featured prominently on the most white-bread hit of the year as well as the one that was, ostensibly at least, the sound of the street. It was also the sound of the future.

APRIL

Marvin Gaye: "What's Going On"

Isaac Hayes: "Theme from *Shaft*"

Gil Scott-Heron: "The Revolution Will Not Be Televised"

Tonto's Expanding Head Band: "Cybernaut"

Sly & the Family Stone: "Family Affair"

Curtis Mayfield: "Get Down"

The Supremes: "Nathan Jones"

Al Green: "I Can't Get Next to You"

Aretha Franklin: "Oh Me Oh My (I'm a Fool for You Baby)"

Santana: "Toussaint L'Ouverture"

MAY

Brown Sugar

On April 4, 1971, an eighteen-year-old from Santa Monica named Glenn Cowan was competing as one of the US table tennis team at the World Championships in Nagoya, Japan. After the day's practice session, he was unable to find the team bus to take him back to the hotel. Spotting another bus bearing the competition's logo, he climbed aboard. There were no free seats and so he stood.

The bus's occupants stared at their exotic new passenger with undisguised disbelief. Cowan was used to this. His long hair, tie-dyed pants, and floppy hats, which attracted attention even at home in Southern California, had drawn crowds in the Japanese city. There was a different quality to the scrutiny on this bus because the occupants were members of the table tennis team of the People's Republic of China, the vast, unknown nation that had shut itself off from the rest of the world in 1948.

Cowan's appearance was no more extreme than any other young American of 1971 hoping to be taken for Keith Richards, but in the Far East of the time it was an outlandish form of fancy dress that demanded an explanation. Cowan asked the team's interpreter to assure the Chinese players that in America many people looked the way he did. This relieved the tension a little.

Eventually, the top player of the Chinese team, Zhuang Zedong, a thirty-year-old who was the star of the world game, came forward and presented Cowan with a silk weaving depicting the Huangshan mountains. Feeling he should reciprocate, Cowan went through his own bag for a gift. He could only manage a comb. He handed it over. When the bus got back to the hotel, the Californian went directly to a shopping center and bought two T-shirts bearing a design that combined an American flag with a peace symbol and the words "Let It Be." It was the kind of item just becoming available in the world's alternative bazaars, a muddled expression of right-on sentiments you could send away for via the small ads in *National Lampoon* or *Rolling Stone*. He presented one to Zedong and kept one for himself.

Following these apparently spontaneous overtures, there appeared out of the blue an unprecedented invitation for the American team to finish their visit to the Far East by spending a few days in China. This was big news far beyond the world of table tennis because it represented the first official contact between the world's most populous nation and its most powerful one since Mao's China detached itself from the rest of the world at the end of the 1940s. The invitation was eagerly accepted, and thus, on April 10, nine American table tennis players accompanied by four officials and two spouses crossed a bridge from the British colony of Hong Kong into the People's Republic of China.

It was, as one of them later recalled, like going to the moon. Their organized visits to the Great Wall, the ballet, and the stupendous republic's handful of tourist must-sees were given prime coverage on nightly TV in China and relayed, with scarcely less pride, into American homes by American networks. It was the most significant piece of sporting diplomacy of the twentieth century. *Time* magazine called it "the ping heard around the world." Within a month of the visit, a poll conducted in the United States found that more than half of the population were suddenly in favor of China's admission to the

United Nations. Its effects were felt far beyond sport. It led to a fundamental realignment of world power and also, eventually, to the iPod.

This apparently impromptu visit had been facilitated at a high level. The green light for the American players' arrival had come from Chairman Mao himself. A keen table tennis player since the 1930s, he had been responsible for making the game the Chinese national sport. In 1971 he knew the US president Richard Nixon was sending out diplomatic feelers. Messages from his consigliere Henry Kissinger to the Chinese premier Zhou Enlai were routed through Pakistan. On the face of it, the two countries were implacably committed to each other's destruction. As the players were being driven down Chinese streets plastered with posters reading, "People of the world defeat the U.S. aggressors and their running dogs," they were unaware that a handful of people at the head of both nations were playing footsie.

Nixon's problem was Vietnam. It was the baby boomers' big issue as well. The military draft was an immediate threat to the life of every young man of military age in the country. In 1971 a twenty-seven-year-old former naval officer and Vietnam veteran named John Kerry faced a Senate committee and asked the members how many young men had to die so that Richard Nixon wouldn't be the first American president to lose a war.

With his stiff bearing and glowering look of disapproval, Nixon was the stereotypical "straight" of every alternative paper illustration, the butt of every Woodstock nation wisecrack, the source of all their discontent. The president cordially returned the favor. The tapes of his conversations with aides in the Oval Office from the spring of 1971 abound with references to longhairs, freaks, drugs, even hot pants, and the part each might have been playing in the imminent breakdown of civilization.

As is often the case in politics, the more Nixon was seen to lean toward one wing, the freer he was to reach out toward the other. His conservative credentials made him the only president who could open up lines to China without being accused of being soft on communism. China needed an outlet for its goods. The United States needed to find a way to get American troops out of Vietnam. Nixon knew the admittance of the table tennis players indicated that his offer of talks would be accepted, and he hoped that he would be able to make the huge step of actually visiting China not long after. "If we get this thing working," he told Kissinger in the spring of 1971, "we will end Vietnam this year."

Nobody knew about Nixon's thoughts on May 1, when thirty thousand hippies descended on Washington, intent on stopping the work of the government. They were entertained on their first day in West Potomac Park by Linda Ronstadt, Charles Mingus, NRBQ, Mother Earth, Phil Ochs, Mitch Ryder (whose pelvic thrusting so offended some of the newly radical feminists that they demanded the right to speak afterward), and the Beach Boys. David Fenton, who reviewed the event for the alternative paper *Ann Arbor Sun*, knew the freaks among his readership would be surprised to see the Beach Boys on the bill but reassured them, "They're freaks now with really long hair and bushy beards. . . . That's an indication of how widespread the changes in this generation have reached."

On May 2 the president withdrew the protesters' permits and ordered the army into the city. So many troops were airlifted into the nation's capital that at one point troop transports were arriving at Andrews Air Force Base every three minutes. Over ten thousand people were arrested or detained. It was the largest mass arrest in American history.

On May 5, 1971, the five members of the Rolling Stones assembled at Nellcôte, the eight-bedroom mansion above the town of Villefranche-sur-Mer on the Côte d'Azur, which Keith Richards had recently begun renting. The tear gas was still hovering over the Washington Mall, but the men who wrote "Street Fighting Man" were settling down to a new life in a millionaire's playground.

That year, 1971, was hugely important for the Rolling Stones. In March they had toured the UK for the first time since 1966, back in the days when the screaming made them impossible to hear. This seventeen-night swing through city halls and theaters was informally known as the "Goodbye to Britain" tour. As it began at Newcastle City Hall on March 4, they announced that when it was over, they would be leaving to become tax exiles. It was the first time those words had been used in the context of the music business. They finished with two nights at the Roundhouse in London and then on March 26 performed at the four-hundred-seat Marquee Club in Soho, the first of the "back to the clubs" shows that were to become a feature of their career. This sentimental homecoming was marred by an incident during which Keith Richards attacked the club's owner with a guitar after he insisted they perform in front of the venue's traditional branding. They did further promotional chores, such as recording a performance of their new single "Brown Sugar" for the BBC's *Top of the Pops*, with Jagger wearing a pink satin suit and baseball cap while singing live over a prerecorded instrumental track.

On April 1, just as the new tax year began, they and their families and retainers left their homes in England and flew out to new ones in France. Charlie Watts and his wife found one in the Vaucluse. The new guitarist, Mick Taylor, whose girlfriend had just given birth to their child, stayed in the Hotel Byblos in Saint-Tropez. Mick Jagger, who spoke French and had a new girlfriend who had lived in Paris since she was a teenager, took a house in the picturesque hilltop town of Biot. The Stones were not exactly close neighbors.

In 1971 very few Englishmen followed their work overseas. Bill Wyman was old enough to realize the move to France might have long-term consequences, though like the rest he had no inkling of what "long term" might mean. He was thirty-five and already had one divorce behind him. Charlie Watts was just on the safe side of thirty. Despite having been at the top of their tree for seven years, Mick and Keith still had their twenty-eighth birthdays in front of them. Mick Taylor was just twenty-two.

The Stones' move to France was made at Mick Jagger's urging. In the world of rock stars, where the ability to balance a checkbook attracts both awe and suspicion, Mick Jagger is often cited as a financial genius. His brief attendance at the London School of Economics rarely goes unmentioned. In fact, what Jagger did in 1971 was no more than what any other bright CEO would have done if he suspected his company was on the brink of falling apart. In doing so, he gave the Rolling Stones an entirely new focus.

Jagger had learned many bitter lessons in the music business, the chief one being that success is only the beginning of a band's problems. In 1965 they had hired the American accountant Allen Klein to bully royalties out of their sleepy British record company. When the contract with that company expired with *Let It Bleed* in 1969, the band found to their dismay that Klein had bought the US rights to their catalog of sixties hits for his own company ABKCO. The rights they thought they had been signing over to themselves they had actually been signing over to a company controlled by him, which is the kind of thing that causes iron to enter even the most forgiving soul. In 1971 Jagger had a new determination that none of this was going to happen again. By moving the band to France, he was doing what no sixties band had managed to do, which was to start again without breaking up.

The previous year, Mick and Keith, the clear leaders of the group since the departure of Brian Jones, had been laying the groundwork for Rolling Stones Mark II. This involved a few different steps. They would sign to a major international label, not one of Britain's pin-striped and risk-averse old firms. It would be a company that would give them a large advance and better royalty rates, spend large sums on promoting their releases, and generally treat them in a manner befitting their self-proclaimed status as the greatest rock-and-roll band in the world.

They would no longer rely on a manager to lead them. Most of the bands who had become successful in the sixties had needed managers to negotiate their fees and operate as an executive nanny service. In Mick Jagger, the Rolling Stones had a leader who realized that the price of remaining in control was a willingness to pay attention in meetings, a skill few of his contemporaries ever acquired. Doing without a manager had an immediate fiscal benefit. A manager's cut turns any five-piece group into a six-piece. The Rolling Stones Mark II had no intention of doing that.

Instead of finding a replacement for Andrew Oldham, who had ceased being involved with them in 1967, Mick Jagger went to see Prince Rupert Loewenstein. Loewenstein was at the time the managing director of the merchant bank Leopold Joseph. His background as a man steeped in the specialist science of wealth management was appealing to a band who needed their wealth managed. The introductions were made by Jagger's art dealer friend Christopher Gibbs, and Loewenstein signed on as their business adviser.

Once he was in post in 1970, Loewenstein, already in his late thirties and healthily incurious about either the music or the celebrity of his new clients, was amazed at how little money the Stones had managed to make out of their fame and how small a proportion of that they'd hung on to. The old saying goes that most people in the music business are either poorer than you'd think or richer than you could possibly imagine. At the time, the Stones were in the former category.

Their situation was a result of low royalty rates, nonexistent merchandising revenues, a career that had been stalled by legal problems, and the slow unwinding of Brian Jones. For the latter part of the '60s, their revenues had been routed through Allen Klein's organization, which reduced them further, and whatever profit they made was being assessed for income tax and surtax at a figure that amounted to anything between 83 and 98 percent. On top of that, they found that they owed back taxes. Bill Wyman alone, who didn't participate in songwriting, the most lucrative seam, owed almost $200,000. This was in 1970, when the average cost of a new car was $2,500. Loewenstein argued that the only way the Stones could pay the back tax they owed was by moving to a jurisdiction where the lower rates gave them a fighting chance of hanging on to more of what they earned in the future. In 1971 the place to go was France.

While there, they would make a record. In 1971 France had the same reputation for fine recording studios as London had for fine dining. The only decent ones were in Paris. The Stones wanted to live somewhere warm like the Côte d'Azur. The compromise was that the Rolling Stones' mobile truck, which had already been used to record at Mick's English country house Stargroves, could be driven down to the South of France and parked at Nellcôte, where Keith, who was emerging as the member who had to be pleased at all times, could record without getting out of bed.

On April 1, 1971, after months of flirtation with Columbia, the only realistic alternative record company, the Rolling Stones announced they had signed with Atlantic Records. A week later their single "Brown Sugar" was released for the first time on their own Rolling Stones label. There was a party at the Cannes Yacht Club to make sure that the business took notice. The man paying for that party, enjoying his share of the limelight, providing both prestige and cash, was, like Loewenstein, a well-dressed individual from an older generation.

Ahmet Ertegun had sold his R & B company Atlantic, once the home of Ray Charles, Big Joe Turner, the Coasters, and scores of other great African American acts, to Warner Brothers in 1967. The forty-five-year-old, impeccably sophisticated son of a Turkish diplomat was, like all the men who built the record business, every bit as excited by money as he was by music. Ertegun recognized that something fundamental was changing in 1971 and that the future was in big-selling, high-margin long players aimed at the white market rather than low-margin 45s for the urban market. What had been about selling to kids was now about selling to adults. What had been about hits was now going to be about careers.

Columbia Records, which had set the pace in the rock album market by signing West Coast acts like Janis Joplin and Santana, was the perceived leader, but it couldn't quite land the Stones. Clive Davis, who ran Columbia, might be a good businessman, but Ahmet Ertegun wrote "Mess Around" for Ray Charles. In the world of the Stones, this counted for a lot more.

Ertegun used the credentials earned in a world that had vanished to put himself at the head of one that was yet to be born. He knew how musicians' minds work, that their motives are colored by sentimentality and ego as well as money. "I think Mick would have liked to sign with Excello," he recalled, talking of the tiny R & B label on which Slim Harpo's "I'm a King Bee" had been released. "We were the closest he could get to Excello and still get five million dollars."

The Stones' own label deal was the template for the record business of the future: funky on the outside, fiscal as hell below. In the corner of the label on "Brown Sugar," unnoticed by most fans, who were too busy smirking at the new jutting tongue logo, were the words "Promotone B.V." This newly founded company, which was owned by the Stones and based in the Netherlands, would own the copyright of any records they put out subsequently and license them to the major record companies, whose job it was to exploit them. The Stones resolved that henceforth they would own their own recordings. They would take advances from record companies for the privilege of distributing them, but at the end of each relationship, they could take their catalog elsewhere. The Netherlands was attractive as a place to base the company because it didn't tax royalties. In every respect, the Rolling Stones were moving upmarket.

This pivotal month in the transfiguration of a scruffy beat group from south London into a grande luxe international attraction was further marked by an occasion that is traditionally every bit as concerned with prestige as it is with romance—a wedding. The May 12 wedding between Michael Philip Jagger and Bianca Pérez-Mora Macias marked the establishment of rock and roll as a viable branch of high society and a recognition on the part of the establishment that the money, fame, and status that the newborn pop industry had brought with it during the sixties was only going to increase in the seventies.

The day before the wedding Jagger chartered a Dan-Air Comet to fly seventy-five UK-based friends to the wedding in Saint-Tropez. These people had been informed of the impending nuptials only twenty-four hours earlier. The newsreel cameras were there to see them off. Old mates from the package-tour years such as Ronnie

Lane, Kenney Jones, Ronnie Wood, Ringo Starr, Doris Troy, and Peter Frampton sashayed across the tarmac at Heathrow in their white suits, clutching amusing presents for the happy couple, trailed by wives and girlfriends in wide-brimmed straw hats and hot pants, some of them hitching newly arrived infants onto their hips, all still giggling at their great good fortune and appearing to the rest of the workaday world like the avatars of a blithe new species.

Ossie Clark, the fashion designer and socialite who was enjoying a new eminence through David Hockney's recently unveiled portrait *Mr and Mrs Clark and Percy*, strode through the terminal wearing a particularly challenging outfit of lemon short shorts and knee-high suede boots, carrying both a doctor's bag and what in years to come would be known as a man bag. Paul McCartney, accompanied by Linda and their two children Heather and Mary, was no less courageously attired in three-quarter-length trousers of the kind that would subsequently become familiar via the Bay City Rollers. Paul was tight-lipped while boarding the plane, worried that he might be seated near Ringo, with whom he was locked in a bitter legal fight. This had been foreseen, and they were kept apart.

At the Hotel Byblos they mixed with their new friends, some of whom, such as the Earl of Lichfield, who gave the bride away, were aristocrats. There were no less than three people on the guest list from the Ormsby-Gore family. One of them, the eighteen-year-old Alice, was the fiancée of Eric Clapton. The daughter of Lord Harlech, the former British ambassador to Washington, she was a member of a group of aristocratic hippies who now found themselves moving in the same circles as the superstars. The old landed gentry was mingling with the new and dealing with some of their old afflictions. Clapton's main concern while attending the wedding party was keeping himself topped up with heroin.

The year 1971 was the high-water mark of rock's overindulgence in drugs. Al Wilson of Canned Heat, Jimi Hendrix, and Janis Joplin had all died within four weeks of each other in the fall of the previous year, their deaths all caused by accidentally miscalculating how much they or their bodies could stand. At this stage, it was still considered unnecessary to keep an eye on anyone who was using. Rose Taylor, who was at Nellcôte almost every day because she had to drive her husband, Mick, there and drive him back, doesn't recall seeing Keith take anything more than Jack Daniel's or marijuana during that summer. "I suppose they were geniuses at concealment," she told Robert Greenfield.

Keith was using in a big way, as was his partner Anita Pallenberg. He moved to France a week ahead of her while she was undergoing the latest of many attempted cures. They weren't the only ones. When John Lennon visited Nellcôte later that week while in Cannes for the film festival, he drank too much red wine and threw up on the steps, which was attributed to the fact that he was being weaned off heroin via methadone.

Among the wedding party there was the drug dealer "Spanish" Tony Sanchez, who dressed as if he wished to be taken for Keith Richards, a personality deficiency that eventually affected hundreds of thousands of young men and women. Sanchez was accompanied by his girlfriend Madeleine D'Arcy, sporting a straw hat and bug-eyed shades, her dancer's body introduced into hot pants, like Jane Fonda as Bree Daniels in *Klute*. Hanging around Nellcôte and also supplying the Stones' friends John Paul and Talitha Getty back in London was Jean de Breteuil, a French aristocrat who Keith called "Johnny Braces" to get round the fact that he couldn't pronounce his name.

A few guests, like the art dealer Robert Fraser, had made their names by greasing the adjoining doors between the high life and the low life, while others, such as the model Donyale Luna, were creatures entirely of their own invention. Bianca Pérez-Mora Macias was a member of that group. She had come to Europe from Nicaragua as a teenager to study at the Institut d'Etudes Politiques in Paris. She took strategic advantage of the blurring effect that often attends the swapping of continents. Her parents had broken up, and her mother ran a shop to make ends meet. She liked to say her father was a well-to-do coffee planter or a diplomat. In fact, the diplomat was an uncle, who was a cultural attaché at the Nicaraguan embassy in Paris and therefore in a position to keep an eye on his bright, willful, and perilously beautiful niece. "I studied hard and remained a virgin until I was eighteen and a half," she recalls with telling precision.

By 1968 the studying was less of a priority. She was living with Michael Caine, not the sort of thing that happens to most overseas students. She was introduced to the actor, already a star, by his tailor Doug Hayward, a key figure in smart London who was the model for the Caine character Alfie and later written into fiction by John le Carré as the title character in *The Tailor of Panama*. Bianca's beauty opened doors and allowed her to present herself as rather grander than she was. The fabled egalitarianism of Swinging London was always prepared to make exceptions for physical attractiveness. In 1970 she was twenty-two years old, spoke five languages, and was already accustomed to the attentions of wealthy, powerful, and significantly older men. She was introduced to Mick Jagger by another of her lovers, the fifty-year-old French record mogul Eddie Barclay.

Like the other members of this long-hair aristocracy, Mick Jagger had grown up in the fifties. Like them, he had traditional expectations of women and a feeling that it was bad form to be without a girlfriend for even a short time. This inevitably resulted in periods of overlap, which could be fraught. Open cohabitation, or "living in sin," as it was known, was still very rare, even among the young and famous. Paul McCartney could get away with living with Jane Asher outside wedlock only because it was under her parents' roof and therefore considered somehow chaste. The eighteen-year-old Marianne Faithfull, who only started making records to get out of doing her A levels, married the art dealer John Dunbar in 1965 because she was pregnant with their child. In the wedding photos, she poses with a soft toy in her lap to conceal her pregnancy. After the child was born, Faithfull embarked on a high-profile affair with Mick Jagger, who was still notionally with Chrissie Shrimpton at the time. Jagger's four-year affair with Faithfull, which made them the iconic couple of the decade, ended in a miscarriage and a suicide attempt while he was filming *Ned Kelly* in Australia.

After Faithfull moved out, Jagger considered marrying the actress and singer Marsha Hunt when she became pregnant with his child. He already had a live-in chef named Janice Kenner at his London house in Cheyne Walk, who slept with him from time to time, on the basis that in those days it would have been impolite not to do so. At the same time, he conducted an affair with Catherine James, an ex-girlfriend of Eric Clapton's who had a child with the Moody Blues' Denny Laine. When Jagger met Bianca, he was impressed and, if it's possible, flattered that she was prepared to ditch Eddie Barclay on their first meeting to go with the younger and more glamorous man.

There was talk of an alternative society in 1971. The enduring alternative was the society inhabited by the rich and famous. While the people in West Potomac Park, the editorials in the underground press, and pockets of dreamy rock fans all over the world mused at what sort of new world might be in the process of being born in 1971, Mick Jagger was determinedly burrowing his way into the old one. Having already seen more sex than a policeman's flashlight during his years as a pop idol, he understood that fame finds money and becomes glamour.

More than any other sixties act, the Rolling Stones had always evoked the exotic world of St. James nightclubs, which the rest of us merely read about in the music papers. Their songs conjured up dreams of models, photographers, and fast cars, of sunglasses worn indoors, of the workaday world surveyed with exquisite boredom through the steamed-up window of the car from the airport. This was a fabulous world of spoiled girls who had grown up in circumstances the rest of us could only dream about, of frisky journalists who needed taking down a peg or two, the heiress who got her kicks in Stepney, not in Knightsbridge anymore, the girl who once had him down but is now under his thumb, sounded far more exciting than the one the rest of us had to live in. At one time, the Stones had merely sung about it. Now, like a few of their peers, they were living it out.

Almost without exception, the rock stars of the sixties married women who would never have looked at them twice had it not been for their wealth and fame. Beneath the veneer of the Aquarian Age, the world beyond the red rope operated according to rules that would have been familiar to Edith Wharton or Thackeray. Here young bucks competed to see who could bed the toniest, the most alluring, the most enviable girl in the rock-and-roll high school, and when they did, they wished to advertise the fact on the biggest stage. That's why everyone was invited to Saint-Tropez. Mick felt he had won the prize and wished it to be known.

The wedding day, May 12, 1971, marks the last point at which he underestimated the power of his own fame and discovered the limits of his own power. It almost didn't go ahead at all, when Bianca discovered on the morning of her big day that French law, as unsentimental in this respect as it is in all others, required that the couple make it clear what property they held in common. Having learned how little this was, she threatened to call it off, facing Jagger with the prospect of the most humiliating reverse in front of his peers. She eventually relented.

Mick, nominally Anglican, had prepared himself for the ceremony, which was to take place in the picturesque fisherman's church of St. Anne, by attending meetings with the pastor. He didn't know that the civil ceremony, which came first, was conducted at the town hall and, by French law, had to be open to anyone who wished to witness it. That meant that hundreds of photographers, many of whom had come over on the flight after the previous day's superstar airlift, installed themselves in the room where the ceremony was due to take place, forcing Les Perrin, the Stones' sober-suited, old-school PR man, to ring Jagger to warn him what to expect. Jagger said he wouldn't get married in a goldfish bowl. This was one of those occasions where the rock star's flounce was countered by the bureaucrat's shrug. Marius Astezan, the mayor of Saint-Tropez, said there was nothing he could do about it. If Monsieur Jagger wanted to get married in France, he must do it the French way. When the bride and groom eventually arrived, late and already perspiring, pushing their way as best they could through the crowds of pressmen, holiday makers, and rubberneckers, they appeared harassed and faintly shocked. The only security for the whole day was provided by Alan Dunn, who worked for Mick, and Jerry Pompili, former house manager of the Fillmore East. It wasn't remotely adequate.

Brides tend to float through their wedding day in a trance of delight, while their grooms are nervous and unsure. This occasion was no different. Jagger appeared more thrown by the chaos than his bride. She was wearing an outfit whose décolletage had clearly been chosen with the express intention of getting a photo of it onto every front page in the world, and also subliminally advertising what nobody but the groom knew, which was that she was already four months pregnant. Jagger wore a suit with shoes that were not yet known as trainers. This was an unprecedented combination of formal and informal, which would be widely copied. They rushed through the civil ceremony to the accompaniment of camera shutters that were never more than feet away. Their union was witnessed by Roger Vadim and Nathalie Delon. Jagger's parents, for whom he was always "Mike," stood in the middle of this mayhem, looking unsurprisingly like people who were watching their son disappear into a mad new world. Their place at their son's right-hand side had been usurped by Ahmet Ertegun. He was the daddy now.

That ceremony alone would have been enough to put most people off public pledges of affection for life. When it was over, Monsieur et Madame Jagger still had the religious one to come. By the time they reached the pretty chapel at the top of the hill, Les Perrin, who by now had added the role of wedding planner and sole responsible adult to his duties as press officer, had decided that the only way he could stop the thing from degenerating even further was by instructing Father Lucien Baud to lock the doors and not admit anyone else. Thus, the least forgiving section of the world's press found, to their delight, that they got a close-up view of the world's number one rock god having to bang on the door and beg admittance like anyone else whose name has been left off the guest list at an exclusive club gig. Inside the church, rock stars and their molls in diaphanous finery lolled around sniggering and bitching, to the understandable discomfort of the priest. Each stage of the ancient Catholic rite was punctuated by a flashbulb broadside from feet away. Nobody could take their eyes off Bianca's cleavage. Keith couldn't disguise his disapproval of the fact that his singer has done something as retrograde as getting married in the first place. Anita Pallenberg couldn't disguise that she loathed Bianca and regarded her as a threat to her role as queen of the court of the Stones. They both sneered at the fact that Bianca, who had even less interest in the music of the Stones than Prince Rupert, had asked the organist to play the theme from *Love Story*. It would prove to be the first and last marriage for both of them, although not in the way anyone thought.

Their union finally consecrated, they stumbled on to the party at the Café des Arts, where Terry Reid, Stephen Stills, Doris Troy, and Michael Shrieve from Santana jammed while the likes of Julie Christie, then at the zenith of her beauty, and Brigitte Bardot, a star so long established that her presence impressed even the Stones, frugged listlessly. Keith Richards would have joined the jam, reported *Rolling Stone*, but by the time it had been organized, he had passed out flat on his back with his mouth open. Mick Jagger's father, Joe, a mere fifty-eight at the time, looked and felt like a stranger at his eldest son's big day. When he left the Café des Arts late that night, he was still carrying the wedding present he hadn't had the opportunity to give to his son and bride throughout the long, trying day, and he confided feelingly to a reporter, "I hope my other son doesn't become a superstar." This last wish was to be fulfilled. Les Perrin later described May 12 as "the most difficult day of my professional career."

Back in London that same night, the groom's forsaken partner Marianne Faithfull was in a cell at Paddington Green police station, sleeping off the effects of a shot of Valium administered by a Harley Street specialist and the three vodka martinis she'd drunk to deal with the fact that Mick was marrying someone else. In her memoirs, she waspishly points to the close physical resemblance between the bride and groom and ascribes the match to his narcissism. "Mick married himself," she wrote.

By the morning, the agreed facts of Mick Jagger's wedding day had already begun to splinter into a hundred, often contradictory accounts. It was such a mess that three men—Keith Richards, the saxophonist Bobby Keys, and Roger Vadim—all claimed to have been best man. A guest later assured me that Keith had decided to liven up proceedings by wearing a Nazi uniform. If so, that's one of the few things the press didn't record. Bianca claims that later that night the bedroom of the happy couple was invaded by Keith Moon. He was actually on his way to play with the Who at the Kinetic Circus in Birmingham.

The Jagger wedding was the shabbiest free-for-all in the history of both rock and marriage and skin-crawlingly embarrassing for all the key participants. It apotheosized the sixties generation's genius for dismantling all the old formality and putting little but inebriation and self-indulgence in its place, perfectly framing the moment at which those who had come to tear down the temple of society were actually caught groping at its open blouse, taking their celebrity and their power and their beautiful girlfriends and their drugs and their tax exile and flaunting it in front of everyone from the World War II veterans looking at the pictures in the *Daily News* to the sixteen-year-old Black Sabbath fans reading all about it in *Rolling Stone*. It ought to have been a *Titanic*-meets-iceberg moment. It should have been the end of the affair.

It wasn't. It was actually a beginning. In a sense, this misfiring spectacular was the perfect launchpad for not only Stones Mark II but also a whole new lease on rock life, one that none of the participants would have been able to imagine. This was due to two things. The first was a record.

Sticky Fingers, **the** group's ninth album in the UK and their eleventh US release, came out in the United States the week of the wedding. It had appeared in Europe earlier, and it was already number one on the UK chart while the single "Brown Sugar" was in the same position on the singles chart. The week after the wedding, the album went to number one on the US chart and stayed there for four weeks.

Both album and single dominated the early summer of 1971, outshining other superstar releases in May, including James Taylor's *Mud Slide Slim and the Blue Horizon,* Paul McCartney's *Ram,* Crosby, Stills, Nash & Young's live double album *4 Way Street,* and Jethro Tull's *Aqualung,* which came out on the day of the wedding. It also overshadowed cult contenders that came out in the same month such as Roy Harper's *Stormcock,* Caravan's *In the Land of the Grey and Pink,* the Flamin' Groovies' *Teenage Head,* and the first stirring of what would later come to be called "world music," the debut release by Osibisa.

Also in May *All Things Considered* was launched as the flagship news program of National Public Radio. Woody Allen stood in for Johnny Carson on *The Tonight Show,* plugging his recently released movie *Bananas* and welcoming Bob Hope as his guest. Hope joked that he couldn't stay long because he had to entertain the troops in Washington. The cover of *Newsweek* wondered if J. Edgar Hoover, director of the FBI since Prohibition, should retire. *Playboy* published a major interview with John Wayne in which he defended his involvement in the expulsion of alleged communists from Hollywood in the fifties and describes films like *Midnight Cowboy* and *Easy Rider* as "perverted."

The hot books were William Peter Blatty's *The Exorcist,* which was at number one on the *New York Times* best seller list for seventeen weeks. Frederick Forsyth was getting rave reviews for *The Day of the Jackal. THX 1138,* the first feature film by a recently graduated George Lucas, was released in the United States. The surprise hit of May was *Summer of '42* starring Jennifer O'Neill as a beautiful woman widowed during the war who introduces the fifteen-year-old hero to sex one wartime summer on Nantucket.

In Britain *Sticky Fingers* was the first Rolling Stones album not to be priced in pounds, shillings, and pence. In the United States the list price was $5.98, but even at the discount price of $3.39 being offered by Gary's on Fifth Avenue, only the wealthiest fans could go straight out and buy it. Most would go and visit it in the record shop, where they might be able to listen to a couple of tracks and certainly gaze in wonder at its cover, which is the thing that really made it such an icon.

Like *Sgt. Pepper's Lonely Hearts Club Band*, *Sticky Fingers* is one of the handful of records as famous for their covers as for what that cover contains. It remains probably the band's most charismatic album thanks to the halo effect provided by the sleeve, which is dominated by a black-and-white picture of the business section of a male stud wearing Levi's jeans, the fly of which had an actual zipper that could be pulled down to reveal an inner card showing a pair of white briefs and a male torso. The card was added late in the design process after it was realized that the zip would otherwise damage the record. The sleeve, a play on the idea of "packaging," which went over most heads, was designed by Andy Warhol. Billy Name, who was a resident photographer at Warhol's Factory, took the picture. Many members of the Factory, including the actor-model-stud Joe Dallesandro, claim the credit for modeling for the picture. (In Spain, which was still ruled by the illiberal General Franco, it was replaced by a photograph of disembodied fingers reaching out of a jar of treacle.)

For the Rolling Stones, the cover was the outward sign of a new confidence, a determination to answer to nobody but themselves. Warhol had originally been contacted by Mick Jagger in 1969 with a view to his doing the cover for their second greatest hits album, *Through the Past, Darkly*. Jagger's letter said, "Do whatever you want and please write back saying how much money you would like." It's unlikely that Decca, the record company at the time, would have signed the purchase order arising from such a brief. The company similarly balked at Jagger's wish to have a lavatory wall on the cover of *Beggars Banquet*. But with the new label, backed by Atlantic, which was in turn part of Warner Brothers, which was ultimately bankrolled by the Kinney Corporation's millions from its parking lots and funeral homes, money was less likely to be a problem. Questions of taste, which had previously been ruled on by their elders, were all theirs. The Man no longer appeared to be in charge.

Sticky Fingers was a transitional record in every respect. When the contract expired in 1970, Decca claimed that it was still owed a single. The Rolling Stones provided one called "Cocksucker Blues," confident that chairman Sir Edward Lewis would never release it. He didn't. It was the first record made without any input from Brian Jones, the difficult young man who had founded the band. In his place they had Mick Taylor, an orthodox lead guitar virtuoso who had come to their attention as the latest and youngest of a succession of featured soloists with John Mayall's band. Taylor made no contribution to the group's image, which may have been one of the reasons they chose him. When a troublesome employee is replaced, it's often by someone from the opposite end of the difficulty spectrum. The soft-featured Taylor was unlikely to get into anyone else's light. He was biddable, and when he left the band in 1974, he had just one joint writing credit to his name.

Sticky Fingers straddled two decades. It was made up of material that had been left over from the previous albums—"Brown Sugar" and "Wild Horses" had been recorded at Muscle Shoals not long after Altamont in late 1969—and during the sessions that took place at Olympic in West London in early 1971, the Stones recorded some tunes that they would hold over for 1972's *Exile on Main Street*. Two of the songs came out in other people's versions before the release of the album. "Sister Morphine," which was cowritten by Marianne Faithfull, first emerged as the B-side of her single in 1969, but then was pulled two days after release when Decca realized what it was about. When the *Sticky Fingers* version came out, her writing credit wasn't on it, a state of affairs Jagger attributes to the desire to keep the publishing out of the clutches of her former manager. Gram Parsons, who had been sent a tape of "Wild Horses" by his friend Keith Richards with a view to getting the Flying Burrito Brothers' Sneaky Pete Kleinow to put pedal steel on it, had realized the appeal of the song, recorded his own version, and then twisted

Jagger's and Richards's arms to allow him to put out his own a full year before the release of *Sticky Fingers*.

Sticky Fingers has more musical range than any other Rolling Stones album thanks to the input of a lot of people who weren't strictly in the band or were new to it: saxophonist Bobby Keys on "Can't You Hear Me Knocking," Memphis maestro Jim Dickinson's honky-tonk piano on "Wild Horses," Billy Preston's churchy organ solo on "I Got the Blues," slide guitar on "Sister Morphine" left over from Ry Cooder's controversial contributions to *Let It Bleed*, and, on "Can't You Hear Me Knocking," a Latin-flavored guitar solo from Mick Taylor that suggested he'd been listening to Santana's *Abraxas*, which had been a huge hit in 1970.

Nobody can remember precisely how the lyrics came along: Marianne Faithfull reckons Jagger had the chords for "Sister Morphine" for six months before she wrote the lyrics; some reckon "Wild Horses" was written by Keith about Anita Pallenberg, but Marianne says it was something she said during a domestic exchange with Jagger. Claudia Linnear and Marsha Hunt have both claimed to be the inspiration behind "Brown Sugar." All the women involved have in their different ways been forced to accept that they owe their fame to their association with a bunch of young men who have, almost without exception, traded them in for younger models. As Faithfull has reflected, it's all very flattering being the paramour of the star and being quoted as the inspiration of his material, but eventually your life is no longer your own, and you end up as the punch line of a piece of rock trivia. At the time, few people pointed out that the exasperated, up-for-days tone of the lyrics could mask a streak of something called sexism. The word was scarcely ever in use and, if anything, as Spinal Tap were later to say, "What's wrong with sexy?" The songs of the Stones might depict a world of predatory women, sleazy businessmen, and straights who weren't with the program. The message of the music was that you can escape all this in the everlasting adolescence offered by the sound the band makes.

Although there are tracks such as the closer, "Moonlight Mile," which were grander and more Gothic than anything they'd done before, the record's heart is in "Brown Sugar," "Bitch," and "I Got the Blues," in which they still sound like the rock-and-roll dance band who made "Around and Around." Anyone seeking to advance the argument that the true leaders of rock bands are the rhythm sections doesn't have to look much further than "Bitch" for the push and pull between Bill Wyman and Charlie Watts, the two members who learned to play rock and roll after they'd already mastered other styles.

"Brown Sugar" was the key single of 1971. I recall Saturday nights that summer turning up to shabbily furnished north London fire-traps lugging a Party Seven of sticky sweet Watney's Red, twenty Benson & Hedges, and a copy of that yellow-labeled mono single with the protruding tongue on it, nights that would climax with the sound of "Brown Sugar" rasping and rattling from somebody's lovingly assembled and nervously guarded component stereo, trainee teachers thrusting their hips in each other's direction with unmistakably carnal intent, while studiously avoiding anything as telling as eye contact, cigarettes held aloft, each recapitulation of the chorus lasciviously lip-synched, temporarily transported to the Dionysian state of peak horn that the Stones achieved more often than anyone else, the rented room gravid with lust and throbbing with abandon. If records do change lives, as editors are always insisting they do, then they tend to do it for only as long as the record runs. "Brown Sugar" changed lives for three minutes fifty seconds, which is the most you can ask of even the greatest record.

In a sense, it was the Rolling Stones' last proper pop hit. "Brown Sugar" was an old-fashioned jukebox record. It worked because it had the power to move a room, any room. Since most 45s tend to be bought by people who like the record more than they like the band, singles sales measure the popularity of the music, whereas album sales measure the popularity of the act. Among those people who laid down their money for that single (effectively an EP with the addition of "Bitch" and a brilliant live recording of "Let It Rock," which may actually have been the best of their many Chuck Berry covers), there was little debate about the subject of the song, a scarred old slaver who whipped and went down on the women in the slave quarters. The whole song, riff and all, was composed by Mick Jagger, who wrote it while killing time between shots on the Australian set of *Ned Kelly* in 1970. It's still a staple of the Stones live set, but when he sings it, he often changes the line "Hear him whip the women just around midnight" to "You should have heard him just around midnight." "I never would write that song. I would probably censor myself," he said many years later.

Sticky Fingers is also the Rolling Stones' most influential album. The boho cowboy pose that people associate with the many heirs of Gram Parsons, that frayed country sound that is apologetically referred to as alt-country, begins with "Dead Flowers" (which has been covered by New Riders of the Purple Sage, Cowboy Junkies, Steve Earle, and anybody else who ever wore buckskin) and "Wild Horses," the latter of which became one of Jagger and Richards's most covered songs with versions by Guns N' Roses, Jewel, Bush, Alicia Keys, and Susan Boyle.

Then there are the groups whose entire careers seem to come in the form of love notes to *Sticky Fingers*. When in 1991 Primal Scream hired the album's producer Jimmy Miller, the result was "Movin' on Up," to all intents and purposes a postdated fan letter to this era of the Rolling Stones. Everything the Verve tried to do is in Paul Buckmaster's strings at the end of "Moonlight Mile." Groups as far apart in time and space as the New York Dolls, Aerosmith, the Black Crowes, and the Kings of Leon have at the very least started their careers as humble footnotes to the Rolling Stones as they were in 1971, at the very peak of their glory.

That the Stones also embodied the look of the year also indicated how far they had bent the world to their will. Mick Jagger had never been considered particularly handsome. When the Stones first emerged, the newspapers liked to contrast them unfavorably with the well-groomed Beatles. Adult eyes failed to register that the Stones put just as much care into their appearance as the Beatles did. In addition, their front man with the wanton, parted lips, the sleepy, insolent eyes, had one of those faces the gaze was quite happy to feast on. Chrissie Shrimpton remembers her boyfriend having vegetables thrown at him in the street in the sixties. In those days, the very way he carried himself seemed like an affront to some people's ideas of maleness. His movements in performance were said to be stolen from James Brown or Tina Turner, but they were transformed by a fresh layer of knowingness, by flickers of camp and the additional dimension of being a member of an outfit that like all great groups carried with it its own internal narrative, a narrative that made everyone else's seem pale and tired. By 1971, thanks to the work of a new generation of portrait photographers like David Bailey and pop photographers like Gered Mankowitz, Jagger had come to represent a new form of androgynous male beauty. (Also in 1971 a young woman from New Jersey transformed herself into a New York scenester by clipping some Keith Richards pictures out of the newspaper and cutting her own hair in imitation. "Machete-ing my way out of the folk era," as Patti Smith later recalled.)

Carly Simon, who was two years younger than Jagger, was in 1971 homing in on the same look from the other side of the spectrum. Carly was regarded as the least beautiful of the three daughters of the prominent New York publisher Richard Simon, one of the partners of Simon & Schuster, and grew up acutely aware of it. However, as she got older, she was also aware that people were beginning to remark that she had a quality of raw sexuality, often attributed to her long legs and wide mouth. In addition, she also had that quality Jagger had of appearing to light up when performing.

The young folkie Simon was fortunate to be signed to Elektra Records in 1970 rather than one of the competitors. Elektra was run by Jac Holzman, who of all the old record businessmen understood that the most powerful marketing tool at his disposal was the twelve-inch-square cover of the album. Album covers had the effect of making their contents seem more important than they were, and Elektra's album covers, which included albums by Love and the Doors, looked more important than anyone else's. Simon's first two albums, which both came out in 1971, put her picture front and center: on the first album, she is reclining on an old couch, her dress pulled taut across her parted legs; on the second, she's standing framed by a gate in Regent's Park, the light from behind silhouetting her legs through a diaphanous peasant skirt. When she appeared at a televised concert in Central Park in July, she outdazzled the rest of the bill, which included Boz Scaggs and the Beach Boys, in a clinging red dress slashed to reveal her interminable legs.

In the week of Jagger's wedding, she was making her first New York appearance, supporting the equally glamorous Kris Kristofferson at the Bitter End. They were both performers you were as happy to gaze upon as you might be to hear. People remarked that Carly looked like Mick Jagger. She was sufficiently connected in New York society to make something of this resemblance. A few days before Jagger's wedding, she interviewed him by phone for the *New York Times*. Their exchanges were flirtatious. It seems reasonable to assume that this didn't come about via the standard PR approach. Jagger probably knew that in the last year Simon had been romantically linked with Kris Kristofferson, Cat Stevens, and Warren Beatty and probably wondered what he'd done to be left out.

A year later the two hooked up at a party thrown for the Stones. She was seeing James Taylor by then, and Jagger was married, but vows rarely get in the way when two centers of ego and beauty wish to merge. They're even more bootless when they appear to be in some senses the same person. Against such forces, the battlements of feminism and hippie culture cannot endure long. They say swans mate for life. Stars mate for glory and their own glamour's increase. The spur for Carly Simon's marriage to James Taylor was Bianca Jagger ringing him up and suggesting his fiancée was having an affair with Bianca's new husband. It seems Bianca was no less persuaded by Jagger's distinctive backing vocals on Simon's huge worldwide hit "You're So Vain" than the rest of us. That record, intoxicating precisely because of the things it supposedly satirizes, comes from inside a new world that was being born in 1971. In this song and its attendant hoopla, the world of pop music merged with the world of Lear jets, and we were all being invited to envy life on the other side of the red rope. As the decade went on, rock and roll's newly acquired glamour would come to make the Hollywood kind look shabby and old.

Following their wedding, Mr. and Mrs. Jagger began their honeymoon on a yacht. Since his new wife had little use for seclusion, they ended up in Venice, never the best place to avoid photographers. The couple were discovering that there is a peculiar mathematics of fame whereby if one famous person marries a slightly less famous but glamorous person, then there is no limit to the amount of fame they can jointly generate or the quantity of publicity they will attract. Modern multimedia power couples like Kim Kardashian and Kanye West, Brad Pitt and Angelina Jolie, Beyoncé and Jay Z, and David and Victoria Beckham are the contemporary heirs of Mick and Bianca. But the photographers who tussled for access had a limited market for their pictures in 1971. Neither the UK nor the United States had any kind of celebrity magazine at the time. Many of the newspapers thought the marriage of a rock star was beneath them. The counterculture publications treated it with lofty disdain.

Meanwhile, the Stones' mobile recording truck had arrived at Nellcôte. A week later the band started playing in the basement. This was the same basement where, according to myths happily promoted by Keith, the German occupiers had kept those they wished to interrogate. It was damp, acoustically poor, and far from ideal for recording, which meant a process that was always likely to be long and drawn out was even more so. Unwilling to pay the normal tariff for electricity, the Stones had somebody shinny up a pole and try to run the mobile off the town's power supply. What they found was that the town was susceptible to the same sudden losses of power as were many southern European communities in those days. This is mildly inconvenient if you're shaving. If you're painstakingly adding a guitar solo on a multitrack recording, it can be

Paul and Linda McCartney attend the High Court in London in February 1971. McCartney's legal action triggered the winding-up of the Beatles. John Lennon's *Rolling Stone* interview (RIGHT) the same month ensured there would be no going back.

1

2

Alfred Hitchcock returns to London's Covent Garden to film *Frenzy* in January, just as developers are planning to flatten the old market.

3

David Bowie (RIGHT) performs at a Hollywood party wearing a Michael Fish gown during his first visit to the United States in February. In June he and Angie and their baby Zowie (LEFT) pose for the *Daily Mirror*. The headline read "Which one is Dad?"

At the same time as Carole King is recording *Tapestry* in Hollywood in January, Joni Mitchell is making *Blue* in the studio next door and James Taylor is cutting "You've Got a Friend" around the corner.

Led Zeppelin's Back to the Clubs tour during the spring allows them to unveil new songs like "Stairway to Heaven" in small venues months before they come out on record.

Nick Drake's reluctance to stir from his room to promote his records means the release of *Bryter Layter* in March goes unremarked. Later in the year he drops off the tapes of *Pink Moon* at his record company and disappears.

The Rolling Stones follow Led Zeppelin into many of the same university halls on their Farewell to Britain tour. Mick Jagger and his girlfriend Bianca let the train take the strain.

Before credit-card booking, rock audiences comprise those willing to stand in line. Stones fans in Manchester show their prized tickets.

Stevie Wonder with his new wife, Syreeta, in 1971, the year he turns twenty-one, renegotiates his Motown contract, and begins working with TONTO, the revolutionary synthesizer invented by Robert Margouleff and Malcolm Cecil (RIGHT).

The true stars of *Soul Train*, the TV show that Don Cornelius takes national in 1971, are the self-taught dancers in the program's trademark "line."

14

13

Motown boss Berry Gordy doesn't think *What's Going On* is the kind of material his leading man Marvin Gaye should be recording but is too preoccupied to prevent it.

RIGHT: In April Francis Ford Coppola finally begins shooting *The Godfather*, with the gunning-down of Marlon Brando on Little Italy's Mott Street.

15

16

"Spanish" Tony Sanchez and dancer Madeleine D'Arcy board the plane sent by Mick Jagger to convey the beautiful people from London to France for his wedding to Bianca Pérez-Mora Macias.

Ahmet Ertegun is at Mick Jagger's right hand when he marries Bianca in Saint-Tropez in May. Keith Richards skulks in the background, muttering dissent.

17

18

19

Unprepared for the level of interest, Jagger makes his wedding vows inches from a battery of cameras. It's the last time he gets married.

LEFT: Julie Christie, fresh from *The Go-Between* and *McCabe & Mrs. Miller,* dances to the hastily convened wedding band at the Café des Arts.

20 The August *Rolling Stone* cover that began the cult of Keef, inspiring Patti Smith and many others to take scissors to their own hair.

U.S. table tennis star Glenn Cowan stops traffic 21 in China during the "ping-pong diplomacy" that eventually opens up relations with the United States.

More than ten thousand are arrested or detained during the May Day Protests against the Vietnam War in Washington, the largest mass arrest in American history.

22

The pyramid stage is built for the first Glastonbury festival in June, which is blessed by good weather and sparse attendance. ²³

During the same summer solstice, hundreds of thousands of young Americans troop to the inhospitable wilds of Louisiana for the misnamed "Celebration of Life." Some don't come back. ²⁴

25

26

The three defendants in the *Oz* magazine trial are ritually sheared while awaiting sentence in June over their controversial "Schoolkids" issue, seen inset in a benefits issue.

The shag hairstyle that Jane Fonda sports in the 1971 hit *Klute* is widely copied. New York is depicted as dirty and dangerous in more than one movie.

27

catastrophic. This was classic Stones: an act of rebellion that ends up making life more difficult for the rebels.

On top of Nellcôte's shortcomings as a place to make music were overlaid intrigues worthy of a Jacobean court as the usual Stones cast of retainers, petitioners, and villains drifted in and out at the volatile pleasure of the house's tenant. The true power center was in the upstairs rooms to which both Keith and Anita would mysteriously repair in order to top themselves up with the heroin, which was, thanks to the proximity of Marseille, in ready supply. Even Mick Jagger didn't dare go upstairs to find out why the guitarist had withdrawn from the session and left the other band members twiddling their thumbs.

Jagger had agreed to site the recording truck at Keith's place because at least it meant nobody would have to get him to the studio. However, Mick underestimated how difficult it could be to get Keith out of bed and, once he was out, to get him to work on a song. The band were hardly ever all present at one time. Charlie lived too far away. Bill didn't like the atmosphere. Mick Taylor could get there only when his wife was available to drive him. The singer was on honeymoon. Jimmy Miller, who had produced *Sticky Fingers*, was heard to plead, "Hasn't anyone got a song?" as the sessions stumbled on as if without end. The record started to sit up only in the fall of 1971, when they moved to Los Angeles and added the vocals.

Exile on Main Street came out in 1972. Like most double albums, it took a while to digest. Even if you could decipher the lyrics through the density of the mix, you couldn't really say that they made a great deal of sense. This no longer mattered. From here on, Stones records seemed to be about themselves, designed to sustain and boost the mystique of the Stones brand, which was to become more important than any individual record. Henceforth, the band lived in a position of gilded statelessness. Their records no longer seemed to refer to London, New York, Los Angeles, or anywhere in the known world but instead seemed to emanate from a Guy Peellaert illustration come to life.

The people who loved *Exile on Main Street* were not the pop pickers who'd picked up *Sticky Fingers*. Instead, they were the people who loved the Stones most. It appeared in the wake of Keith Richards's "Lennon Remembers"–type interview, which got him on the cover of *Rolling Stone* and established the idea that he somehow was the true spirit of the Rolling Stones, an idea he has never been in a hurry to discourage. In 1971 the Rolling Stones became a brand, and Keith was elevated to the position of being that brand's key spokesman.

In a sense, the pictures taken at Nellcôte that summer by French photographer Dominique Tarlé matter as much to the legacy of the Rolling Stones as anything they recorded there. These images of unshaven young men so confident in their appearance that they can afford to be slovenly about it, their clothing apparently made up of whatever garment had been at the end of the bed when the noonday sun tickled them into wakefulness, drifting around the halls of this antique pleasure palace holding precious Martin guitars by their necks, long cigarettes dangling from their mouths as they reach for the first coffee or cognac of the day and make their way down to the villa's dank cellar to fall in with whatever subset of heavy friends happened to have either got up early or remained there from the previous night—this elegantly wasted look became the new hippie fantasy.

In the background, like so many extras, were their lissome blond girlfriends and their tousle-haired children. It was a dream of a new form of living, a fantasy in which you could live the life of a hippie on the budget of a banker, like Manet's *Le Déjeuner sur l'herbe* as reimagined by the advertising department of *Rolling Stone*. It became, through the photographs of Dominique Tarlé, the earthly dream of a whole generation of young men, and also, because it was the most photographed recording session of the era, fixed a visual idea of how creativity should look in the rock era. As Mick Jagger later said, it didn't really happen that way, but the look of Nellcôte couldn't help but make us believe that it did.

It was the year that they established the mystique on which the Rolling Stones have run ever since. Very little has happened with the Stones since that summer that is all that interesting musically. If you went to see them today and their repertoire didn't go beyond 1972, you'd still feel you'd got the Stones. The rest is pyros. Since that time, the main interest has been in them as a brand, a soap opera, a sitcom, a group of wealthy men fighting the depredations of age, an international attraction that is not, as you might imagine, hanging on by its fingernails but instead remains ready to roll through any frontier you put in front of them and set records wherever records are to be set. The move to France didn't just give them another five years. It gave them another forty-five.

Mick and Bianca divorced in 1978. Mick has never formally remarried. Nixon and Mao have gone to their graves, as has Glenn Cowan, the long-haired table tennis player, Ian Stewart, Gram Parsons, John Lennon, Jimmy Miller, and many others who drifted through Nellcôte that summer. John Kerry, the young man who addressed the Senate committee, is at the time of writing, 2015, the US secretary of state. In 2006 Nellcôte was sold to a Russian, who reputedly paid a hundred million euros. Prince Rupert Loewenstein died in 2014, having given up looking after the Stones affairs in 2008. He had proposed that the Stones sell their business, when they received an offer that amounted to double their net worth in cash in their pockets. They were going to take it until Mick Jagger changed his mind at the last minute.

We will never know what combination of musician's nervousness and businessman's hard-nosed calculation made him withdraw. One of the reasons his group has now been going longer than most record companies is that they haven't entered into any relationship they couldn't walk away from. Over the more than fifty years that they've been trading, they have seen the business change to the point where hardheaded investors will pay many millions of dollars for the rights to exploit in the future songs and likenesses that were once thought to be the definition of ephemeral. In this marketplace the Rolling Stones have a value greater than anyone else for the simple reason that through all that time, through good times and bad, whether relationships were cordial or poisonous, no matter what waves of musical change threatened the cliffs of tradition, they never broke up. This, above all, is what made them unique. As they used to say about the Windmill Theatre, which stayed open through the London Blitz, they never closed.

The small step that took the Rolling Stones from the home counties to the Côte d'Azur coincided with the People's Republic of China making another small step that led to their eventual emergence as the powerhouse of the world economy and began the global tilt that has seen it become the world's manufacturing base, the source of all the expensive digital toys that keep the youth of the world amused, and the world's biggest market for luxury goods. Back in 1971 even Mick Jagger, who's never been one for predictions, wouldn't have dreamed that the band he moved across the English Channel in order to preserve their finances would still be functioning over forty years later or that he as a great-grandfather would be leading them.

The music doesn't belong to the past. On July 27, 2013, Taylor Swift introduced Carly Simon to duet with her on "You're So Vain" in front of fifty-five thousand predominantly teenage girls in Foxborough, Massachusetts. All those girls, whose mothers weren't born when the original came out, knew the words. Meanwhile, Georgia May Jagger and the Richards sisters have lent their version of the Rolling Stones brand to the marketing of Sunglass Hut. Bianca Jagger is fronting the Bianca Jagger Human Rights Foundation. Mick Jagger was on the front page of Britain's biggest newspaper when he was photographed entertaining a twenty-seven-year-old companion he had met on tour in Switzerland, only a month after the death of his longtime partner L'Wren Scott. The only surprising thing is that we find it surprising.

On March 12, 2014, the Rolling Stones played their second show in China in front of a modest crowd, by their standards, of ten thousand at the Mercedes-Benz Arena in Shanghai. Like any other international luxury brand, the Stones were building up their business in the world's biggest market for luxuries. They played a few tunes from *Sticky Fingers*, which is probably the album you would use if you wished to explain them to a Martian. The first time they played China, in 2006, they brought on local star Cui Jian to sing "Wild Horses" with them. The censors wouldn't allow them to do "Brown Sugar." They didn't complain. They played "Dead Flowers" instead. As Prince Rupert was clear-eyed enough to see back in 1971, rock bands don't change the world. The world changes without their help. Writing in the British underground magazine *Oz* in July 1971, Richard Neville said that the Jagger wedding was "public confirmation of the growing suspicion that Mick Jagger has finally repudiated the possibilities of a counterculture of which music is a part," which was another way of recognizing the same thing. By the time that line was published, Neville and the other *Oz* editors were in the dock of Britain's highest court.

MAY

Rolling Stones: "Brown Sugar"

Serge Gainsbourg: "Ballade de Melody Nelson"

Carly Simon: "Anticipation"

Randy Newman: "Tickle Me"

James Taylor: "Hey Mister, That's Me Up on the Jukebox"

David Crosby: "Laughing"

Paul McCartney: "Uncle Albert/Admiral Halsey"

Elton John: "Tiny Dancer"

Colin Blunstone: "Say You Don't Mind"

Stephen Stills: "Change Partners"

JUNE

Won't Get Fooled Again

On May 1, 1971, a bomb exploded in a storeroom at the Biba shop in Kensington High Street. Responsibility for it was claimed by the Angry Brigade. Since the previous targets of Britain's only homegrown terrorist cell had all been political—ministers' homes and foreign embassies—the decision to extend their campaign to one of London's most popular fashion outlets was particularly puzzling to the generation of pleasure seekers who had grown up in the sixties, a few of whom might even have had some distant sympathy for the brigade's radical objectives.

The Angry Brigade explained its action as follows in a communiqué, which had a twist on a Bob Dylan song: "If you're not busy being born, you're busy buying. . . . The only thing you can do with the modern slavehouses—called boutiques—is WRECK THEM. You can't reform profit capitalism and inhumanity. Just kick it till it breaks."

In 1971 the loose alliance of groups and individuals who had rallied under the banner of the alternative society splintered into different factions, ranging from people who wished to bring about the violent overthrow of the state through those who considered themselves in permanent opposition to bourgeois values to those who simply wanted the right to pursue their lives free from postwar strictures. It also saw the severing of what had previously been seen as natural bonds between rock and rebellion. People who'd been reading the Marxist philosopher Herbert Marcuse's *One-Dimensional Man*, whose publisher announced it as "the most subversive book published in the United States this century," argued it was no use looking to rock to bring down society because this allegedly repressive society used things such as rock to neuter the urge to protest. The record business was clearly happy to deal with anything provided that it sold. In May John Lennon's single "Power to the People," which had been dashed off in response to reading an interview with the radical Tariq Ali, was still on the charts. The same message from less familiar sources fell on stony ground. In June a full-page advertisement appeared in the *Melody Maker*. It was for a new album by a group called Third World War and the ad copy foreshadowed the punk rock movement of the late '70s. "This is class rage, class anguish," declared the ad. The record didn't sell, and it wasn't for want of trying.

In the film of the rooftop concert that climaxes the 1970 Beatles film *Let It Be* there is a cutaway of an older gentleman climbing up a fire ladder to the roof to find out where the noise is coming from. He is wearing a buttoned overcoat, horn-rimmed spectacles, and a trilby hat and in his mouth is jammed a pipe. Even in the few seconds that he is in shot, it is possible to read the hint of the military in his bearing and the disapproval he can't help but radiate. The world in 1971 appeared to be run by men like that. They had wives who wore twin sets and kept their hats on while drinking Brown Windsor soup in stuffy hotel dining rooms. There was nothing in their manner or appearance that suggested they had ever been young. And why should there? When they had been in their late teenage years, they had been in some godforsaken barracks or living a stultifying domestic existence in which the best they could hope for at the end of a week was powdered egg. These people had grown up believing that pleasure was something that could be snatched only in tiny increments. It was something that was delivered only when the requirements of duty had been fully satisfied. Like a day of sunshine at an English coastal resort, it was the exception rather than the rule and was appreciated as such. Pleasure, like freedom, was far from a right.

During the fifties and sixties, these people had worked diligently to ensure that their children, the baby boomers, would have a different kind of life. They then reacted with hurt surprise when their offspring turned out to be entirely different kind of people. My own father could simply never understand why a generation who could afford to wear smart clothes should instead decide to deck themselves out in denim. This feeling of incomprehension was even more pronounced when we would wear army surplus jackets or long naval greatcoats, the kind of clothing that he and his generation associated with getting shot at or shouted at. When he said Bob Dylan "wasn't music," that wasn't an indication of intolerance so much as a poignant statement of sincere belief. How could he possibly be expected to surrender to this, he who was tuned so differently, he who was built for duty rather than fun? The generation that had grown up since the war had little sense of duty. They weren't particularly interested in jobs, career, money, security, or the future. Since there was a feeling that this would all magically work itself out, they didn't really need to.

The thing they asked most of so-called straight society was that it should leave them alone. As soon as they could, they grew their hair long and shacked up with boyfriends or girlfriends in distant cities, often without telling their parents. For the majority of baby boomers who were in London during this period, that was how they spent their time: growing their hair and having sex. There wasn't an awful lot else to do, and both activities were free.

In 1971 there seemed to be two separate worlds. One was dominated by serious people who had fought in the war, had short hair, and ran things. The other was dominated by pranksters with long hair who just wanted to enjoy things. The idea that those two worlds would not be in permanent opposition to each other seemed far-fetched. The idea that politicians could ever have wished to tap into the enthusiasm that attended rock and roll, other than in the clumsy manner that Harold Wilson had used to sidle into the spotlight of the Beatles, seemed ridiculous. In fact, it wasn't even thought about. In modern parlance, it wasn't even a thing.

On the other hand, these fun seekers weren't wildly interested in material things because there weren't an awful lot of them. Their desires in this direction tended to be focused on two particular areas: records and clothes. On Saturdays it would be perfectly normal to go into the West End and just spend the day in the company of records. Shops served as libraries, places of association, and churches as well as retail outlets. You could wander around the West End, from the twinkling array of imports at Musicland or Harlequin to the severe-looking old blues and jazz albums in Dobell's on Charing Cross Road, from the soul singles outside Cheapo Cheapo Records in Rupert Street to the tiny kiosk opposite Finsbury Park station out of which reggae singles would be heard blasting. Music wasn't simply a pleasure. Record shops weren't just a place to buy things or to associate with other people who wanted to buy things. They were an education in themselves.

The smart magazines were trying to get a handle on the world of liberated London, to turn revolt into style, and therefore they studied the alternative press, which was enjoying a small boom. In London the products of the alternative press could be found if you knew which specialist store in which area of town to look in. In the United States these papers sprang up all over the country, usually in college towns, galvanizing opposition to the war in Vietnam. The alternative press attracted disproportionate profile by their willingness to publish words and images that the grown-up press wouldn't go near and in some cases, such as the *Los Angeles Free Press* and Boston's *Real Paper*, prospering because they had a near monopoly on local music and entertainment listings and the advertising that came in its wake.

Given the limitations of their distribution, these titles didn't sell many copies, but since a great deal of the material they published was the kind of thing that would never have made it into print in the standard outlets, they were much talked about. They lived in the netherworld of the media, with all the attendant dangers. A steer too far in one direction or another might attract the attentions of some guardian of public morals, a printer demanding to be paid up front, or a distributor requiring indemnification against possible legal action.

The subliminal message that came through the damp pages of these titles, a message eagerly devoured by those of us who were too young and provincial to actually take part, was that somewhere in Kensington or San Francisco a handful of privileged souls were living in a kind of saturnalia where the music was the very choicest, the whole way of speaking and behaving was being changed from top to bottom, nobody had anything more important they ought to be doing, and the joints were being rolled by beautiful long-haired girls who didn't think it necessary to get dressed because within the next half an hour they were bound to be taking you to bed. These magazines would have hated to be described as "lifestyle" titles, but that's inevitably how they were read.

The people who wrote for them may have prided themselves on their willingness to publish rambling, discursive pieces on drugs, politics, and "the war," pieces that were often rendered illegible as well as unreadable by being laid out in broken type on colored backgrounds on over-absorbent paper. What they didn't like to talk about was the extent to which their sales relied heavily on sex, whether in the humorous form of Germaine Greer reaching inside Viv Stanshall's pants to grab his penis, the recurrence of the popular cliché of a bare-breasted black girl cradling a machine gun, any of the walnut-nippled hot mamas drawn by Robert Crumb, or the crudely cut-out Amazons who ended up on the cover of the notorious "Schoolkids" issue of *Oz*, which eventually landed its editors in court in June and brought the carnival to an abrupt halt.

The *Oz* trial of June 1971, in which the editors of the UK's most prominent underground magazine were accused of seeking to deprave and corrupt public morals, was the climactic event of Britain's Great Hippie Scare. It marked the point at which tweedy, horn-rimmed, pipe-smoking, car-washing, lawn-mowing, hat-wearing respectable Britain decided that it was no longer prepared to tolerate the provocations of a bunch of long-haired, loudmouthed libertines—many of whom were foreign, damn it, all of whom seemed determined to mock everything that they and their good lady wives held dear—and was going to give them the metaphorical and actual buzz cut their behavior was so clearly crying out for.

Mounted in the august theater of the Old Bailey, with characters wearing either the fancy dress of hippiedom or the wigs and gowns of the age of Pitt the Younger, the *Oz* trial brought the awful majesty of one of the oldest legal systems in the world to deliberate upon the sexual readiness of a cartoon bear and its likeliness to deprave and corrupt children of school age who would never have heard of the scandal had the law not chosen to intervene. Meanwhile, in the streets outside, lissome daughters of the gentry in hot pants and mini-skirts addressed their supporters through megaphones, bemused bobbies moved in to extinguish halfhearted fires lit by supporters a hundred yards away from where in centuries past enemies of the realm would have been actually burned to death, former members of the Beatles led processions nowhere in particular, representatives of the popular press, some of them in actual mackintoshes, lingered in the hope of an aristocratic nipple, while the overwhelming mass of the population of London reacted to the entire hoopla with the grumbling indifference that is their ancient birthright. Clive James memorably described it as "a fair to middling episode of *Monty Python* running at the wrong speed."

It made celebrities of everyone involved: counsel such as John Mortimer, who went on to become Britain's most famous barrister, witnesses like DJ John Peel, jazz singer and art critic George Melly, drug law activist Caroline Coon, and comedy writer Marty Feldman, who started a whole seam of British thinking by describing the judge, Lord Justice Argyle, as "a boring old fart." Most of all, it made the defendants famous, far more famous than any of them wished to be.

Richard Neville was a handsome Australian closing on the age of thirty and feeling it. Neville had the precious gift of being able to talk a good fight and, as far as the press were concerned, the further advantage of a beautiful girlfriend named Louise Ferrier. Jim Anderson was a lawyer by training and had come over with Neville from Australia where their magazine *Oz* had been a succès de scandale. One of their friends was Martin Sharp, a gifted illustrator who ended up sharing a flat with Eric Clapton, writing the lyrics for Cream's "Tales of Brave Ulysses," and designing the cover of *Disraeli Gears*. The only non-Australian in the dock was Felix Dennis, a twenty-four-year-old former musician from outer London who had come to the notice of the other two through his success in selling *Oz* and had hence become the magazine's publisher. Anderson was the organization's conscience, Neville its propagandist, and Dennis its engine.

Oz had no particular agenda, and its lead times were too long to allow it to cover the convulsions of the scene as the weekly *International Times* did. Consequently, it relied to a large extent on stunt issues devoted to themes. The "Schoolkids" issue, which came out in 1970, was one such wheeze of Neville's. Noting his thirtieth birthday on the horizon, he complained that he was feeling old and irrelevant, and therefore it might be a good idea to invite a number of schoolkids in to edit the magazine. The editors advertised in their own pages and, given the rather narrow nature of their demographic, got a lot of well-connected kids from Notting Hill Comprehensive, the odd precocious scion of libertarian stock, and from Reading the teenage tyro rock writer Charles Shaar Murray.

Between them, they produced an issue that featured among other things the well-loved children's character Rupert Bear, the copyright of Express Newspapers, in priapic engagement with Gypsy Grandma, the copyright of Robert Crumb. The cover, which was ripped from a book that happened to be in Jim Anderson's flat, was originally intended to be a center spread. Only when Felix, demonstrating the nascent flair that would eventually make him a multimillionaire as a publisher of men's magazines, insisted that the center spread be used to sell back issues (of which they presumably had a warehouse-full) was this provocative picture promoted to the cover. Hence, the juxtaposition of mountains of naked flesh with the words "School Kids Issue" ensured that any intended subtlety would be lost, and the die was cast. It was neither the first nor the last time that a magazine's cover arrived at on a whim would have serious repercussions.

The indictment read: "The Oz Publications conspired together with Vivian Berger and certain other young persons to produce a magazine containing divers obscene lewd sexually perverted articles, cartoons, drawings and illustrations with intent thereby to debauch and corrupt the morals of children and young persons within the Realm and to arouse and implant in their minds lustful and perverted desires."

This was the kind of sonorous and rarely used charge that could in theory result in ten years in prison. The argument was that this was a magazine aimed at children rather than one put together by teenagers, who were a bit more than children. In 1971 there wasn't the moral panic about corrupting the young that exists today, but the charge was serious enough to carry the threat of real jail time with it. For all that Neville and his fellow defendants dressed up as schoolboys for the committal or as barristers in wigs, for all that they tried to turn the event into a giant prank at the expense of the establishment, they knew that this was serious. Had a similar case been brought today, more would probably have been made about the piece on student agitation at various London schools being placed opposite a photograph of a uniformed teenage schoolgirl captioned "Jailbait of the Month." Jim Anderson's time in the witness box was additionally tense because he feared that he would be asked whether he was homosexual. He had decided to answer this question honestly if it was put, even though he knew he would be laying himself open to further suspicion of corrupting minors and would also break the heart of his mother at home in Australia.

After a trial lasting almost two months, the defendants were found not guilty of conspiracy but guilty of two lesser charges. Prior to sentencing, their hair was cut for them by the prison authorities, a judicial shearing that sent a shiver of dread through every student in Britain. The sentences were overturned on appeal, with everyone from the *Listener* to the National Association of Probation Officers condemning the sentences as heavy-handed and pointing out that nobody had been corrupted. The view outside London might have been different. In his diaries, Michael Palin recalls having dinner with some teacher friends of his wife's in Surrey while the trial was going on and finding them critical of the permissive ideas that they associated with smart London folk.

The magazine boomed on the back of the publicity that attended the trial, but by 1973 it had blown itself out, and *Oz* was closed. Neville and Anderson went back home. Felix Dennis, stung by the judge's description of him as "the least intelligent of the three," started on the road to a publishing empire, most of which would be anything but alternative.

John Lennon had helped put together a benefit record for *Oz*, which like most benefit records didn't make enough money to benefit anyone. He also wrote a check for the *Oz* defense fund and told Neville, "Don't ever let lawyers into your life," the key learning gleaned from the endless meetings the Beatles split had mired him in. Lennon, newly shorn and holed up in Tittenhurst Park recording *Imagine*, claimed that Mick Jagger had been on the phone offering to help out if it went wrong. Bands did gigs for *Oz*. The re-formed Traffic took some of their live album *Welcome to the Canteen* from one such benefit performance.

In the summer of 1971 the alternative press treated rock stars as unpredictable uncles who might occasionally be touched for a donation, but still weren't sure whether rock and roll was part of the struggle or something you amused yourself with after the struggling was over. While the trial had been going on, Richard Neville managed to persuade Jim Anderson that it wouldn't look good if he were to slip away at the weekend to go to a rock festival.

* * *

In June 1971 Andrew Kerr was thirty-eight. Wellborn and privately educated, Kerr had spent ten years working with Randolph Churchill, spendthrift eldest son of the wartime prime minister, as they penned Randolph's father's official biography. Kerr was far from the standard clubman. Coming from farming stock himself, he was of the bohemian tendency among England's landed gentry. These were people who saw the possibilities of a conjunction between their traditional duty to steward the land and the more nebulous aims of the long-haired tribes who were beginning to leave the cities to establish a new way of life in England's countryside.

Returning from 1970's Isle of Wight Festival, Kerr felt there ought to be a gathering that did more than draw six hundred thousand rock fans to a massive field to bob their heads in time to Jethro Tull and Johnny Winter. He craved a festival with a nobler purpose. Unlike most people returning from rock festivals, Kerr didn't forget the idea after a good bath and a hot meal. The first thing he looked for was a site, and he wanted a site with significance. He inspected Stonehenge, not yet fenced off from visitors, and rejected it because it was surrounded by arable land. He was eventually directed toward Worthy Farm near the village of Pilton in Somerset. Here, the farmer, the thirty-six-year-old Michael Eavis, had organized a very small rock festival in 1970 in the vain hope of paying off his mortgage. The entrance fee on that occasion was one pound, the headliners were Tyrannosaurus Rex, and the handful of campers were invited to buy their morning milk from the farmhouse door. This venture didn't clear Eavis's mortgage and actually left him with more debt to pay off. Welcome to the festival business.

Kerr reached an agreement with Eavis to mount a second festival in 1971 at Worthy Farm and moved in to begin planning. He invested his own money and brought on board Randolph's daughter, Arabella, who did the same with a small family bequest. In 1954 *Time* magazine had proposed the infant Arabella as a future bride for Prince Charles. By 1970 she had swapped debutante's pearls for the kind of hippie chic, which only a handful of hippies could actually afford, and joined the trickle of upper-class dropouts in the direction of the Vale of Avalon. The Irish writer George Bernard Shaw had astutely remarked that it is impossible for one Englishman to open his mouth without another Englishman hating him, and the Aquarian Age didn't change this. Eavis regarded Kerr and Churchill with the inverted snobbery that is the standard English response to those whose speech brands them as toffs. All this was relative. For singer Linda Lewis, who was born in the East End of London and joined the throng, Eavis was, by some distance, the poshest person she had encountered in her twenty-one years.

Pilton is seven miles distant from Glastonbury, the storied settlement where Joseph of Arimathea is said to have journeyed after donating his tomb to Christ. Kerr decided that was close enough to justify calling the new festival Glastonbury Fayre. In making this kind of stretch, he was only following in the footsteps of Woodstock, which actually took place at Bethel, New York. Kerr and Churchill attempted to organize the succession of new agers, chancers, and sundry lost souls who began to arrive. Some were in place months before the festival was due to start on the summer solstice on June 20, 1971. These pioneers included Bill Harkin, who devised the pyramid stage, a one-tenth scale version of the great pyramid at Giza. This was placed on the site of an ancient spring located by dowsing. It was that kind of festival. People came from all over the world to join the effort. The Brazilian musicians Gilberto Gil and Caetano Veloso, who had been exiled to London by the military government in their home country, turned up and injected ideas from their national tradition of carnival. Jeff Dexter, former mod and now DJ at all of London's "head" concerts, used his contacts to secure the services of major bands. He approached Pink Floyd and the Grateful Dead, both of whom appeared well qualified on the grounds that their music seemed to be reaching for some higher consciousness. They also had a reputation for occasionally playing for free, which was bound to help.

A key part of Kerr's plan was that everything should be provided for free. The idea that musical performances should be available without payment had gained sufficient ground since the fence came down at Woodstock in 1969 that some bands had, at least in public, meekly succumbed to the idea. This was regardless of the fact that it was clear to any sentient observer that, whether you wished to pay the performers or not, rock shows incurred considerable expense. As if to drive home this point, Pink Floyd had lined up all their equipment on the runway at Biggin Hill airport for the cover of the 1969 album *Ummagumma*. This seemed like an unprecedented arsenal of gear at the time because it required as many as two roadies to look after it all. In the event, neither Pink Floyd nor the Grateful Dead did appear at Glastonbury, though the latter donated some live recordings to the album that was subsequently released to pay off the inevitable debts incurred by the allegedly free festival.

Glastonbury's infrastructure was very basic. The stage cost £1,100, which seemed like a great deal. However, during the set by Quintessence, who could always be relied upon to arrive accompanied by everyone in Notting Hill with nothing better to do, it was moving so much that the designer was forced to wander among the musicians requesting that those not directly related to the performance get down. The lavatories were holes in the ground above which the patrons perched on scaffolding poles. The stage lighting was inadequate unless boosted by the arc lights that David Puttnam and Nic Roeg's film crew brought along with them. Viewed today, their documentary film *Glastonbury Fayre* appears to depict an event on the same scale as one might find in a suburban park during the summer months. The attendance was sparse by Isle of Wight standards, possibly as few as ten thousand people, which left ample elbow room for idiot dancers to do their thing and adequate parking space for those bikers who wished to drive right up to the stage with their bare-breasted old lady on the back.

In Glastonbury's chaotic fields—among the head bangers, tribal drummers, mud sliders, face painters, geodesic dome dwellers, exotic religionists, naked exhibitionists, boy mystics in patent leather shoes, bewildered children, pert-nippled girls rehearsing their music and movement lessons in the open air, ravishing film superstars and rake-thin models rarely seen more than a few yards from the Chelsea Drugstore, puzzled musicians surveying the bobbing heads of gibbering loons, their brains fried with acid—here, on the week beginning June 21, 1971, a cultural phenomenon was born that continues to this day, attracting hundreds of thousands of people, monopolizing hours of airtime and newspaper space, and turning over many millions of pounds.

This was the week when, according to the people closest to him, David Bowie ceased his dabbling and got serious. Bowie's stock had been rising since his return from the United States in February. He'd appeared on *Top of the Pops* the week before Glastonbury, miming the piano part on Peter Noone's hit recording of his song "Oh! You Pretty Things," and had recorded an *In Concert* for BBC radio, where he appeared in public for the first time with his new group with Mick Ronson, Woody Woodmansey, and Trevor Bolder. Bolder, having only previously seen him as a normal bloke in shirt and jeans and assuming him to be just another band leader, had been amazed to see Bowie get changed into a gown before the show. Bolder came from Hull, where such sights were rare.

Bowie and his wife Angela, who had evidently found someone to park their three-week-old son on, made their way to Glastonbury by train, alighting at a remote country station and then attempting to walk to the festival site. This was made more difficult by the costume they had decided upon for the day, which was Oxford bags, unsuitable shoes, and Three Musketeers hat. Bowie was supposed to go on in the early evening of the twenty-second, but delays and Kerr's fear of the neighbors meant that Bowie didn't appear until the dawn of the following day. He performed as a duet with Ronson, unveiling most of the songs from *Hunky Dory* for the first time. He had already started recording this at Trident Studios in Soho. He played "Kooks," the song inspired by the birth of the child he and his wife had left behind, the song that was a hit for Peter Noone, "Changes," and "Song for Bob Dylan." Arabella Churchill remembers his performance of "Memory of a Free Festival," which unfolded as the sun came over the hill to warm those who had endured a night on the cold, hard ground, being a particularly magical moment. The song had actually been inspired by a far less grand occasion that had taken place a couple of years earlier on a recreation ground in Croydon. That Sunday evening as Bowie was traveling back by train, his platform shoes hurting as the feather in his hat was doubtless drooping, Radio 1 broadcast the *In Concert* show that he had recorded the week before. It felt to Bowie and his retinue, who included Dana Gillespie, his manager Tony Defries, and his publisher Bob Grace, as though things might be finally falling into place.

In the afternoon sunshine, Terry Reid—the man who had left school at fifteen to play with a show band, the man who turned down the chance to be the singer with Led Zeppelin, because he wanted to make a different kind of music with his new band of friends from America, including slide guitarist David Lindley—made the sound that wouldn't be heard for another couple of years on his album *River*. It was a fervent, passionate strain of jammed-up rock, which seemed to be able to do without words or riffs. It seems fair to assume that the most beautiful woman there was Julie Christie, and the most beautiful man was Terry Reid. In the full splendor of his handsomeness, he carried himself like a leading man, exuding such powerful rays of attraction that Linda Lewis appeared unbidden at his side to add backing vocals, drawn by the powerful need to be in his vicinity. They were both just twenty-one.

In the evening, the extended lineup of Traffic played. They were newly energized by the success of *John Barleycorn Must Die* and about to record "The Low Spark of High Heeled Boys," with Jim Gordon on the drums and Ghanaian Rebop Kwaku Baah on percussion and both Dave Mason and Chris Wood back on the strength. Riding atop the foaming swell of "Gimme Some Lovin' " was their leader Steve Winwood, who had already known three years as a scream idol, two as a hippie princeling, and one as an unhappy member of the first band to be formed largely for lucre, now returning to his first love and still only a few weeks beyond his twenty-third birthday. Both acts hit the top of their curve in the fields of Glastonbury in 1971.

Although Andrew Kerr was inevitably left with bills that took him years to clear, Glastonbury was deemed a success. This was the week when the sylvan memory on which Glastonbury has traded in the years since was first planted. Not that the media or music business took much notice. Frank Sinatra had announced his retirement the same week. He was fifty-five, which seemed a sensible age to knock it on the head, even for a crooner. Michael Parkinson hosted the first of his chat shows on BBC television. His guest was the gap-toothed cad of a hundred cozy comedies Terry-Thomas. Glenn Frey and Don Henley played their first show together as members of Linda Ronstadt's backing band. The contract with Disneyland, part of an initiative to attract young people to the park, stipulated that Ronstadt must wear a bra. In the same week the South African Broadcasting Corporation revoked its ban on Beatles records. In his message to Congress, Richard Nixon declared the United States' first war on drugs.

Andrew Kerr was really fortunate in that the two elements that most govern the perception of a successful festival worked in his favor. The weather was good and not too many people turned up. The same could not be said of Stephen Kapelow, who chose the very same summer solstice to launch his Celebration of Life Festival in Louisiana. This is less fondly remembered than Glastonbury, for good reason.

Kapelow was the thirty-year-old heir to a New Orleans property company who decided to get into the rock-and-roll business via an eight-day festival in the country near Baton Rouge, Louisiana. There were very few rock festivals in the United States that year because city authorities had seen what had happened at Woodstock and at Altamont and knew that there would be stiff local resistance to bringing hundreds of thousands of fun seekers to their communities. Nonetheless, Stephen Kapelow used his connections to get permission to promote a festival near the town of McCrea.

Many thousands of young people made their way to this remote corner of rural Louisiana attracted by a bill featuring the Allman Brothers, the Rolling Stones, the Beach Boys, Miles Davis, Sly & the

Family Stone, Pink Floyd, and, inevitably, Richie Havens and Ravi Shankar. Most of these names obviously didn't appear. Some of them were never going to. Kapelow further promised a spiritual dimension with teachers, healers, and consciousness-raising sessions. What he delivered was hell on earth.

The hundreds of thousands of people naive enough to make the journey to the Cypress Point plantation in the month of June, a time when no sane Louisiana native would ever stray far from a block of ice, found themselves camping on a mosquito-infested swamp with no facilities. The site was more like a refugee camp than a pleasure ground. The temperatures were so high that the few bands who turned up to play couldn't perform until after sundown. Security was provided by the Galloping Gooses, a biker gang from New Orleans, with predictable consequences. During the day, the only way the fans could cool off was by swimming in the treacherous depths of the Atchafalaya River. Three deaths were recorded, and the suspicion is that others went unnoticed. More than one bather waded out to cool off and was never seen again. A boat was sent out to recover a drowned man and returned tugging a corpse by its arm. When the boat reached the shore, it was surrounded by curious hippies, some of whom were naked. The body was carried away by six African Americans, a reminder that in this part of the world things were not much touched by the Aquarian Age. The stage collapsed, and one man was taken away with a metal pole right through his body. By some miracle it did not breach any internal organs. Over a hundred kids ended up in local jails. They were the lucky ones.

The myth of Woodstock was that if a large mass of long-haired people gathered in the country to listen to their rock heroes, then they would not need regulating, policing, organizing, and placating because they would be carried through the experience by dint of their magical cohesion as a group. The argument went that they were qualitatively different from a mass of people gathered to watch football or displays of marching, that people from the alternative society were somehow alternative people. Those who attended the Celebration of Life knew this was not the case. When the entertainment got started, three and a half days late, it began with one Yogi Bahjan taking the stage and asking the audience to "meditate for one minute for brotherhood."

A voice from the crowd rejoined, "Fuck you! Let's boogie!"

A week later the Newport Jazz Festival, which had been put on in the tony coastal resort in Rhode Island since 1954, was visited by a similar crowd. Promoter George Wein, like many middle-aged jazz aficionados, had hopes that the rock fans' apparent taste for improvisations might introduce new blood into the jazz family. In 1971 he had booked the Allman Brothers Band to play on a bill that also included Gerry Mulligan, Dave Brubeck, and Dizzy Gillespie. All the longhairs in that part of the country duly headed for the site, aware that the Allmans played loud enough for them to be able to hear the music even if they were not inside the festival grounds. By Saturday night they had tired of being outside the festival and destroyed the fence, demanding the entertainment be provided for free. This insurrection took place as Dionne Warwick was onstage warbling "What the World Needs Now Is Love," a song that proved somewhat unequal to the occasion. Some of them invaded the stage and stamped on the keyboard of the piano, destroying equipment and entertaining the crowd with an interminable, bongo-based version of "Land of a Thousand Dances." The festival had to be called off on Saturday night, two whole days before it was due to finish. The following year George Wein moved his festival to New York. He didn't return to Newport for ten years.

As all this was happening, John Lennon was sitting down at the white grand piano in the garden room of his house at Tittenhurst Park to mime his new song "Imagine" for the promotional video. Rarely has a song seemed so out of touch with the realities of everyday life. Rarely has an artist allowed himself to be seen singing it in a setting more remote from the ones familiar to the people who were watching. Rarely has it mattered less.

In the same week, Joni Mitchell released *Blue*, which seemed better tuned to the times. This was her sparest album yet, full of songs that were either openly autobiographical, such as "My Old Man" about her former lover Graham Nash, secretly autobiographical, such as "Little Green," which concerned the child she had given up for adoption five years earlier, or perfectly attuned to the creeping mood of disenchantment of many who remembered the sixties and were already hankering after them. One line in the title song seemed to resound more than most: "Acid, booze, and ass / Needles, guns, and grass / Lots of laughs / Lots of laughs."

A week after the festivals at Glastonbury and Cypress Point, the Who released their new single, "Won't Get Fooled Again." The version that was played on the radio was a three-minute edit of a recording that would run for eight minutes on their upcoming record *Who's Next*. The music was the sound of the Who at their imperious best. The message was one that could be traced back to Woodstock, when Abbie Hoffman interrupted the Who's set to make a statement about the imprisonment of John Sinclair, an interruption that ended when Townshend attacked him with his guitar and told him to "Get the fuck off my fucking stage." The key word in that sentence was the possessive pronoun. What rock stars really resented, and resented far more than people realized, was the assumption that they could be used, their platform appropriated, their music co-opted to serve the purposes of some of the most self-interested exhibitionists who ever drew breath.

In July the Who held a party to mark the release of the album at Tara, Keith Moon's new home in Chertsey, Surrey. Here, Townshend was cornered by various members of the underground press, who demanded that he clarify what, if anything, the lyrics of "Won't Get Fooled Again," with its line about meeting the new boss, same as the old boss, said about how the Who related to the Movement. He responded in full in a piece in *International Times*. Talking of Roger Daltrey's climactic scream, he said, it "screams defiance at those who try to tell us what we have to do with money that's not ours, a power that belongs not to us but to our audiences, and lives that long ago were handed to the rock world on platters. . . . You have no need to fret. You're not gaining new leaders. You're keeping The Who."

JUNE

Plastic Ono Band: "Power to the People"

Traffic: "Gimme Some Lovin'"

Terry Reid: "Dean"

John Martyn: "Glistening Glyndebourne"

Flamin' Groovies: "Teenage Head"

Genesis: "The Return of the Giant Hogweed"

Pink Floyd: "Echoes"

Alan Stivell: "Ys"

Bob Marley: "Acoustic Medley"

Fairport Convention: "Bridge Over the River Ash"

JULY

Every Picture Tells a Story

On Saturday, July 3, 1971, the *New York Times* carried news of the latest hijacking of an airliner. In this incident an armed couple had taken control of a plane operated by the Texan airline Braniff, demanded $100,000 in cash, which the company paid, and forced the flight to divert to Monterrey in Mexico, where they released one hundred passengers and then took off again. On the same day Evonne Goolagong, described by the paper as "the 19-year-old daughter of an Australian aboriginal sheep-shearer," had won the women's singles title at Wimbledon. The big new movie reviewed inside the paper that day was *Shaft*. The big new album of the week was Joni Mitchell's *Blue*. Across the Atlantic, Grand Funk Railroad had embarked on the latest stage of their campaign to broadcast their apparently great popularity by playing a free concert in Hyde Park in front of many holidaying Americans and a few curious Londoners.

Given the time differences, it's likely Jim Morrison was already dead in Paris by the time that edition of the *Times* went to press. According to those close to the singer, his body had been found in the bath of a rented apartment in the Marais district in the early morning of Saturday, July 3. The first news of his death didn't reach the United States until after the weekend, when Clive Selwood, who ran the Doors' label, Elektra, in London, responded to phone calls from the music weeklies asking if he could confirm the rumor of Morrison's death. He called the band's manager, Bill Siddons, in Los Angeles. Siddons called Morrison's girlfriend Pamela in Paris and was told to get on a plane and "take care of arrangements." Morrison had already been dead for forty-eight hours, but no announcement had been made. The British music paper *Melody Maker* passed on the rumors to its readers in the issue of July 8 but wasn't able to confirm the death until a week later.

When Siddons arrived in Paris, he was met with a closed coffin, which subsequently encouraged those who preferred to believe that Morrison wasn't actually dead and had somehow slipped away. There was no inquest because the French authorities believed he had died of a heart attack. Nobody in his circle pressed for one because they knew from his usual behavior and the company he was keeping that drugs were involved. Forty years later Marianne Faithfull claimed that Morrison had been given heroin that was too pure by her former boyfriend Jean de Breteuil, who had been one of the guests at Mick Jagger's wedding six weeks earlier. Other, more outlandish stories claimed that the singer had actually died in a nightclub, and his body had been spirited away so that the club could retain its license. Morrison was twenty-seven, the same age at which Jimi Hendrix and Janis Joplin had died in circumstances of similar carelessness only a few months earlier.

The cult of Jim Morrison turned out to be even more powerful than those of the other two. As Bill Siddons later reflected, Morrison was an alcoholic, but he nevertheless had the kind of public personality that made people wish to project their own hopes and aspirations onto him. They couldn't believe that his death could be quite as tawdry as it appeared. He was coming off a well-received album, *L.A. Woman,* and his image had been preserved for all time in a series of powerful photographs in which he looked like Don

Draper's idea of a rock god. (Ten years after his death one of those pictures made a memorable cover of *Rolling Stone* with the line "He's hot. He's sexy. He's dead.") Morrison's elevation into a cult hinted at a new truth about the music business, which was becoming even more apparent as it turned into an industry. It was no longer strictly necessary for its performers to be alive. In a handful of cases, it was probably better if they weren't. "Live fast, die young, and leave a good-looking corpse" was the traditional advice. In Morrison's case, the doctor who examined his body rather than his publicity photographs deduced that he was nearer fifty-seven than twenty-seven. Thankfully, the publicity pictures told a different story.

The official statements about Morrison's death seemed calculated to mislead. When Morrison's girlfriend registered his death with the US embassy, she said he had no known relatives. This was not the case. She knew it was not the case. Some members of Morrison's family were too prominent to be easily overlooked; his father was still serving as a rear admiral in the United States Navy. *Rolling Stone*'s headline said, "James Douglas Morrison, poet: dead at 27" and said that he had died peacefully, which suggested its editors had a liberal definition of the term. Bill Siddons's statement said, "He died in peace and dignity," without explaining how he could possibly know. By the time Siddons arrived, he had to take the word of Morrison's friends for that. Still, the young manager could have been forgiven his naïveté. He was only twenty-three.

Three days after Jim Morrison's death, Louis Armstrong died at the age of sixty-nine. He was still living in his modest home in Corona, Queens, New York. Here the king of jazz could be found in his later days out on the street playing with the neighborhood kids. When asked why he never moved to somewhere more grand, he said, "We didn't think we could have any better neighbors any place else so we stayed put," a policy that no rock star has ever seen fit to pursue. Armstrong's obituary made the front page of the *New York Times* and appeared three days before the announcement of Morrison's death. The latter was a small story on an inside page that pointed out to its middle-aged readers that the Doors were a rock group who played loud, amplified music, still a minority taste.

There were even signs that the era of the rock group, which had been the totemic performing unit of the previous decade, was passing. In the UK chart for the week ending July 18, 1971, solo albums began to outnumber albums by bands. This was the week Carole King's *Tapestry* made its first appearance at number thirty-two, and Joni Mitchell's *Blue* went in at forty-two. Leonard Cohen's new record *Songs of Love and Hate* stalled at thirty-one, but his debut record had reentered the chart due to the use of its songs in the recently released Robert Altman movie *McCabe & Mrs. Miller*, which starred Warren Beatty and Julie Christie. James Taylor had two albums in the top twenty. Neil Young's *After the Gold Rush* was climbing the charts again in its thirty-second week. Graham Nash's *Songs for Beginners* was at number fifteen.

The breakup of the Beatles, which was still slowly being accepted as a reality, seemed to be echoed in every area of the music business. In 1971 name musicians were increasingly expected to be able to behave like jazz players, turning up in different lineups as mood and personal ambition dictated. While this provided the music papers with the excuse for endless speculation about who was about to join whom, it couldn't entirely compensate for the fans' resulting loss of belief in a group as the teenage gang of their dreams. Into this post-Beatles vacuum came a new breed of individuals, either single performers in their own right or people so charismatic they were clearly going to burst the bounds of any band that sought to contain them. Three of these individuals, all of whom put their mark on the summer of 1971 in their different ways, were Londoners born and bred, and they all carried within them some of the worldliness and humor that is the birthright of all Londoners. None of them came from Cockney stock. They were all, in one way or another, the children of immigrants, all were indulged youngest children, all had left school as soon as the law allowed, and all had entered the music business in order to avoid being condemned to a normal job. In July 1971 they all still lived in the city.

One of them lived right at its heart. If the theatergoers who were flooding out of the Saturday evening performance of *Hair* at the Shaftesbury Theatre in July 1971 had looked up as they crossed the road, they might have seen a light burning in one of the rooms on the third story of a building housing a popular tourist restaurant called the Moulin Rouge. This was run by the Greek immigrant Stavros Georgiou and his Swedish ex-wife, Ingrid. The couple had divorced but remained together to run the business. Their three grown-up children were all involved in keeping the place going. The most reluctant of the three was their youngest, Steven.

Steven always thought he could be a pop star and had grown up close enough to London's Tin Pan Alley to have some idea how to go about it. Because at the time there was no precedent for anyone with a foreign-sounding name ever turning up among the would-be pop stars on *Ready Steady Go!* or *Thank Your Lucky Stars*, Steven had changed his name to Steve Adams and then, in a further, curious jump, to Cat Stevens, in which guise he had his first hit, "I Love My Dog," in 1966.

Cat had a flair for writing pop songs that seemed more substantial than the standard fare. He had a good, romantic voice and the looks of a leading man. The sixties had been mainly about groups. At the time, even the best-looking male solo artists still seemed like spare parts, mincing around for the TV cameras, shooting their lace cuffs, dandling microphones at the end of leads, simpering at the camera, and, finally, railroaded into awkward, stool-perching duets with the variety stars who inevitably topped the bill on the TV shows on which the singers guested. Cat had further hits, "Matthew and Son" and "I'm Gonna Get Me a Gun" among them. He joined the last of the great ill-matched package tours, where he appeared with Jimi Hendrix, Engelbert Humperdinck, and the Walker Brothers, before, weakened by overwork, he collapsed with TB and was hospitalized, thus bringing his first career to an end.

When Cat reemerged in 1970, he was a regular James Taylor, newly legitimized via an actorish mustache. Now he played a guitar, sat on a stool, used his deep, dark eyes to project sincerity, and sang older but wiser songs with names like "Pop Star," about his past experience in the star-maker machine, and "Lady D'Arbanville," inspired by his girlfriend, the nineteen-year-old American model Patti who had appeared in Warhol's film *Flesh* when she was just sixteen. Cat wrote the first of these songs when she left him to go back to the United States for a few weeks. In a world moving as fast as his was in 1970, such separations seemed endless. It wasn't until 1971 that you could place an overseas telephone call without the help of an operator. Even for a jet-setting rock star who was selling records by the millions, the other side of the Atlantic was as remote as the moon.

For Cat there wasn't even time to find the luxurious pop star pad that his earnings would no doubt have bought him. Thus, he remained living above his parents' restaurant on the edge of Soho as he moved to follow up his success with *Tea for the Tillerman*, his second album of original material in 1970, with *Teaser and the Firecat* without pausing for breath. He was twenty-two. Between the spring of 1970 and the summer of 1971, an interval of barely fourteen months, Cat Stevens recorded and released "Where Do the Children Play?," "Wild World," "Father and Son," "Tuesday's Dead," "Morning Has Broken," "Moonshadow," and "Peace Train." These are the songs that formed the core of his repertoire. These are the songs that people still turn out to hear him sing almost fifty years later.

Cat Stevens became enormously popular in 1971 for a number of reasons: he had a lovely voice, the kind of voice that was easy to live with, and an angel face, the kind that seemed to match the sensitivity of his material. Many of these songs, such as "Remember the Days of the Old Schoolyard," "Oh Very Young," and "Father and Son," had a rueful tone to them, which made them appealing to people in their midtwenties who were suddenly discovering the hitherto unknown sensation of nostalgia. Songs like "On the Road to Find Out" and "Miles from Nowhere" hinted at an interest in matters of the spirit, which would eventually become more explicit. Cat's position as the harbinger of consciousness raising was further underlined in 1971 when he provided the songs for Hal Ashby's much-applauded *Harold and Maude,* in which young Bud Cort has a romance with seventy-nine-year-old Ruth Gordon. Cat's song "Trouble" carried the weight of a memorable and wordless final scene. (Interestingly, this was one of a number of films released in 1971 that played upon the subject of May–December love affairs. Others were *The Last Picture Show,* in which high school senior Timothy Bottoms made love to Cloris Leachman, the neglected wife of his teacher, and *Sunday Bloody Sunday,* in which Peter Finch and his wife, Glenda Jackson, were both having affairs with young artist Murray Head. Even more interestingly, this second film also featured the first kiss between two gay characters in a mainstream movie. It was directed by John Schlesinger, who nonetheless felt it best not to declare his own sexuality. Minutes before they were due to shoot the scene, the crew approached the director and asked in a pained manner, "Is this really necessary?")

For all his interest in spirituality, Stevens was no more above the pleasures of the flesh than his more obviously libidinous peers. Lots of beautiful women wanted to sleep with Cat, and being a gentleman he didn't like to let them down. Carly Simon's big break came when she got the job of supporting Stevens at the Troubadour in Los Angeles in April 1971. On the same night, Stevens introduced her to her future husband James Taylor. But before that, Stevens and Simon were briefly an item, at least in London, where she had come to record her second album with Stevens's producer Paul Samwell-Smith. She wrote its title song, "Anticipation," about the experience of waiting for Stevens on their first date and subsequently also penned "Legend in Your Own Time" about him. Within weeks she was sitting in a suite at the Gramercy Park Hotel in New York while a drunk Kris Kristofferson, whose songs "Help Me Make It Through the Night" and "Me and Bobby McGee" lorded it over every other singer-songwriter's music on the airwaves in 1971, sang a song he had composed just for her. It was called, for the avoidance of doubt, "I've Got to Have You."

The 1971 generation of singer-songwriters, finding themselves the biggest show in town, were increasingly infatuated with each other and with the idea of figuring in each other's songs. They measured their success in terms of pulling power, in the bedroom as well as the concert hall, and didn't hold back from writing about it. This was powerful medicine for those doing the writing as well as those being written about. In Sheila Weller's *Girls Like Us*, Carly Simon describes the experience of seeing herself through Stevens's eyes. "He would look at me and it would be dazzling, the reflection of all things miraculous."

In the same year, Leonard Cohen penned "Chelsea Hotel #2" about his experience of sleeping with Janis Joplin. Many years later, in a more modest time, he would apologize for the indiscretion. According to the song, Joplin was prepared to break her rule about only sleeping with handsome men in Cohen's case. Janis used her celebrity to sleep with men who would ordinarily have been out of her league. According to Peter Ames Carlin's book about Bruce Springsteen, Joplin wasn't choosy about how famous her lovers were. She went looking for the then unknown musician after spotting him backstage at a show in Asbury Park, and she wasn't after a long-term relationship. In the higher echelons of the music business, there had always been predatory alpha males. Now they were joined by a handful of females no less keen to leave their mark. As Joni Mitchell sang on the title track of her new album, "songs are like tattoos." In Cohen's song he further comforts Joplin with the disingenuous "We are ugly but we have the music." Most of these performers were far from ugly, and they had the music as well. The looks of artists like James Taylor, Cat Stevens, and Carly Simon may not have been as labored over as they might be nowadays, but they were as much a part of their appeal for the fans, who would have been horrified to be characterized as such, as for the teenybop stars they were all so happy condescending toward.

TV was important to finding Cat Stevens a place in the hearts and homes of his audience. In July 1971, three months before the release of *Teaser and the Firecat*, he recorded a BBC TV special with producer Stanley Dorfman. Dorfman, who had come up through *Top of the Pops*, had carved out a niche at the BBC with half-hour TV specials that used the new color technology on the new wave of solo artists. In 1970 he had recorded similar specials with James Taylor, Elton John, and Joni Mitchell. In 1971 he recorded Neil Young when he was in the middle of touring the UK with the songs that turned up the following year on *Harvest*.

"Cat Stevens Sings Cat Stevens" was a classic of the genre. Its title was classic Dorfman, underlining the small miracle that these talented, charismatic people were also self-sufficient. Stevens was accompanied by Alun Davies, the guitarist who worked closely with him through this period, and bass player/percussionist Larry Steele. Nothing proclaimed Stevens's membership in the new generation of singer-songwriters as powerfully as the fact that he performed sitting down, something few had done in the hectic decade in which he had first made his name. Like Carole King's performances of *Tapestry*, Stevens's BBC show seemed to be less a performance than a session to which the audience were invited to eavesdrop. In Dorfman's programs the audience were often seated behind the performers so that they could be seen only occasionally. The girls nodded sympathetically behind their shiny curtains of hair. The men, with their horn-rimmed spectacles, wispy mustaches, and heavy corduroys, composed themselves into postures indicative of sage appreciation. This was not *Ready Steady Go!*, but it was no less au courant. Some of the songs Stevens played on that show were, in his words, "really old." They had been recorded as long as four years before. His songs still had the simple hooks and sentimental appeal that they had when Stevens had no pretense to anything other than hit singles, but this time they seemed to have more weight.

Dorfman's was a format that framed the singer-songwriters of the time perfectly by allowing that they were interesting enough to be able to carry half an hour of TV time—inclusive of tuning up, unrehearsed patter, and mumbled asides, which were all part of the package—and flattered the audience by suggesting this music was worthy of the serious attention of adults like them. The deliberate modesty of the visual presentation was as important to the appeal of the music as the time-honored razzle-dazzle of Ike and

Tina Turner had been to theirs. Artistes appearing to reverse away from the limelight can be just as magnetic as those seeming to rush to embrace it. The new Cat Stevens albums all had cover paintings done by the artist rather than photographs of him. This achieved the double miracle of putting his artistry front and center while appearing to withdraw his personality from the equation.

In late 1971 Penny Valentine interviewed Stevens for *Sounds* at the place in Fulham that he'd finally moved into and asked him how he felt about the shift from groups to solo performers. "The barriers have been broken down now, there aren't so many false idols," he said, sounding all his twenty-three years. "Musicians are now like friends of the people they play for. It's now like the complete expression of an artist that is becoming the medium, a period where Carole King emerges because she's beautiful but very plain and simple lyrically, where James Taylor becomes huge even though his voice isn't anything ultra-extraordinary, where Joni Mitchell and all these people can simply express themselves. So instead of the music holding them up, they hold the music up."

Cat was describing the stardom that didn't appear to be stardom, which is what made it the most powerful form of stardom of all. It's the kind of stardom that keeps him in the public eye almost fifty years after he made the records on which that stardom was initially based. In his case, the audience's sense of connection with that music has survived retirements, more than one religious conversion, a further change of name, and repeated attempts on his part to deny the music and put it behind him. What Steven Georgiou did in the frantic eighteen months between spring 1970 and autumn 1971, now regularly used on the soundtracks of smart postmodern films and TV programs beloved of Generations X and Y, has come to define him in a way that he will never grow out of or get away from. Nothing Cat Stevens has done since July 1971 has counted half as much as what he did then.

Like Cat, the second of the triumvirate of London boys who wrote their names across 1971 was the descendant of immigrants. Marc Feld's father was of Polish/Jewish extraction, and his mother was a market trader. Marc was cut from different cloth. He embraced the soft science of salesmanship as much as Steven Georgiou searched for an answer within himself. At the same time as Stevens had made the change from prancing pop idol to sedentary troubadour, Marc Bolan, as Feld had called himself since he made the mental move from Stoke Newington to Soho in the midsixties, was making a journey in the opposite direction.

In the winter of 1970 he was twenty-three and had been in and around the music business for seven years, trying to find a vehicle for a talent as much for chutzpah as for music. A genius when it came to matters of presentation, Bolan had devised Tyrannosaurus Rex back in the hippie days as an act who played sitting down. He got this idea from seeing a Ravi Shankar concert. Sitting down lent them the air of supplicants, and their music, acoustic strums, and sub-Tolkien doggerel delivered in a simpering tone was the sound for which the terms both "airy" and "fairy" could be usefully employed. There was something in their album titles, *Prophets, Seers & Sages: The Angels of the Ages* and *My People Were Fair and Wore Sky in Their Hair . . . But Now They're Content to Wear Stars on Their Brows*, which seemed to defy the market to accept them. For over a year Tyrannosaurus Rex were an appendage of the DJ John Peel, following him as he spun records in the lower common rooms of colleges and universities the length of the land, sitting cross-legged on their rug with their bongos and acoustic guitars, looking for all the world like people who were simply too fine and pure to be bothered by the prospect of worldly success. The events of the year 1971 would render that idea hilarious.

Regardless of how long a pop career may be spun out for or how inflated the reputation that is constructed on its back, both career and reputation are still owed to a period of inspiration that is relatively brief. The music business is one in which it is so hard to catch a break that all performers, no matter how elevated the claims they make for themselves and their art, are opportunists at heart. Once that opportunity is spotted, they tend to pursue it with the single-minded determination of sharks, often in direct defiance of every claim they have made for being above such petty distractions. One of the key lines in John Lennon's interview with *Rolling Stone* in February had been "You have to be a bastard to make it . . . and the Beatles were the biggest bastards on earth." This rule applies to all performers, no matter how charismatic or deficient in charm, but none more than Marc Bolan in the year 1971.

They had something they could trade on. Even at their daffiest and most effete, Tyrannosaurus Rex always had hooks. Beginning in 1971, the newly abbreviated version of the group, now trading as T. Rex, placed those hooks in the shop window. *T. Rex*, the first album to appear under the more consumer-friendly brand name, was released a week before Christmas 1970. The cover showed Bolan and new percussionist Mickey Finn as pinups rather than hippie idols. For the first time, he was carrying an electric guitar, a signifier like a Kalashnikov propped against the cave wall behind a contemporary holy warrior. The record did well, despite the fact that "Ride a White Swan," which eventually rose to number two on the UK charts, wasn't on it. Bolan continued playing for the longhairs with his new partner and a bass player, but he was beginning to attract a different audience, one that was younger, more female, and not overly bothered about the music he had made in the past.

In mid-January 1971, just three weeks after the release of the last album as a duo, the three of them plus drummer Bill Fifield went into Advision studios and recorded two songs. One of them, "Hot Love," a title that had previously seemed about as likely to be applied to a Tyrannosaurus Rex song as to a Virginia Woolf novel, came out as his next single just two weeks later. One week after that, it went on the chart at number thirty-one, rising to seventeen, then seven, and then climbing to number one, where it remained for no less than six weeks, selling over a million copies in the UK alone. From this position, it lorded over the tawdry chaos of the British singles chart, over Ray Stevens's "Bridget the Midget," Judy Collins's "Amazing Grace," Neil Diamond's "Sweet Caroline," Perry Como's "It's Impossible," and the inevitable singles by John Lennon, Paul McCartney, and George Harrison. For a younger generation who felt the sixties had never quite belonged to them, T. Rex at number one felt like the harbinger of a new age.

With the pressing prospect of an American tour to undertake in April, Bolan decided to make the drummer permanent. While "Hot Love" was riding high and Bolan was doing his victory lap of press interviews, the band was frantically rehearsing in the basement of an estate agent in Pimlico. The make-do-and-mend, seat-of-the-pants reality of the way Bolan operated was always at odds with the grand pronouncements he would make in interviews. He decided to make a virtue out of improvisation. "I love putting singles out," he told *NME*. "Lennon's into that and 'Hot Love' is so right because it's so new."

The American tour, which was made up of support slots way below the likes of Mountain, Johnny Winter, and Humble Pie, could not have been further removed from the world of TV shows like *Top of the Pops* and magazines like *Fabulous 208*, which were already banking on the emergence of Bolan to boost their ratings and circulations. This wasn't a struggle he was built for. Bolan was not one for building a career one brick at a time. Nothing sticks in the craw of a rising musician quite like the hopelessness of trying to convince people in one territory just how popular he is in another territory. The Atlantic seabed is littered with the whitened bones of those acts who thought their celebrity in the UK entitled them to a free pass in the United States. All too many have retreated as soon as it didn't work out, disguising their hurt pride behind a veil of Old World condescension. T. Rex were like that. They were altogether too thin a prospect to make their name on the concert stage. They needed a single market, preferably an overcrowded island overserved with media and with a fatal taste for triviality; they needed the unclouded focus of an entire family looking at the same flickering box on a Thursday night, ideally with father arriving in time to snort, "Is that a boy or a girl?" And it needed to happen quickly. Marc's pop appeal was fading almost from the moment he realized he had it. Youth's a stuff will not endure, and no pop star seemed more built for youth than Marc Bolan.

Nonetheless, he used his brief time well. Things were so busy for T. Rex in 1971 that there were no proper recording sessions for their breakthrough album *Electric Warrior*. Bolan's producer Tony Visconti simply pursued him as he toured America, slotting in sessions as and when the schedule allowed, very much as Ahmet Ertegun had done with Ray Charles ten years earlier. The songs were worked up in hotel rooms and on buses, arranged in the studio, and put on tape while they were still hot.

They recorded "Jeepster" and "Monolith" at Media Sound in New York, with Robert Margouleff engineering as he was doing with Stevie Wonder at the same time. In Los Angeles they hooked up with backing singers Flo & Eddie, the former Turtles Howard Kaylan and Mark Volman, who got them into Wally Heider's Studio, there to add the swooning harmonies that made sure the finished records soared from jukebox speakers. This latter session produced "Get It On," which went to number one in the UK in late July and remained there for four weeks. Renamed "Bang a Gong," it also became a top ten record in the United States.

Although the records were full of smart touches, such as Rick Wakeman's piano glissando at the beginning of "Get It On," T. Rex were underpowered as a live proposition, and without the double-tracking, the singer's voice was clearly inadequate. But in the studio Visconti turned the weaknesses into strengths. Bolan's head may have been full of Tolkien, but his heart was in the 1950s, and he had a gift for retooling old riffs. "Beltane Walk" was a straight pinch from Jimmy McCracklin's 1958 hit "The Walk." "Get It On" quoted the line "Meanwhile, I was thinking" from Chuck Berry's "Little Queenie." When Tony Visconti asked him for the title of the tune they were about to cut during a session at Media Sound in April, Bolan said "Monolith," which seemed consistent with the self-importance of the time, but then couldn't stop himself adding, "or the Duke of Earl" with a snigger that gave away his teddy boy self.

Bolan's attitude to the fruits of success was similarly old-fashioned. That spring he and his wife, June Child, moved from West London to a chic address in London's Little Venice. He bought a white Rolls-Royce, which he couldn't drive. At the same time he betrayed most of the people who considered themselves his patrons and all the things that people had assumed were his principles. John Peel, who had previously been his meal ticket, was dismissive about "Get It On" in public, and the two never spoke again. David Platz, the man whose Fly label had introduced him to the pop charts, was another he turned his back on. Bolan reneged on his contracts, and in a few months that summer his new manager Tony Secunda managed to score huge advances for his artist from overseas territories on the back of the major success he was having in the UK. Everyone who worked with him that summer has memories of the charm wearing thin as success piled on success. He stopped talking about the power of meditation and openly espoused the joys of having lots of money. He began drinking and drugging, which had an immediate effect on his looks, his key currency. He began speaking in quotes. When he was trying to be serious, he talked the most frightful balls. When he was talking about the glory of pop, he sometimes seemed like the only sane man in town.

What particularly disturbed the conservatives of the hippie press was the way he cavorted for the cameras and the fans as if it was no longer enough to just play the music. "I've always been a wriggler," he told Keith Altham. "I just dig dancing. It was just a bit difficult to wriggle when I was sitting cross-legged on the stage." Most of those who had been Marc's patrons during his hippie days recoiled at his new Becoming. Peel was foremost among them. He confessed himself puzzled as to why Marc had chosen to take this amplified route to stardom and said that he simply didn't think he was as good at the pop stuff as he had been at the material of his student union days. It's tempting to wonder whether Peel, like many members of a generation suddenly experiencing the disagreeable sensation of being made to feel old by the emergence of new youth, actually found himself liking the stuff and just couldn't bring himself to admit it. Like the students who had been interviewed storming out of Bob Dylan's concerts five years earlier, the critics had turned that feeling into an elaborate moral fable where their beloved had been led astray by the money changers in the temple, and the inevitable outcome had been betrayal. The truth, as vouchsafed to the young fans who went and bought *Electric Warrior* in droves when it came out in the fall of 1971, was that T. Rex, insubstantial though they might be, sounded just fine, and "Get It On," "Hot Love," and "Jeepster" soundtracked the youth club dances of the kids who were born in 1958 every bit as well as "Satisfaction" had done for the people who'd been born in 1950.

This was the beginning of the era when you started to read about music before hearing it, particularly in Britain, where the radio outlets were so limited. So a whole generation of music buyers grew up forming opinions about music and the people who played it that were based on how the musicians set out to justify that music in print. In print it was easy to build an argument that Bolan's music was infantile because it saved you having to respond to it as pop music was surely intended to be responded to—in the moment, over the air, into the ears, via the pleasure centers, and up from the floor through the feet. It wasn't music you could take seriously unless you considered the business of having a good time a serious business, which of course is one of those divides between rock fans and real people. The argument that raged over the corkscrew curls and be-glittered visage of Marc Bolan in 1971 is the same one that kept the British music press going for the rest of the century—the struggle between the instincts and the intellect, between pop and rock, between Roundheads and Cavaliers, if you must, the fight between what we think we ought to like and what we actually do like and the refusal to recognize the fact that this is music and in music the right sound will ace the correct thought every single time.

Those two ways of looking at the world collided over the head of Marc Bolan in a field in Essex on the weekend of the August Bank Holiday of 1971. The Weeley Festival began as the initiative of local councilors who wanted to put their small town on the map and raise some money to relieve suffering in Bangladesh. They staked out ground, identified the weekend of the bank holiday, and put out some feelers for talent. The next thing they knew they seemed to have signed up most of the longhair bands in the UK. They booked far more than the running order could ever accommodate. Band followed band remorselessly all the way round the clock with no respite. Status Quo played at six o'clock on Friday morning. At three on Saturday morning some poor souls were voluntarily submitting themselves to the Groundhogs recital of their new album *Split*. Rory Gallagher played his amplified blues at five in the morning, an hour no blues was ever intended to see. Tens of thousands of people turned up with home-forged tickets, thus saving themselves the two-pound entrance fee. The Hell's Angels, who had been charged with security, clashed with the market traders, who had paid money for the concession to sell burgers. The stage was inadequate, the performers invisible to anyone farther back than fifty yards. The bill was packed with proven crowd pleasers like Mungo Jerry, Arthur Brown, and Edgar Broughton. The audience were, like all festival audiences, sick with exhaustion. Only a sucker for hubris like Marc Bolan would have wanted to be top of this particular bill.

When he took the stage late on Saturday night, he knew that the crowd was a disgruntled animal, made up of people inclined to regard him as a sellout or somebody who appealed to their younger sister. They were tired and had used their last reserves of enthusiasm on the band who'd come on before him. "Hello," he said, introducing himself. "You may have seen us on *Top of the Pops*." This passive-aggressive stance was not the way to get the audience on his side, and his band weren't powerful enough to win them over either. At Weeley he was eventually forced into the humiliation of asking those in the crowd who clearly didn't like him to "make love somewhere else," a choice of words that perfectly captures his combination of hippieness and conceit. Had he ever thought that he could be the new Beatles in the sense of being able to unite a disparate audience, his nine songs at Weeley disabused him of it. As he tried to push his performance uphill in the face of the indifference of what was not his crowd, he must have known that he had made the cardinal error of thinking he could go on after the third of our trio of London boys—someone who burst out in the summer of 1971, came as close as anyone to filling the shoes of the Beatles, and, had the expression existed, went viral.

Our third London boy had also been born above the business premises of a small tradesman of immigrant stock, in his case Scottish; he was also the youngest and most indulged of the family, but he was slightly older than the other two London boys. He had come along three years earlier, during the Battle of the Bulge, when the outcome of World War II was not yet certain. He was a very different sort of personality. Any bohemian tendencies were kept well in check. Any spiritual yearnings were on tight rein. His choice of a new home said a lot about him. While Steven Georgiou wished to remain where he had grown up, at the center of the known world, and Mark Feld was keen to live in a part of London that seemed appropriate for someone of his grooviness, the third of the London-based musicians who lit up the summer of 1971 had moved in that year to a half-timbered detached executive home in Winchmore Hill, a north London enclave noted for its air of bourgeois respectability and freshly made millionaires. His neighbors were footballers and car salesmen, not fashion designers and poets. This suited Rod Stewart just fine.

At the age of twenty-six, Rod Stewart could afford the property, thanks to his earnings as lead singer of the Faces, who were a strong live attraction in both Europe and the United States, and to the fact that he'd released two solo records that had been popular in the United States. His solo albums showcased him as a great interpreter of other people's songs, particularly the folkie ones. He was steered toward these tunes by Paul Nelson, the rock journalist who looked after him at Mercury Records and had previously had a great effect on the young Bob Dylan. *Every Picture Tells a Story*, Rod's third solo album, which came out on July 9, 1971, was about to propel him into a different orbit as a solo artist.

When success occurs in the music business, it makes the person to whom it has happened feel as if he's woken up on a runaway train with no choice but to keep looking forward and hope that the impact when it comes isn't fatal. At a time when musical taste seemed on the point of splintering along tribal lines, Rod Stewart's *Every Picture Tells a Story* was the record that everybody seemed to buy. *Rolling Stone* magazine named it the album of the year, one of the last times the critics' favorite was also the market's. By the end of 1971 Rod was making so much money that his accountant urged him to get rid of some of it by buying a house fit for the multimillionaire that he had now become. The workload of that year had been so intense that he had scarcely had time to see the inside of the Winchmore Hill property.

The year 1971 was Rod Stewart's shining moment. It was not unpredicted. It was clear to everyone who had heard him since the midsixties that Rod Stewart wasn't just an exceptional singer. He also had a genuinely distinctive instrument, a real voice, the kind that was capable of carrying a record on its own. There was something in the rasp at the back of his throat, the vibrancy of his middle range, and his uncanny ability to put over a song instead of merely singing it that meant he would probably outgrow any group that would have him, whether that was the Shotgun Express, the Jeff Beck Group, or, latterly, the Faces. Rod had a gift that he shared with people like Sinatra and his own hero, Sam Cooke, in that his singing voice sounded like the perpetuation of his speaking voice by other means, which meant that through music he was able to express the personality he had and build another one that people could grow to love. He modeled his singing style on Cooke, who used to sing above his natural register. It could have been this that made him sound as if he was reaching for something, gave him the yearning, little-boy-lost quality that struck such a chord, and made people overlook the fact that a little boy lost was clearly the very last thing he was.

Everything Rod sang sounded like an old song, and everybody prefers a song they already know. Even the new ones, like "Mandolin Wind," sounded as though they'd been found rather than composed, which seemed to suit his artisan's attitude to his work. Possibly because he saw himself as a singer who could turn his hand to writing if need be, the standard of his songs was higher than those of his contemporaries who were contractually obliged to believe themselves capable of coming up with a dozen good new songs every time they went into the studio. Rod had the gifted hack's quality of being able to lend instant authenticity to songs. "Gasoline Alley" was an expression he'd never heard until a girlfriend threw it into conversation, but by the time he put it in a song, it sounded as if he were singing the story of his life. Everything he did seemed human scaled. There was nothing macho or aggressive about his voice. He sang songs for people rather than critics. He made everything sound like a campfire sing-along. His delivery was an open invitation to join in.

At the time lots of other musicians seemed to be making things darker and more complicated than they needed to be, and when *Every Picture Tells a Story*, with its cozy art deco cover, appeared in the summer of 1971, it bridged the worlds of Tony Blackburn and John Peel, of AM and FM, of the *Record Mirror* and *Rolling Stone*, of the hippie record shops and the Woolworth singles counter, of Cat Stevens and Marc Bolan, in a way few acts had done since the Beatles. At a time when pop songs seemed increasingly opaque, dealing in windy abstractions, confected memories of frontier America, or described worlds and feelings most people couldn't recognize, Rod's songs all made perfect sense to people. In the world of Rod Stewart, your dad handed down his old suit and gave you some good advice about how you shouldn't let the ladies get to your money. The alternative society had clearly never penetrated the world around Rod Stewart's parents' sweetshop in Archway.

As John Mendelsohn said when reviewing the record in *Rolling Stone*, "He has it in him, has Rod Stewart, to save a lot of souls, to rescue those of us who are too old for Grand Funk but not old enough for those adorable McCartneys from being nearly consummately bored with the current rock and roll scene. It's not inconceivable that he could do it without even opening his mouth: He's physically sensational, the idols of perhaps three continents' heavy trendies, the most profound influence on rock and roll fashion since the Stones tour. He's the single most glamorous rock figure rolling."

Every Picture Tells a Story distilled the promise of its two predecessor records. Its title song was a picaresque account of the sexual adventures of his late teens, the breakout hit, "Maggie May," recollected the delighted joy of being used as a plaything by a fleshy older woman, the story of "Mandolin Wind" was less easy to discern, but nobody ever went bankrupt singing about a man's debt to a woman, and the rest came from the same songwriting mills that supplied Motown, Elvis Presley, and the public domain. You could have played that record to anyone, and they would have found something to like on it and be pulled along in its genial wake. Rod knew that pop shouldn't seem like work. *Every Picture Tells a Story* was the creation of a man of the world. In its tunefulness and easy universality, it was the nearest 1971 would get to the way 1969 had felt about *Abbey Road*.

When *Rolling Stone* called it the album of the year, there was no rejoicing in the ranks of the Faces. All groups contain within them the seeds of their own demise, and the appeal of Rod's voice made the Faces a classic case. By 1971 his stature in the United States made it inevitable that the Faces would turn up in a city to find that the local promoter had billed them as Rod Stewart and the Faces, a red rag to any bull. All bands have within them a burning issue, usually involving credit and attention, and the way they invariably deal with this is by doing anything but talking about it, instead conducting their negotiations behind their hands, via barbed lyrics or messages sent through managers, producers, or girlfriends. The Faces were no exception.

Rod's position within the group was made even more parlous by the fact that he didn't play an instrument but did compose. When he went in the studio, he relied heavily on the musicians' ability to just vamp something that he could add words to. That's how "Maggie May" was written, if written is the expression. He used members of the Faces, with whom he was spending most of the time on the road and with whom he had developed a clumsy, appealing, but characteristically British style. It would have been surprising if the repertoire of one didn't leach into the other.

Every Picture Tells a Story changed the lives of most of the people who contributed to it, but it was only a net gain for Rod Stewart. Martin Quittenton, a former member of Steamhammer, who was responsible for the acoustic stylings that showcased Rod's voice best, ended up cowriting two of Stewart's biggest hits and then effectively retired from the music business. The man whom the artist credited ungraciously on the sleeve as "the mandolin player out of Lindisfarne whose name I can't remember" was Ray Jackson. He got a twelve-pound session fee for playing the intro without which "Mandolin Wind" is inconceivable. Before he finished the session, they asked him to add some decoration to another song they had recorded but didn't feel would make the cut for the album. "Maggie May" was included on the record only because it was running short. The feeling of the musicians and the record company was that it didn't have enough tune, and it was pushed out as the B-side of the first single from the album, Tim Hardin's "Reason to Believe," where it remained until a radio station in Milwaukee flipped it and started playing "Maggie May."

"Maggie May" marked the beginning of his career as a mainstream superstar (and "superstar" was a term that was just coming into use) and the end of his career as the kind of rock star who found favor with the people who like to feel they decide on these things. It was responsible for Ronnie Lane leaving the Faces, which made their eventual breakup inevitable. It defined the Rod Stewart persona, the lairy lad on the lam, with the roving eye, the heart of gold, and an almost total lack of introspection.

Rod Stewart's 1971 workload beggars belief. The Faces toured the UK in January and then the United States for February and March, by which time their second album, *Long Player,* was released. In April they were back in the UK playing universities and recording TV appearances. In May Warner Brothers released *It Ain't Easy,* an album by Rod Stewart's and Elton John's old boss Long John Baldry. Stewart and John, who had been in bands led by Baldry, each produced a side, and the album was recorded during a week's break in the Faces' February tour. *Every Picture Tells a Story* came out on July 9, at which point they went back to the United States to play. At the end of August, when "Maggie May" was number one, they returned to England to play the Weeley Festival in Essex, where they so comprehensively upstaged the headliner Marc Bolan. Two weeks later they played alongside the Who at the UK's answer to the Concert for Bangladesh at the Oval cricket ground. In his autobiography, Rod Stewart remembers driving to his home in Winchmore Hill after the show with his posh girlfriend at his side, realizing that he was now truly the rock star. Two weeks before December, the Faces released *A Nod's as Good as a Wink to a Blind Horse*, their second album of original material in a year. Nobody could recall precisely how it came to be recorded. Stewart's next solo album, which appeared a year after *Every Picture Tells a Story*, was called with heavy sarcasm *Never a Dull Moment*.

Apart from the music, Rod Stewart projected back to the music-buying public two great British passions that had never really been significant in pop music before: football and drinking. The football was a big part of Rod Stewart. Despite coming from the most football-crazed city in England, the Beatles never advertised any interest in the game, nor were they expected to. By the time, many years later, that Rod Stewart had installed a full-sized football pitch at one of his homes in Epping Forest, British rock stars were expected to make a fuss about their attachment to the national game, even if they had to have a team suggested for them by a PR agent. It was one of those interests that was supposed to root them in everyday life, even if their everyday life had been spent in the back of a Transit. Elton John and Robert Plant both had history with football, but Rod Stewart was the first rock star to use it as a way to define what he was and what he wanted from life. He had been good enough as a schoolboy footballer to have a trial with Brentford, which was certainly enough to establish his bona fides in the sport. He would turn out for charity matches, boot plastic footballs from the stage during Faces gigs, and have his photograph taken in his Scottish strip. His love of football was sincere, but it also helped seal him in the affection of a mass audience in Britain, a mass audience who were inclined to find the pronouncements and pretensions of the big bands increasingly baffling.

He had a look as well. The younger Rod Stewart had followed the dress codes of first the beatniks and the mods, but in the Faces he slowly adopted a style of his own, which was more than merely a set of clothes. It was a look that was widely followed. He dressed like a disreputable clerk out of Dickens, with his coxcomb of hair, his Fair Isle sweaters slightly too short, and his shoes unsuitable for heavy work. Onstage he planted the microphone stand like the spike on a pair of compasses and looked out at the crowd with the impudent air of a pitch invader that the authorities have been unable to eject. He seemed to be perpetually in the process of falling over, and the quality he seemed to value most in the Faces was that they stopped him doing just that. In their pictures they were always tumbling, leaning on each other like Edwardian bucks who had overindulged in strong waters, as they clearly had. Blue Nun, Guinness, Green Chartreuse—they liked their drinks like they liked most other aspects of their life: lush and highly colored. Now that the Rolling Stones had left the UK, the Faces seemed the only gang in town, and they were enjoying the role in big style. It couldn't last forever. There was no clear decision to render unto the Faces the things that were the Faces' and unto Rod the things that were Rod's. The Faces played Rod's songs as part of their stage act. They even backed him up when he appeared on *Top of the Pops* promoting his own singles. In later years Ronnie Lane said that Rod stole "Mandolin Wind" from him. It would be impossible to prove that there wasn't some truth in this.

At the end of July 1971, the Faces were playing in Long Beach, California, and their record company threw the inevitable party for them. Dee Harrington was twenty-one, and she was the kind of girl that only wealth and celebrity could have provided Rod Stewart with the chance to meet. The daughter of an RAF officer, she was the well-bred totty who does something to boys like Rod Stewart. She claimed that she was not familiar with his music, though girls like this, who are hanging around the film business and picking up a little modeling work, are old enough souls to understand the power of not letting on that they have. She must have known that he had the means to show her a good time because he produced a model of the yellow Lamborghini Miura that he had at home, a move that was both gauche and worldly. She left the party with him and within a month was installed in the house in Winchmore Hill. Not long after, he proposed marriage. It never happened. She was Rod's starter blonde. There would be many others.

By the summer of 1971, Cat Stevens, Marc Bolan, and Rod Stewart had been in the music business for five years and in that short time had banked a lifetime of false starts, setbacks, and hard lessons. They all had ambitions to make albums yet were astute enough to know that their careers depended on hit singles. Because they rose to fame in the densely populated hothouse of the UK, where the entire population was getting used to sitting down every Thursday evening to watch *Top of the Pops*, they knew the importance of being able to put themselves over on the small screen. A year before David Bowie appeared on *Top of the Pops* singing "Starman," Bolan, Stewart, and Stevens were already learning that it paid to flirt with the camera. They were the first generation of TV-savvy rock stars.

When the Beatles first arrived in New York in 1964, an American journalist had remarked that they were "new kind of people." Bolan, Stewart, and Stevens, the London boys of 1971, were further varieties of new kinds of people: Bolan, the little guy whose talent could never measure up to his ambition; Stewart, the gifted cynic who knew the arts of survival and played his public image to the hilt; and Stevens, the genuine seeker trying to conceal the fact that behind his good looks he could be a little dull. Britain has produced many other pop stars in their image—fabulous nine-day wonders who deliver less than meets the eye, twinkling old-fashioned entertainers who the audience is convinced are singing for them, and patently sincere while painfully vague singer-songwriters. Before these three performers came along, there was nobody to compare them with. They established new archetypes.

Marc Bolan never did make it internationally, and he was not the kind of person to settle for reduced circumstances. When he died in a car crash in 1977, he was a disappointed man. Cat Stevens's spiritual quest climaxed on a beach in California in 1978 when a near-death experience led him to a religious conversion, which twenty years later was to make him one of the few Muslims that people in the West would know by name. By 2015 he was making a comeback, still performing the songs he unveiled in 1971. The third of the trio of Londoners doesn't find a comeback necessary because he has never been away. Every year since 1971 has been a further victory lap celebrating his unsinkable popularity. Rod Stewart has had the life that his school friends at William Grimshaw Secondary Modern could only dream of. It's to his credit that he always looks as if he can't quite believe it. He's been a household name for over forty years, longer than Louis Armstrong. Like Louis, his move into the role of all-round entertainer tended to make people underestimate the unique talent that had earned him the right. He still goes on tour, and "Maggie May" is still the song he plays more than any other. Not far behind it is "The First Cut Is the Deepest," a tune written by Cat Stevens. To his great surprise and ours, the job that he took on to avoid having to take a proper job, the job that was supposed to offer the life expectation of a mayfly, has turned out to be the most enduring occupation of all.

JULY

Rod Stewart: "Every Picture Tells a Story"

T. Rex: "Jeepster"

Cat Stevens: "Tuesday's Dead"

Leonard Cohen: "Dress Rehearsal Rag"

Graham Nash: "Wounded Bird"

The Doors: "Riders on the Storm"

Shuggie Otis: "Strawberry Letter 23"

Alice Cooper: "I'm Eighteen"

Dave and Ansil Collins: "Double Barrel"

Harry Nilsson: "Without You"

AUGUST 8

Wild Night

In years to come, the Concert for Bangladesh, the benefit concert that took place at Madison Square Garden, New York, on the first day of August 1971, would come to be viewed as one of the defining events of the era. It marked the emergence of a new senior league of rock stardom, as illustrated by pictures of George Harrison, Bob Dylan, Ringo Starr, Eric Clapton, and Leon Russell performing together in a new ecumenical spirit. The event also provided the blueprint for every subsequent effort to harness the popularity of rock music and the perceived moral stature of the people who play it to benefit some sort of deserving cause. This was the kind of thing that folkies had always done. They were always ready to gather to protest this or propose that and had a long tradition of linking arms at the end to belt out songs of unity and brotherhood. However, they were just folkies, and it was unlikely that anything they did would move the dial of public attention in the wider world or end up on the front pages that landed on America's porches. But once a Beatle was involved and the show was at Madison Square

Garden, all that changed. This was rock turning respectable for the first time.

The Concert for Bangladesh was as hastily improvised and as ill considered as every other decision made in the accelerated atmosphere of 1971. The conflict between Pakistan and its reluctant citizens in faraway East Bengal had been simmering ever since the Indian subcontinent was partitioned at the end of British rule at the end of World War II. The declaration of the state of Bangladesh in March 1971 had been followed by a combination of massacre and natural disasters that left thousands dead and millions displaced or threatened with starvation. It's likely this would have had no more effect on George Harrison than any of the other convulsions the wider world was going through in 1971 if he hadn't noted the effect it had on his friend and teacher Ravi Shankar, with whom he was collaborating on the soundtrack of a documentary called *Raga*. The Indian maestro's father had been born in Bengal, and he felt the events keenly. "Bangla Desh," Harrison's song about the catastrophe and the need to draw the West's attention to it, began, "My friend came to me with sadness in his eyes." Over ten years later, when Bob Geldof felt similarly moved to do something to alleviate the suffering in Ethiopia, the only musician he could go to for advice was George Harrison. Harrison's advice was "Do your homework"; he knew that's what he had failed to do.

In the summer of 1971, the twenty-eight-year-old Harrison was uniquely well placed to make a big gesture on behalf of rock. He was on his way to selling three million copies of an album that had no obvious precedent. *All Things Must Pass* wrapped its message of the mutability of the material world in swooning pop anthems multilayered to such a degree that the entire universe seemed to be humming in accord. All summer you could walk under ladders at the top of which decorators would be distractedly singing the "hare krishna" refrain from "My Sweet Lord," try on clothes in boutiques to the accompaniment of "Art of Dying," or pay ten new pence to hear "What Is Life" from the pub jukebox. The message may have been profound by pop standards but at its core it was the same kind of elementary pop tune that had inspired the Beatles ten years earlier, this time arrayed in acoustic finery and presented as a serious work of art. The other thing that made *All Things Must Pass* unique was that it was three records in a cardboard box. Never mind that the third record had only studio jams, which were shabby even by the complacent standards of the form, the sheer bulk of the package seemed to match the heft of Harrison's ambitions. John Lennon may have been the one shouting his message from the rooftops, but if anybody could be said to have been carrying the weight of the Beatles into 1971 it was the group's youngest member.

It was Shankar who first had the idea of doing a fund-raising concert. As soon as Harrison said he would like to join in, it became a rock concert, and because he was a Beatle, it could only be a big one. When the papers found out that Harrison was going to appear, speculation began about the chance of a partial or complete reunion of the band that the world seemed to be missing like a phantom limb. In 1971 the mainstream media, as represented by the newspapers and television, didn't care about pop music. The serious papers didn't cover it, and even the popular press rarely went near. What the media did care about was the Beatles. The prospect of their reunion was a story that they could run endlessly, and the upcoming concert, which was announced in mid-July, only a couple of weeks before it was due to happen, gave them fresh license. The first person who agreed to play was Ringo, even though he was in the middle of shooting the spaghetti western *Blindman* in Spain. The second was Klaus Voormann, the old Hamburg friend who was widely tipped to replace Paul in the event of the Beatles re-forming. The third was an Oklahoma-born pianist and bandleader who had spent the last few years laboring in the mills of the Hollywood session scene and was finally emerging as one of the key figures of the year. In his book *The Tipping Point*, Malcolm Gladwell theorizes that to start a cultural epidemic you need three types: mavens, who know a lot of things; connectors, who know a lot of people; and communicators, who know how to frame a message. In that sense, Leon Russell was a one-man epidemic.

Russell had been the opportunist behind Joe Cocker's Mad Dogs and Englishmen tour, the hottest ticket of 1970. He was the sloe-eyed figure with the Old Testament hair and ringmaster's top hat who looked as if he ought to be wrestling snakes in a revival tent. He was the musician whose signature rolling piano, fervent tambourine, and chorus line of wailing hot mamas seemed to bridge the divide between the barrelhouse and the Pentecostal church and satisfy what was a contemporary taste for a sound that seemed both comforting and social. He also made the sound that the young Elton John was, by his own admission, emulating on his records *Tumbleweed Connection* and *Madman Across the Water*. Russell wasn't bothered about that as long as his telephone kept ringing.

One of the people who rang him was Bob Dylan. "Watching the River Flow," the Russell-produced and -accompanied single that was Dylan's first release of 1971, is a rollicking repudiation of those people who gathered round Dylan's door insisting he had a duty to be the spokesman for a generation. It began with the line "What's the matter with me? I don't have much to say," which made his position very clear.

Having secured the services of a safe pair of hands like Leon Russell, Harrison decided that he wanted Eric Clapton to play guitar, a comparatively high-risk decision. Nobody knew better than Harrison that Clapton was holed up in his country house at Hurtwood Edge, devoting most of his energy to killing himself with heroin. He knew this because Clapton was laying siege to Harrison's wife, Pattie Boyd, and had taken to snorting heroin when she declined to leave her husband and join him. While this was going on, Clapton was also conducting affairs with Boyd's older sister, Paula, and Alice Ormsby-Gore, the teenage daughter of Lord Harlech. Alice was drinking two bottles of vodka a day because there was not enough junk to feed both his habit and hers. Clapton's depression, which was rarely far away, had come in like a storm front following the unaccustomed experience of being rejected by both Pattie Boyd and the record-buying public, who had failed to purchase his 1970 album *Layla*, possibly because they weren't altogether clear who Derek and the Dominos were. Since Harrison was the one who had suggested the band should give themselves a tongue-in-cheek name, it's possible that he felt some guilt about that. Despite the possibilities for disaster that might come with his involvement, emissaries were dispatched from the Beatles offices to go round to Clapton's house and convey the troubled guitarist across the Atlantic.

Those applauding this noble fund-raising endeavor might have narrowed their eyes had they known that Clapton would come to New York only if it could be guaranteed that he would have access to a supply of his favorite junk, known as White Elephant. Hence, while Harrison was appearing in front of the world's press and talking about peace and brotherhood, he had minions running round the less salubrious parts of New York City trying to make sure that the aristocratic teenage girlfriend of this overprivileged English guitar player would be able to secure his supply of drugs. Most people would have been shocked if they had known how closely the underground had come to depend on the underworld. The public associated heroin with the parts of New York in which the average person would never dream of setting foot, districts such as those visited by the young Al Pacino in the 1971 film *The Panic in Needle Park*. Movie theaters were simultaneously showing the trailer for *The French Connection*, a new Gene Hackman–Roy Scheider film in which they play two disgruntled New York City cops condemned to spend hours drinking bad coffee in nasty cars on garbage-strewn streets as they stake out a gang of French criminals who plan to bring a shipment of drugs into the city. New York has never seemed a less glamorous, more threatening, more charmless place than it did in that summer thanks to movies like *The French Connection* and *Klute*.

Harrison took out insurance against Clapton's nonappearance by getting Peter Frampton along to rehearsals. He didn't tell Frampton, who had just left Humble Pie, that he was being used as first reserve. That's something Frampton only figured out later. The beauty of having a Beatle at the top of the operation was that everybody else fell into their place in the hierarchy. Other spear carriers included members of Badfinger, one of the acts Harrison was supposed to be piloting through the uncertain waters of Apple Records, where they were invariably the victims of well-intentioned interference. They were called upon to play some of the banks of acoustic guitars that made up the *All Things Must Pass* sound and to provide backing vocals. Jim Keltner was brought in as second drummer to provide backup for Ringo, Billy Preston to play the organ, the rest of the holes being filled by members of Leon Russell's big band. Nothing apart from the hiring of Clapton was being left to chance.

This commitment to bringing in as many musicians as it would take to reproduce the sound of a highly processed studio album like *All Things Must Pass* was without precedent. By the time the Beatles had got round to building up their records layer by layer, they were no longer intending to play them live, and so the need never arose. The Concert for Bangladesh set the template for what became the rock recital, a presentational approach that was to grow in direct proportion to rock's sense of self-importance, the audience's demands that performances sound like the record they heard at home, and the extent to which it was felt that the occasion demanded some sort of grand gesture.

In 1971 there was no template for doing this kind of show, but necessity dictated that decisions had to be reached quickly. The story was that August 1 had been chosen for the concert date because a mystic had decided it was a propitious date. In fact, it was the only date that was available, Disney on Parade being due to open in Madison Square Garden the following day. It was decided that there would be two shows, which had been a standard way of presenting concerts in the sixties. The first would be at two thirty on Sunday afternoon. The following one would begin at eight o'clock the same evening. There were no plans to broadcast the show live on radio or to record it for TV. None of the US or British networks were set up to do such a thing, nor would they have had the technical capability. The show was eventually captured by three movie cameras for a possible cinema release. The master shot from the back of the Garden was largely unusable, as was the angle from the side. What survives is largely thanks to the camera that was in the pits.

The anticipation around the show was largely because it was going to have two Beatles onstage together for the first time since 1966. Harrison did talk to Lennon about his playing, but as soon as Lennon said there had to be a role for Yoko, Harrison wisely stopped raising the subject. He knew that people would be less kindly disposed to the charitable intentions of the show if Yoko Ono was ululating in the vicinity. Having instigated the painful and protracted effort of dissolving the Beatles, McCartney clearly could never have been involved.

The appeal of the Beatles getting back together or at least not splitting up didn't have much to do with nostalgia, which was yet to be seen as something applicable to pop music. (In 1971 the only compilation of the Beatles' greatest hits was *A Collection of Beatles Oldies,* a record put out in 1967, only about a year after the newest of the so-called oldies had been recorded. Catalogue marketing was undeveloped.) Pop music lived in the present, and it was expected that if the Beatles did ever perform again, something they hadn't done for more than five years, it would be to play their new tunes, not their old favorites, much as most other bands did.

The ghost of their old group hovered over all four individuals that summer. It didn't matter how much they protested. They were locked together from the point of view of business whether they liked it or not. In light of this, the success of "My Sweet Lord" wasn't merely of interest to Harrison. John Lennon might not like the idea of Harrison selling more copies of *All Things Must Pass* than he'd managed to sell of his *John Lennon/Plastic Ono Band,* but he knew that as one of the directors of the record company, he profited from those sales, just as he was credited as the cowriter of such McCartney tunes as "Yesterday" and others that he would have been mortified to have been associated with.

Sitting athwart their joint fortunes was Allen Klein. He was the only source of advice and counsel for John, George, and Ringo. McCartney had failed in his attempt to get his brother-in-law John Eastman put into Klein's position and had therefore taken steps to dissolve the partnership. While the lawyers were arguing the rights and wrongs, all that joint money was frozen. Meanwhile, the record business was becoming bigger and more profitable than it had been at any stage in the previous decade. The big money was in advances against future royalties, based upon the promise of what might happen rather than the reality of what had already happened. Klein knew that the one product he would always be able to get a huge advance for was a new Beatles album. Therefore, he was concentrating on performing the key duty required of the manager of any group, which is to prevent a group doing what all groups are always on the point of doing, which is splitting up.

Everybody within the Beatles orbit at some point in 1971 would have imagined that an album containing "My Sweet Lord," "Isn't It a Pity," "Jealous Guy," "Imagine," "Another Day," "Back Seat of My Car," "Admiral Halsey," and Ringo's "It Don't Come Easy" would be, if anything, better than *Abbey Road*. During the spring of 1971, the press filled the news vacuum with speculation that the three of them might re-form with Klaus Voormann as bass player, speculation about which meant the blameless German had to temporarily go into hiding. It was the era of supergroups like Blind Faith, Crosby, Stills, Nash & Young, and Ginger Baker's Air Force, when stars could be traded from one band to another as simply as pro athletes might be shipped from one team to another. The idea that groups could be reduced to separate atoms was brilliantly expressed in the English rock magazine *ZigZag*, where editor Pete Frame put his draftsman's skills to good use in sprawling family trees that traced the constantly changing lineups of such restless aggregations as John Mayall's Bluesbreakers or Jefferson Airplane.

Some people saw this as a healthy symptom of the overdue jazz-ification of rock, in which a group was merely a temporary alliance. The members of the Beatles had never looked at life like that, and from the moment the group broke up, George Harrison was uncomfortable with life on his own. The Beatles' performing experience had been as narrow as it was deep. When Lennon played the Toronto Rock and Roll Revival with his hastily assembled Plastic Ono Band in 1969, he threw up before going onstage because of his nerves. He'd spent thousands of hours onstage, but he'd never spent any time with anyone but the Beatles. He'd always looked to his right and seen the same faces. George felt much the same. Although all of them took every opportunity to describe what they had created as "just a band," at the same time they had great faith in the power of that band's brand and worried that people would not accept them as readily if they were out on their own.

Harrison's junior position in the Beatles' second line had given him the opportunity to shine without needing to be a load-bearing wall. As soon as he was free from the Beatles, he rushed to join Delaney & Bonnie's Friends, where his contributions were largely unheard as he merged among the teeming multitudes at the back. His comparative youth had allowed him to play the mulish adolescent when it suited him. The fact that he was in a group with the two most talented and productive songwriters of the age meant that only his best songs got on their records, which shielded him from criticism. Unlike Lennon and McCartney in their very different ways, he was not a leader. All groups pretend to be democracies while depending on one member being prepared to endure the derision of the others by taking a lead. Harrison was never comfortable being that person.

As the prime mover behind the Concert for Bangladesh, Harrison was in an even more exposed position. Had he been a few years older, he might have been sufficiently cautious not to take the risk. In this situation he had to advocate for something that had never been tried before—putting on a high-profile charity concert featuring rock superstars while keeping those rock stars happy even though many of them, like Clapton, were wrestling with terrors of their own, and all of them were entertaining the single thought that goes through the mind of a performer once outside their familiar zone of operation—how will this make me look? Whatever anxiety they felt could only be a fraction of what Harrison was feeling. When Bob Dylan said he was nervous about going out in front of the twenty thousand people in Madison Square Garden, Harrison reminded him that he had never been out front in the Beatles and that the few steps toward the microphone at center stage was going to be a very, very difficult journey for him to make.

Bob Dylan's appearance at Madison Square Garden on August 1 would prove to be a pivotal moment in his career. Dylan had just moved back to New York City after spending five years living in Woodstock in upstate New York. In these sylvan surroundings, people sometimes broke into his house in the middle of the night, so his wife and children lived in fear of nutcases, drug casualties, and random truth seekers. He wasn't alone. Rock legends didn't yet have security. On May 22, 1971, the staff at John Lennon's house found one such wide-eyed apostle sleeping in the grounds of his house in Tittenhurst Park, where he was recording his new album. The meeting between Lennon, who was, by his own admission, "just a bloke who wrote some songs," and this desperate man, who believed that all those songs were addressed specifically to him, was filmed. In the man's beseeching eyes, where the childish hopes of the revolution jostle with years of drug use and probably mental illness, it's possible to see what made people like Lennon and Dylan determine that in future they would build higher walls and remain behind them. The demands of fans were made even more ridiculous and frightening by the fact that in 1971 people still thought they had a right to demand things of rock stars, things they would have never considered demanding of elected politicians. At a launch party at Keith Moon's house on July 14 for the Who's "Won't Get Fooled Again," Mick Farren and other members of the underground press surrounded Pete Townshend and demanded that he explain where he stood in relation to the revolution. The gist of Townshend's response was that he was reasserting control over his own life.

Dylan tried to do something similar by moving back to New York, taking a town house at 94 Macdougal Street, close to the folk haunts of his early Greenwich Village days. The real estate decisions of rock superstars frequently betray how far removed they can be from normal life, and this was one such. This attractive, commodious, double town house had the notable disadvantages of having tenants in the basement and a front door that opened directly onto the street. This alone would have made life difficult enough, even without the attentions of A. J. Weberman. He came into Dylan's life in 1971 and became a byword for the vampiric tendencies of people who think their affection for songs grants them ownership of the person who writes them.

No accounting of the wages of fame has ever dared invent a pest like A. J. Weberman. Nowhere in the history of film or sport do you find people like the vampires who began to attach themselves to rock. Weberman was a ghoul, a bore, and an unbalanced person, who felt the imminent arrival of the alternative Jerusalem licensed him to suspend the laws of human decency. In early 1971 he felt entitled to lead demonstrations outside Dylan's Macdougal Street house with other members of his self-styled Dylan Liberation Front and, on occasion, to actually enter his house without an invitation, then to go through the things in his garbage and attempt to decode where Dylan was "at," as if that could be done and as if the location of Bob Dylan and his mental disposition were something that could be said to have an urgent bearing on the lives of people all over the world.

People like Dylan and George Harrison were used to attention, but this was a new dimension of torment. Most of their lives as public property had been spent in the back of large cars or in hotel suites where they suffered along with comrades-in-arms who had signed up for the same life. Now that they were married and were attempting to spend more time at home building a family life, they saw these threats through the horrified eyes of their wives and children and wanted nothing more of them. Weberman's demonstrations didn't simply disturb Dylan's peace and frighten his children; they also made him a pariah among his neighbors. Dylan tried to build a wall at the back to protect his children's privacy. He had no permission to do so, and when he came back one weekend, he found his neighbors had knocked it down.

Because Dylan had been largely out of sight for five years and had made regular adjustments to his appearance with beards and spectacles and had never been a big TV star in the first place, his name was more famous than his image. He hired John Cohen, the photographer who had taken pictures of him when he first came to New York, to take pictures of him back in the city. He made sure Cohen brought a long lens camera with him so that he could be photographed from across the road, apparently merging with the crowd. Throughout his life, this has been his dearest wish, to escape observation in order to be able to observe. To an extent he had succeeded. In its report on the Bangladesh concerts, the *New York Times* stated that one of the security guards looked at this man in his late twenties who was walking onstage to such tumultuous applause and asked if this was a member of the Beatles that he didn't recognize. At the end of May, Dylan went to Israel for a few days and was photographed at the Wailing Wall in a skullcap, which fueled speculation that his next "thing" might be religion. On the beach at Tel Aviv, he was buttonholed by the *Jerusalem Post*. Even the Israeli licensee of his recordings invaded his privacy by taking an ad in the paper congratulating him on his thirtieth and welcoming him to the country. There seemed to be no escape from attention. If that was the case, he may as well go back to work.

Dylan was turning thirty years old, one of the first of the famous names of the sixties to reach this watershed. His father had recently died, which gave him something further in common with Harrison, whose beloved mother had died the previous year. He didn't release a new album in 1971, though he did put out *Bob Dylan's Greatest Hits Vol II*, which was to become the best-selling record of his career. One of the reasons it sold so well, apart from providing the new generation of rock LP buyers with a rock LP by Dylan, was that it was packaged in color pictures of Dylan taken at the Concert for Bangladesh, in which he appeared with his trademark corkscrew curls, denim jacket, and harmonica holder, like an older but wiser version of the man they had once regarded as the spokesman for a generation. He wasn't singing country. He wasn't doing anything odd with his arrangements. On August 1, 1971, he sang "A Hard Rain's a-Gonna Fall," "Blowin' in the Wind," "It Takes a Lot to Laugh, It Takes a Train to Cry," "Love Minus Zero/No Limit," and "Just Like a Woman" and could not possibly have been more "on brand." When

Harrison had turned to the wings to introduce "a friend," which was soon adopted as the folksy way to refer to a superstar, he hadn't been at all confident that Dylan would be there. When Dylan went off half an hour later, the Concert for Bangladesh could be officially declared a success, and Dylan suddenly saw a way that he could present himself in the new world of enormous halls and crowds that stretched to the horizon.

The Concert for Bangladesh did more for the careers of the people who appeared on the stage and for the profile of the nation it was named after than it did for the people it was intended to benefit. Even the most successful benefits don't come close to equaling what governments and relief agencies can mobilize. Money went missing, either into the pockets of security guards who let fans in without tickets, into the accounts of agents and middlemen, or, most notably, to the tax collectors of the United States and the United Kingdom. Harrison had assumed that his sincere desire to raise money to benefit the people of Bangladesh would overcome all obstacles. But the record companies didn't see why they should be compelled to release the music packaged in the way that Harrison wanted, particularly with an emaciated child on the cover. The IRS took the view that since the charity wasn't chosen until after the concert, the revenue from the concert was income and as such had to be taxed. The British Treasury didn't see how it could waive the purchase tax on the live album just because a Beatle asked them to. Accustomed to being able to command and make it so, Harrison was suddenly discovering a world of adults where his writ didn't run.

This confirmed a lot of his suspicions about the way the world worked. He was already watching the extraordinary worldwide success of his hit "My Sweet Lord" turn into a legal and financial quagmire. He had started composing "My Sweet Lord" while on tour with Delaney & Bonnie in 1970. It was initially worked up with Delaney Bramlett, who expected to have some share of the songwriting credit. Bramlett was the first one to point out that it sounded like the 1962 Chiffons hit "He's So Fine." This was drawn to Harrison's attention more than once, but he kept going, probably hoping that wiser counsels would intervene to keep him from himself. After all, Phil Spector, the man who had produced the Chiffons tune, was also overseeing the Harrison sessions. Early reviews also pointed out the resemblance, but nothing was done to avert the problem, which was more certain to loom the more successful the record became.

The old music business saw "where there's a hit, there's a writ" stresses the importance of timing and captures the time-honored wisdom that says lawsuits arrive only once there's a large pile of cash on the table. On February 12, when "My Sweet Lord" had been number one in the United States, the UK, Spain, Sweden, France, Germany, Ireland, Norway, New Zealand, Australia, Austria, and the Netherlands, lawyers representing Bright Tunes Music began an action for plagiarism of their property, which had been apparently written by Ronald Mack, who had been the manager of the Chiffons in 1962. At what point in the process the grace note upon which the eventual court case subsequently hinged had been introduced and by whom nobody would ever know. By 1981 the case had become pop music's equivalent of the *Jarndyce v. Jarndyce* case in Dickens's *Bleak House,* a remorseless engine of profit for the lawyers and a source of unending pain for the participants; it was a machine with a pitiless will all its own.

Accusations of plagiarism are occupational hazards for successful songwriters, particularly prominent ones. There are only a limited number of combinations of chords, only a certain number of ways you can push around one-syllable verbs and personal pronouns to form them into a twist on a well-known phrase or saying and then mold it into three choruses, a verse, and a bridge before somebody somewhere thinks or pretends to think you have deliberately sat down and copied their previous composition and tried to pass it off as your own. If that was his intention, Harrison would probably have chosen one of the thousands of great girl group records that never troubled the charts and languished in undeserved obscurity. If that were the case, Harrison would not have begun "Something," his most successful song, with a line straight out of "Something in the Way She Moves" by James Taylor, an artist who

The Weeley Festival begins as a local fund-raiser for those affected by the war in Bangladesh but is soon swamped by every long-haired band in the land.

The news of Jim Morrison's death in Paris in July takes days to come through. His posthumous *Rolling Stone* cover begins his iconic era.

Marc Bolan, the UK's new king of pop, gets a lukewarm reception at Weeley. He is more at home in the *Top of the Pops* studio. Elton John is seemingly at home everywhere.

In a year when attractive singer-songwriters sleep with each other and write songs about it, it's almost inevitable that Carly Simon should stop off at Cat Stevens en route to James Taylor.

5

Rod Stewart's solo success guarantees that his days as lead singer of the Faces are numbered. Even before "Maggie May" is a huge international hit, that success had brought him a grand home with luxury cars in the drive. By the end of 1971 his accountant is telling him to move to somewhere bigger.

6

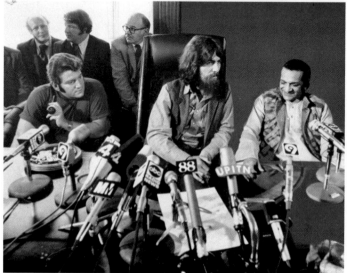

Taking on the leadership of the Concert for Bangladesh in August places George Harrison between the spiritual world, as represented by his mentor Ravi Shankar, and Mammon, as represented by his manager Allen Klein.

7

Bob Dylan's appearance alongside George Harrison and Leon Russell at Madison Square Garden, sporting the denim jacket and harmonica holder of his protest era, makes the Concert for Bangladesh a triumph.

8

In the autumn of 1971 the newly formed Big Star are thrown the keys of Ardent Studios in Memphis and allowed to make their own record.

9

In Hollywood, David Geffen (RIGHT) is gathering a stable of winsome acoustic stars like America to exploit the young adult market opened up by Carole King.

10

Van Morrison, seen here in the studio in 1971, turns a rare period of domestic contentment into hit singles and also inspires the young Bruce Springsteen.

11

The unknown Jackson Browne is composing so many great songs he can afford to gift "Take It Easy" to the equally unknown Eagles.

Neil Young in the barn on his northern California ranch where he completes *Harvest*, the key album of his career, in September.

1

13

14

Rick Wakeman's transfer from the Strawbs to Yes is headline news in progressive-rock circles.

15   With *Hunky Dory* recorded and plans for *Ziggy Stardust* already hatched, David Bowie plays an acoustic show at Friars in September. Tickets are less than a pound.

16

Sly and the Family Stone's long-delayed album *There's a Riot Goin' On* is at number one on the *Billboard* charts soon after Attica prison in upstate New York is consumed by a disturbance (BELOW). At least thirty-eight people, both prisoners and guards, lose their lives.

17

LEFT: The affluent Loud family of Santa Barbara, California, are the first to submit to "reality TV." The cameras track them throughout 1971 and they never once ask for privacy.

RIGHT: The *Rolling Stone*'s Beach Boys cover in October accompanies the release of *Surf's Up* and depicts them as wistful elders of the church of fun.

19

18

ABOVE: Elton John poses with his mother and stepfather in Pinner for a major *Life* magazine feature, while Frank Zappa entertains his parents, Francis and Rose Marie (RIGHT). The photographer notes that all his subjects are on their best behaviors in front of their parents.

The Who at the launch of *Who's Next* in the garden of Tara, Keith Moon's bizarre playhouse in the Surrey suburbs.

RIGHT: When Led Zeppelin mark the release of *Led Zeppelin IV* by playing Wembley Arena, still known as the Empire Pool, it represents a dramatic increase in scale for live rock in Britain. *Melody Maker* (LEFT) is wondering if the release of "George Jackson" means Dylan is getting back to protest.

Elvis Presley's
1971 shows are
premium-priced,
heavily ritualized
celebrations of his
own magnificence
rather than musical
events. They point
the way to the
future.

26

LEFT: The all-conquering Alice Cooper arrives at London airport with his trademark snake. David Bowie models the look of his new band on the just-released film *A Clockwork Orange* (BELOW).

happened to be signed to a label of which Harrison was a director. If that were the case, he would have taken steps to cover his tracks. He didn't.

The argument with Bright Tunes was purely about dollars. Allen Klein tried to set up a deal whereby Harrison could buy Bright Tunes, but the owners had no incentive to sell and certainly not quickly. The case didn't come to court until 1975 and was not concluded until 1998, by which time Harrison had severed his relationship with Klein, and Klein had secretly bought Bright Tunes for himself. He was the only person in the whole deal who knew how much "My Sweet Lord" had earned and therefore knew how much his former client, who had been forced to admit to "unconscious plagiarism," would eventually have to hand over to the company he now owned. Whether this was duplicitous or not, it was presumably not what George Harrison had in mind when he went along with John Lennon's wish and handed over the direction of his career to Klein.

All Things Must Pass was the biggest success any former member of the Beatles would ever put his name to. It was critically acclaimed and commercially successful. It was one of the few rock albums that can claim to have combined a certain amount of wisdom with old-fashioned pop catchiness. It was the high-water mark of a sound that married the euphoric drive of early '60s jukebox music with the dense thick rock sound of 1970. When George Harrison stood there at the end of the Concert for Bangladesh at 10:55 p.m. on August 1, 1971, at what seemed like the midpoint of the year, he was the biggest solo star in music. Had he been a politician, his approval ratings would have been off the chart. People had always loved his music, but now they felt that he had elevated pop above its tawdry history into something altogether finer and more noble. He had done something that nobody had ever done before, and he had apparently done it on his own. He had, temporarily at least, eclipsed the Beatles.

But if for Bob Dylan the experience of going onstage at Madison Square Garden provided a glimpse of a future for him, a future in which his legend grew in direct proportion to the size of the audience, for George Harrison it was more like an ending. The amazing thing is that he would never do anything quite so resounding again. It was difficult to tell whether he was trying. Everything Harrison recorded and wrote after 1971, with the possible exception of the first Traveling Wilburys album, released in 1988, was pale and tentative. It was as if he no longer entirely believed in himself, as if he was no longer capable of playing the confidence trick of writing a fresh song. All songwriters like to ask, "Where did that come from?" when a new song strikes them. They joke that if the song is any good it must have been written already. For George Harrison, thanks to his bittersweet experiences with the "My Sweet Lord" case, that could never be a joke again.

He wasn't the only one for whom August 1, 1971, was an ending masquerading as a beginning. For the week of the Bangladesh concert, Badfinger appeared to have it made, rubbing shoulders with superstars, going to the after party at Ungano's, and getting mentioned in all the press coverage. The tragic thing was that none of this star power ever actually transformed their fortunes, and the comedown was cruel. Badfinger's first gig following Madison Square Garden was at Huddersfield Polytechnic. Their whole subsequent career was to be dogged by the worst kind of luck.

They had been the first group signed to the Apple label and were widely regarded as having some of the DNA of the Beatles with two strong songwriters. Paul McCartney had written their first hit, "No Matter What," but they really didn't require star patronage. Then Harrison had taken a particular interest in them. When in 1971 he offered to rerecord some of the tracks from their new album *Day After Day* with him as producer, they canceled an Australian tour so that they could fit around his schedule. In the end he didn't have time, and so the album, which had been begun with Beatles engineer Geoff Emerick, was completed with the new whiz kid Todd Rundgren and was released just ten days before Christmas, which is as good a guarantee of oblivion as anything.

Badfinger's biggest score of 1971 came in Harry Nilsson's version of Pete Ham's "Without You," which was number one in the UK at the end of the year. The Concert for Bangladesh made them well known, but they never recovered their momentum, and what money they did make was salted away by their new manager Stan Polley. In 1975 their leading songwriter Pete Ham killed himself, accusing Polley in his suicide note of being a "soulless bastard."

The shadow of 1971 didn't stop there. Eight years after Ham's death, Tom Evans also committed suicide following a bitter argument with the other two members of the group about the money from "Without You," which was a huge hit all over again in a version by Mariah Carey. The legacy that was the cause of such pain and destruction continues to mount up remorselessly. "Baby Blue," which comes from their 1971 album *Straight Up*, was the final song on the final episode of the hit TV series *Breaking Bad* in 2014, and in this form will play forever on the Internet, far too late to benefit any of the people who wrote it.

A great deal of the music recorded in 1971 has had an afterlife that none of the people who played it could have predicted. As the giant hits of that era become dulled by familiarity, there's an increasing demand for less well known songs that nonetheless seem to share some of the same DNA. In the case of Badfinger, the years of retrospective success have if anything caused more anguish than the years of obscurity.

The day after the concert a report appeared on the front page of the *New York Times* along with a picture of George Harrison, Bob Dylan, and Ringo Starr. This was a significant departure for the Gray Lady, which rarely touched upon pop music. Even the London *Sunday Times,* which was comparatively breezy, touched rock only via the condescending forceps of its popular music critic Derek Jewell. The *Guardian* had just begun taking the reviews written by a student named Robin Denselow, who had berated the paper for its lack of interest in what seemed to him a vital part of the life of young adults. The editors were more likely to let him review rock bands if he told them they were folk. The adult world regarded mainstream pop music as primarily of interest to teenagers, a tribe who didn't read newspapers.

The *New York Times* report used the word "Beatle" eleven times, a clear indication of its angle on the story, which was in the nature of an anthropological report on a visit to a strange tribe of erstwhile screamers, all wearing dungarees and T-shirts. "I'm shaking like a leaf," confessed seventeen-year-old Debbie from Brooklyn, who had gained entrance by paying eighteen dollars to an official who sneaked her and a friend past the ticket takers. The paper also got a quote from the policeman in charge, who provided the obligatory reflection on the miracle that so many people should require so little arresting.

The concert was well received, as much for the worthiness of its objectives as the power of its performances. Given the seriousness of the cause that had brought them there, this seemed only right. Given the fact that the main players were, by the standards of the time, staring at the prospect of middle age, it also felt right for them. What nobody noted was what was going on beneath the surface, which was the introduction into pop of a number of values that hadn't been evident before. Instead of screams and hysteria, there was reverence, continuity, respect, formality, even worthiness. For the first time, some of the songs of the Beatles were being performed outside the context of the Beatles. At the same time, Bob Dylan was taking some of his songs that were most associated with the ferment of the sixties and performing them as if they were classics. Leon Russell was doing the same with the Coasters' "Young Blood," a song about underage sex. The whole show had the feeling of a ceremony with both performers and audience getting used to changed roles and the establishment of a canonical view of rock.

Not all the people running the American music business that week adopted the same selfless note, nor did the people packing the record shops have their thoughts on higher things. James Brown had the number one soul single with "Hot Pants (She Got to Use What She Got to Get What She Wants)," which encapsulates his trademark marriage of carnal and mercantile. *Switched-On Bach* was at the top of the classical listings, although it was expected to make way for the newly released soundtrack of Luchino Visconti's *Death in Venice*. (The popularity of this owed less to the ethereal nature of the music than the vision of Björn Andrésen, who played Dirk Bogarde's teenage love object in the film.) The Bee Gees were at the top of the US singles chart with their soupy "How Can You Mend a Broken Heart." T. Rex were at number one in the UK with their bouncy "Get It On."

A world away from all this, in Los Angeles, Joe Smith was building a record company that seemed removed from the razzle-dazzle of the record business as it was known in New York. His Warner Bros. Records operation carried itself more like a prestigious publisher of books for the discriminating reader or a boutique advertising agency than a mere vulgar peddler of pop tunes. Under the guidance of Smith and Mo Ostin, who were both Sinatra-generation ring-a-ding-dingers by upbringing, the company was signing up maverick talent with little regard for its immediate commercial prospects, and it was marketing that talent via a wry, self-deprecating house style subsequently aped by hundreds of independent labels.

Warner Bros. began truffling for that talent within a hurled newspaper of their Burbank headquarters, which is how it came to recruit such an interesting bunch of movie business brats, showbiz kids, beatnik progeny, and willful eccentrics. There was songwriter Randy Newman, whose uncles were giants of movie theme music, Lowell George of Little Feat, whose dad sold furs to movie stars, Bonnie Raitt, whose dad had been a star of musicals on stage and screen, Ry Cooder, the one-eyed son of a folk-music-singing lawyer from bohemian Santa Monica, and, strangest of all, Van Dyke Parks, a child prodigy of classical music who'd come from the South to star opposite Grace Kelly and wound up writing the words to Brian Wilson's rococo "Heroes and Villains." They were all absurdly talented and utterly intractable. They made brilliant records of the kind nobody had made before, records that came in striking covers and attracted glowing reviews but sold only a handful of copies. Warner

Bros. sold so few copies of Van Dyke Parks's lushly orchestrated song suite *Discover America* that one of its adverts boasted about how much it cost the company. Randy Newman's voice was so difficult to market that Warner's advertising genius Stan Cornyn took an ad saying, "His voice is quite something—when you get used to it." The company was introducing into the marketing of pop records a quality that had never previously been thought relevant—good taste. Its marketing challenged you to share it.

The first Little Feat album, which came out in January 1971, was gloriously all over the place, from a raging medley of two Howlin' Wolf tunes, featuring George and Ry Cooder locking antlers on the glass finger guitar, through "Brides of Jesus," which proposed a previously unmapped connection between Procol Harum and the Band, to the almost Brechtian knockabout of their own "Crazy Captain Gunboat Willie." According to Ben Fong-Torres's book about Little Feat, that first album sold only twelve thousand copies. Nevertheless, in 1971 the world of rock was small enough and the fact that their bass player Roy Estrada was a former member of the Mothers of Invention counted for enough, and the cover, which saw them in front of a Santa Monica mural, was cool enough that it seemed everyone who cared about that kind of thing had heard it. Warner Bros. was even prepared to have a go with avant-garde blues shouter Captain Beefheart, who had already tested the courage of even the most forgiving longhairs with *Trout Mask Replica* and *Lick My Decals Off, Baby*. For a short while in the early seventies, it didn't seem entirely beyond the bounds of possibility that Warner might be able to get him on the radio and into the charts.

It's unlikely that Steve Ross ever heard Captain Beefheart or Van Dyke Parks or Ry Cooder. Ross was the person responsible for underwriting this unprecedented flowering of creativity within the record business. No hipster he. Forty-four at the time, he had been born Steven Rechnitz in Brooklyn, married into a funeral home business, and then diversified into limousine hire and car parking. By 1969 his company Kinney was big enough to be able to buy Warner Brothers–Seven Arts, which encompassed an ailing movie studio and a directionless record operation. Noting that the growth was all in music—even Warner Brothers' biggest movie hit when he took over was *Woodstock*—he put all the emphasis on that side of the business. Most of Ross's background was in businesses with small margins. He loved the idea that entertainment was all about sudden windfalls, and therefore he paid his record company executives handsomely and encouraged them to bet big.

The person who probably saw the future most clearly was actually working on the company's lowest rung at the time. Ted Templeman had been the drummer in Harpers Bizarre, a preppy close harmony group who had hits with cotton-candy revivals of "Anything Goes" and "The 59th Street Bridge Song." When the group broke up, he got a job as a "tape auditioner" for Warner Brothers for seventy-five dollars a week. Nobody really knew what Templeman was up to, but every chance he got he would slip into sessions for people like Frank Sinatra and Elvis Presley to learn different ways of doing things.

Templeman had a feeling he knew how to produce records and could help bands sound better. He eventually heard a biker band called Pud from the Bay Area that he thought had potential. He produced their first record, which flopped in April 1971, but it was cheap enough for Warner Bros. to give them another go. At the same time, Templeman had been brought in to handle the already impossible Van Morrison. Van had done his album *His Band and the Street Choir*, which contained the airplay favorite "Domino," in Woodstock, and Warner had released it in November 1970. Like Bob Dylan, Morrison decided there were now too many tourists in Woodstock, and under the spell of his new wife, Janet Rigsbee, who had changed her name to Janet Planet to signify her oneness with the universe, he moved against his will to the other side of the country and settled in Marin County, north of San Francisco. Here the couple briefly lived in a sylvan fantasy with a horse called Moondance, a fantasy rather awkwardly celebrated on the cover of his 1971 album *Tupelo Honey*.

Like its predecessor, *Tupelo Honey* showed the tuneful, relaxed side of Morrison. Templeman had a combination of skills rare in a producer: the ears to recognize good tunes and the diplomacy to be able to handle the people who came up with them, even if they were people that most producers would be tempted to punch. Templeman was smart enough to know he had to record the vocals during the brief window before Van lost his patience, and then he could deal with everything else when he had gone back home. It was the sound of first *Street Choir* and then *Tupelo Honey*, and the blithe spirit of "Domino" and "Wild Night," plus that Irish show band lineup with horns, that caught the imagination of lots of other musicians that year, most notably young Bruce Springsteen back in New Jersey.

Looking back in later years, the equable Templeman vows, "I would never work with Van Morrison again as long as I live. He's a marvelous talent, but he's fired everyone who's ever worked with him, and he understands nothing about the recording process." He remembers that when *Tupelo Honey* was finished, he spent two days working on what he considered a perfect mix of the album, only to have Morrison put out an earlier, rougher version. Two days after the record came out, Morrison rang him in the middle of the night to say that he'd been wrong. "I could have wept."

The lessons Templeman learned in 1971 were paid back when he worked with more pliable talents as the record business continued to turn into an industry and learned how to turn inspiration into formula. One of the guitarists on Morrison's album was a young San Francisco player named Ronnie Montrose. In 1973 Templeman recorded his band Montrose, developing a signature pop metal sound that the producer later took to the bank with Van Halen. The second album he made with the biker band, now called the Doobie Brothers, started off with a song called "Listen to the Music," the first of a string of Templeman productions that would go on to enjoy a seemingly eternal commercial life. It was formula music but done in the best possible taste.

Warner Brothers wasn't allowed to enjoy its position as the sole artist-friendly record company for long. In August 1971 David Geffen was preparing to launch his own Asylum label. Geffen was twenty-eight and had already made the first of many fortunes as the manager of Laura Nyro and Crosby, Stills, Nash & Young. In a milieu where most people prided themselves on a laid-back approach, Geffen was a bulldog. Attempting to get a deal for his new client the twenty-three-year-old songwriter-performer Jackson Browne, he took him to play for Columbia president Clive Davis in his New York office. Halfway through the meeting, Davis's secretary came in to say that his boss was on the phone. Geffen turned to his client and said, "Pack up your guitar."

Geffen was a grandstander. That's why acts like Joni Mitchell and Crosby, Stills, Nash & Young were eager to work with him. He might have been a jackal, but he was their jackal. They would go into his office just to hear him shout at people on the phone on their behalf. Geffen spent months shopping Browne around to the majors and got nowhere; finally, he did as Ahmet Ertegun suggested, which was start his own label. The September 11 *Billboard* announced the establishment of Asylum Records. Joni Mitchell would be moving there from Warner, but Geffen's protégée Laura Nyro, who had been rumored, wouldn't. The item said Joni would be joined by Jackson Browne, John David Souther, and an "as-yet unnamed group featuring Bernie Leadon, Randy Meisner, Glenn Frey and Don Henley."

Asylum was so named because it was supposed to represent a shelter away from the depredations of the majors. Since in each case Geffen was the manager, the music publisher, and record company, which is rarely in the best interests of the artists, the wheels were bound to come off at some point in the future, but as 1971 drew to a close the David Geffen–Eliot Roberts management firm and their accompanying Asylum label were the pinnacle of the new funky glamour.

Jackson Browne was sent into Crystal Sound Studios with the engineer who had recorded James Taylor, the top male solo act at the time, and the rhythm section that had played on Carole King's *Tapestry*, the top female solo record. Browne took a break in the middle of recording to take his jeep through Utah and Arizona and came back with the basic idea of a new song, which began, "Well I'm runnin' down the road, trying to loosen my load." When he played it for his neighbor and fellow struggler Glenn Frey, the latter was desperate to have it for his new group, who by now had fresh dentistry thanks to Geffen and were called the Eagles, and so with Browne's permission he finished it. He took it to London in February 1972, where the Eagles recorded it for their first album.

The window of opportunity that opened in 1971 for anyone who could be described as a singer-songwriter allowed entry for musicians from every point of the compass. One of the breakthrough albums released that month was *Just As I Am*, the debut of the gifted, diffident, entirely gimmick-free Bill Withers. Thirty-three-year-old Bill was still working on the payroll of an aircraft construction firm in 1971 as his song "Ain't No Sunshine" began climbing the charts. The whole first album, which also included "Grandma's Hands" and "Harlem," was recorded in just three sessions of three hours each. The record label thought it would take four sessions, but so apparent was the perfection of what they had achieved that producer Booker T. Jones was able to cancel the last one.

Bill had wise eyes, wore a granddad vest, and carried an acoustic guitar, which he hadn't actually owned a year before he was at number one. His songs about economically disadvantaged, honest people in the ghetto, people who were sometimes weak and sometimes strong, people who sometimes drank too much, went off the rails, and in one extreme case killed themselves, weren't aimed at a pre-existing category. This new market for long-playing albums was still too new to have become crisscrossed with familiar tracks for future marketeers to follow. Record companies, management firms, producers, and artists themselves hadn't yet set themselves up to base the new thing on the old thing. Most of the things being done were being done for the first time. In the case of Bill Withers, they were also being done for the last time.

Warner Brothers even decided to take a risk on a solo album from Gram Parsons, who was best known at the time for his drinking and drugging and had been asked to leave Keith Richards's rented home at Nellecôte because he was preventing the guitarist from concentrating. In October in New Orleans he got a call from Chris Hillman, in the midst of a tour with the Flying Burrito Brothers, during which they recorded the ragged but appealing *Last of the Red Hot Burritos*. Hillman suggested Parsons come out and join them for a couple of shows in Maryland. Hillman also suggested Parsons investigate the lissome, long-haired folksinger he had seen a week earlier in a club in Washington. The folksinger, who had a child to look after, wouldn't take the train to Baltimore, and so Parsons, accompanied by his model wife, Gretchen, whom he'd recently married, was compelled to go to Washington. It was there he met the woman on whom his legend eventually came to depend, Emmylou Harris.

The year 1971 was full of such accidental meetings between troubadours. Kris Kristofferson was on a flight to Chicago when he met the sixties balladeer Paul Anka, who told him he had recorded one of his songs. Once in Chicago, Kristofferson went to see Anka's show in the lounge of an expensive hotel. In return Anka came to see Kristofferson in a club, where he was being supported by a local songwriter named Steve Goodman. Anka was impressed by Goodman's own "City of New Orleans" and a song about a returning Vietnam veteran called "Sam Stone," which was written by Goodman's friend. Goodman took Anka and Kristofferson to another club, where the friend, a mailman named John Prine, was having a nap between sets. As a result of that encounter, both men got record deals. When Atlantic released Prine's first record in the fall of 1971, critics were caught between applauding him for his compassionate portrayal of real American lives and adding him to their list of new Bob Dylans, alongside Loudon Wainwright III, whose second album, featuring such songs as "Saw Your Name in the Paper" and "Motel Blues," was satisfying the market's need for sardonic story songs in the style of old Bob Dylan.

Wainwright was married to Kate McGarrigle, the Canadian folksinger whose sister Anna had written a song called "Heart Like a Wheel," which she played at the Philadelphia Folk Festival of 1970.

The Texan singer Jerry Jeff Walker was in the audience, and he subsequently sang it for Linda Ronstadt, who instantly recognized it, even in his truncated, dimly remembered version, as being something that she needed to do. In 1974 it became the title track of her biggest album. The days of double-platinum and adult-oriented rock were far away in the future. This was the last summer of the folk club, when you could still find extraordinary talent, talent apparently without precedent, growing wild at the side of the road.

These folkies and roots-music kids were different stock. Unlike the Bangladesh stars George Harrison, Eric Clapton, and Leon Russell, they were often middle-class kids whose parents had encouraged them in buying a guitar and learning folk songs on the grounds that these songs had to be better than "Twist and Shout." They had different hinterlands, and in their efforts to map a place for themselves in this new post-Beatles world, they went searching in the heritage. Hence American music in 1971 suddenly had room for all sorts of arcane styles, for Taj Mahal's country blues, the antic cowboy jazz of Dan Hicks & His Hot Licks, Bette Midler's campy torch songs, the art songs of David Ackles, and the a capella of the Persuasions, Laura Nyro, and Labelle. Promoters and press were prepared to give anything a go, and the audience would apparently try anything once. It was the best of times because in many respects it seemed to be the first of times.

The 1971 level of productivity was never going to be matched in the future. It took another five years for the silky soul of Boz Scaggs to break into the charts, but a lot of the elements were in place in 1971 when he put out one album, *Moments*, and recorded another, *Boz Scaggs and Band*, at Olympic in London. Bands like Scaggs's, even more than Van Morrison's, were introducing elements of all kinds of American vernacular music, from the big band stylings of Bobby Bland to the country of George Jones, and seemed to have polish bands hadn't previously had. Members of Jefferson Airplane, who only two years earlier had been putting America up against the wall at Woodstock, were now members of Hot Tuna playing "Candy Man" and "Keep Your Lamps Trimmed and Burning" in a style that owed a lot to traditional fiddle music and at the same time didn't sound the same at all. Similarly, the Flying Burrito Brothers supercharged their honky-tonk music with the steel guitar of Al Perkins and were touring with a set that combined bluegrass protest songs with barroom versions of Wilson Pickett. The new favorite of the stoner set was the first album by Commander Cody and His Lost Planet Airman, who sang in praise of the life of the working man and his hot rod Lincoln. In August Gene Clark released *White Light*, a solo album that was finally worthy of his uniquely moving singing style. Commercially, it didn't amount to much, but it was well received, as was the first album by Judee Sill, which came out with the first Asylum releases in September. The world of rock was still small enough for a song like Sill's "Jesus Was a Cross Maker" to become familiar to most people who read the music press and listened to the right radio programs.

The world of rock musicians was small enough to ensure that the prodigiously talented player and singer Nils Lofgren was constantly in demand; in 1971, having just come from working with Neil Young on *After the Gold Rush*, he released *1 + 1*, the second record by his band Grin, while also becoming a temporary member of Crazy Horse, whose first album had been released in February. This featured the first version of Danny Whitten's song "I Don't Want to Talk About It." Almost ten years later this would be an enormous hit for Rod Stewart. At the time, it went largely unnoticed. Like "Heart Like a Wheel," "City of New Orleans," "Life on Mars?," "Doctor My Eyes," "Tiny Dancer," and scores of others, it was one more letter posted in 1971 that didn't arrive until years later. It would take the world a long while to catch up with the number of great songs that were strewn right across 1971.

George Harrison: "What Is Life"

Bob Dylan: "Watching the River Flow"

Leon Russell: "Stranger in a Strange Land"

Crazy Horse: "I Don't Want to Talk About It"

Little Feat: "Willin'"

Judee Sill: "Jesus Was a Cross Maker"

John Prine: "Hello in There"

Gene Clark: "For a Spanish Guitar"

America: "Ventura Highway"

Neil Diamond: "I Am . . . I Said"

SEPTEMBER

Family Affair

Not all the fresh music made in 1971 made an impact in that year. Some of it didn't come out until years later, by which time the people who made it had moved on, become different people, or died. Early in September 1971, a young man named Stuart Love, who worked for Warner Brothers in the New England area as a promotion man and talent spotter, booked a day in Intermedia Studios at 331 Newbury Street in Boston. The studio had opened only the year before, bringing sixteen-track recording to the Boston area for the first time. One of the albums that had been recorded there earlier in the year was the second one by Loudon Wainwright III, which featured "Motel Blues," "Saw Your Name in the Paper," and "Nice Jewish Girls," and led, via the inclusion of one song on a budget sampler album in the UK, to his first UK tour, during which he supported Status Quo, presumably a surprise to both acts.

There were four young men in the band that Love planned to make a demo with that day in September. They were Jerry Harrison, a twenty-one-year-old keyboard player studying architecture at Harvard; his friend and fellow student Ernie Brooks, who played bass; David Robinson, who had grown up locally and played drums; and the guitarist, singer, and leader, also a local, a clean-shaven, rangy, and clean-living nineteen-year-old named Jonathan Richman.

Collectively, they were known as the Modern Lovers, a name that hit an unusual note. At a time when new bands tended to pick names like Gentle Giant, Supertramp, Little Feat, America, and Atomic Rooster, any name that began with the definite article seemed attractively retro and intriguingly arch. Formed the previous year, the Modern Lovers' performances at local colleges and clubs had left audiences more puzzled than excited. The group's lean, driving sound, which owed something to one-off hits of the sixties like "She's About a Mover" and "96 Tears," was placed at the service of Richman's unique vision, which had been shaped under the spell of the Velvet Underground.

The Velvet Underground had been formed in 1965 by Lou Reed and John Cale. Reed had worked as a jobbing songwriter in New York's Tin Pan Alley while Cale studied the music of the avant-garde. Via this unique combination of limitations and inclinations, they arrived at a droning sound that appealed very strongly to a very small group of people, one of whom was Richman. Jonathan had been so smitten by the unvarnished realism of the Velvet Underground's songs that at the age of eighteen he had moved to New York in order to be near them. But whereas most people who moved in the Velvet Underground's orbit had tastes and sometimes vices that placed them beyond the pale of so-called straight society, Jonathan Richman had first become known in the Boston area for taking his guitar to Boston Commons and singing in a style halfway between skiffle and Tiny Tim, a style that defied people to decide whether or not to take him seriously. Speaking to Joe Harvard of the *Boston Rock Storybook* website in 1997, Jonathan talked about how he developed his unique style, which was the pop music equivalent of the naive school of painting: "You feel kinda naked and everything. So you just sing. But actually it isn't that you just sing. You just SING. Because it's life and death. You just SING like you're in a bullring. You don't care if you're on-key or off."

The songs that Jonathan sang were similarly out of step. Many repudiated the alternative society that had grown up since Woodstock. In fact, if Jonathan was rebelling against anything, it appeared to be rebellion. One of his songs, "I'm Straight," was a direct plea to a girl, beseeching her to ditch her hopeless hippie boyfriend and accept Jonathan's suit for the good reason that he didn't do drugs. Another was about still loving his parents and the old world, a genuinely revolutionary sentiment in the Age of Aquarius. Another was such an artless hymn to the delights of driving around Boston and calling at his favorite shops that even the people who liked the song, having grown so used to a life of ease that they no longer ascribed it any value, could only assume that he was being ironic. He wasn't. Jonathan looked at seventies America with the hungry eyes of a third-world asylum seeker. The big song was called "Roadrunner."

The Modern Lovers recorded three tunes that day in September 1971, "Roadrunner," "Someone I Care About," and "Hospital," and the tape impressed Love's bosses at Warner Brothers sufficiently that the following year they invited them to California to record with the Velvet Underground's John Cale, by then working for the company as an A&R man and making his own record, *Paris 1919*. By the time Warner Brothers made up its mind to take up the option in 1973, two years after Love had first flagged them, Richman had lost interest in the sound of the original Modern Lovers and preferred to make quieter, more consoling music.

When Jonathan got to California in 1972, he was introduced to Gram Parsons. The two bonded over their admiration of the simple sentimental songs of the Louvin Brothers. The friendship between the two is more of a surprise to latter-day scholars of American music than it was to the two musicians. In 1972 this pair had no idea that the open terrain over which they ranged so freely would one day be crisscrossed by the barbed-wire fences between categories, and every shade of musical style would become a "format." At the time, Gram wasn't aware he was singing something that would come to be called "alt-country." For his part, Jonathan had no idea that what he was doing would one day be called "punk rock."

Richman wasn't the only category pioneer trying to get noticed that summer. One evening in the summer of 1971, the *Melody Maker* journalist Richard Williams came home to his London flat to find that somebody had visited and left a tape with his girlfriend. The reel of tape was in a small box labeled "Roxy" and bore the name "Bryan" and a phone number. Bryan Ferry, the would-be rock star who had dropped the tape off, had chosen Williams because he was a journalist who had a reputation for appreciating musical experimentation. Ferry suspected that the music on the tape was the kind that might benefit from being explained. He was working as a ceramics teachers at Holland Park Comprehensive school and living in a rented flat near Kensington High Street. What Williams heard on the tape seemed promising enough for him to phone Bryan and arrange a meeting at the Golden Egg in Fleet Street. This led to a short feature in the *Melody Maker* at the beginning of August, which focused on the fact that the members of Ferry's group, still called Roxy, were the kind of people who wouldn't normally be found in rock bands. For a start, their average age was twenty-seven, and at least two of them had a background in the art world.

Some rock musicians have spent time at art college before, but they had usually dropped out when presented with the option of life on the road. The members of Roxy hadn't simply come to pop following art school. They had deliberately chosen pop as way to pursue their career in art, which had certain implications. They were threatening to bring art school to pop. The year 1971 seemed like a propitious time to make that switch. The palaces of high culture were finding room for the products of cheap media (the exhibition *AAARGH! A Celebration of Comics* was running at the Institute of Contemporary Arts at the beginning of 1971), and it seemed only right that pop should open its glittery portals to many of the ideas being promoted in the art schools, particularly since those schools seemed less concerned with teaching students how to produce something than with teaching them how to think.

The members of what was then called Roxy (it would be changed to Roxy Music to avoid problems with an American act called Roxy) had not come together in the usual way. They hadn't spent much time in the back of vans. The leaders were Ferry, who had studied fine art under Richard Hamilton at Newcastle University, and Brian Eno, who had studied art at Ipswich and Winchester and had an interest in music despite not being able to actually play an instrument. Eno could operate a rudimentary synthesizer, and he made tapes, which were as important as anything else to a group wishing to apply the montage approach to music. They were joined by Andy Mackay, who was classically trained and also taught at Holland Park, and later on by accomplished guitarist Phil Manzanera. The last member to join the group was drummer Paul Thompson, who was laboring on a building site at the time. Thompson had a very different background. In the end it was his driving drumming on songs like "Virginia Plain" and "Do the Strand" that made Roxy Music popular, every bit as much as any of the clever cultural steals or kinetic presentation.

However, as they developed in late 1971, they were careful not to position themselves as just another rock band, notable for a particular soloist or the qualities of its vocalist. They wanted to be appreciated as an art project might be appreciated. Roxy Music were producing music by people who had spent a lot of time listening, reading, watching, and thinking; therefore, the appropriate selection from their library of influences mattered as much as anything, the right thought aced the right performance, and the right gesture aced everything. Ferry was not really a musician. He had not played any kind of musical instrument until a few months before the band began gigging. All the conversations about Roxy Music that took place in 1971 as they found management in the shape of old Harrovian David Enthoven and a record company in the shape of Island took place against a background of references: not just the obvious ones like Motown but also the avant-garde ones like the Velvet Underground, the nonmusical ones like Richard Hamilton, and the prerock ones like Ethel Merman. It was an inclination that was to become even more explicit as they became more visible. It was clear that Roxy Music's hair styles and clothes had been thought about every bit as much as the sound. This was pop as a branch of the gestural arts.

This was a new aesthetic at work, in which qualities like authenticity and sincerity were no longer self-evident virtues. Indeed it was possible for things that were plastic and fake to be just as admirable. They had been talking like this in the art schools for some years, but in the world of pop music, which liked to think of itself as having graduated from an obsession with surfaces to a more mature understanding of what was important, this was all new. The art graduates weren't the only people from the so-called legitimate world of the arts to start trying the doors of pop. At the same time that Bryan Ferry was selling his vision of a new kind of pop music in London and David Byrne was meeting up with Chris Frantz at the Rhode Island School of Design and thinking about a band called the Artistics, other people were moving into the direction of pop, from the world of classical and avant-garde music.

Also in 1971 Ralf Hütter and Florian Schneider, who had studied classical music at the Schumann Conservatory in Düsseldorf, moved into a workshop space in Cologne in Germany to start making the second record by their group Kraftwerk. The process of making this music had more in common with the workshopping approach of improvised theater than the performance-oriented approach of traditional rock. As was the case with Roxy Music, it was difficult to know whether the name applied to the group or the project. And also like Roxy Music, rhythm was eventually the key element with Kraftwerk. Since they didn't have a drummer at that point, they started to experiment with a cheap drum machine.

At the same time, the two principals of Germany's senior group Can, Holger Czukay and Irmin Schmidt, who had studied under Stockhausen and had already made two albums, were given free use of a castle in Westphalia by a wealthy patron. They moved in and, free of noise restrictions, played all day and all night. What came out of it was a double album called *Tago Mago*. Like the Rolling Stones, who were doing roughly the same thing a few hundred miles nearer the Mediterranean sun, this band was making music that was more about the groove than songs. This music, which was increasingly known as "krautrock" and even marketed as such by the people who made it, was taken up by John Peel and others. What nobody for a moment suspected was that this music being made by these balding beatniks with their rehearsal room pallor contained the spoor that would lead to the dance music of the twenty-first century and a revolution quite as big as the one that had brought along rock and roll.

These new directions didn't have much in common with the romantic flourishes of what passed for "progressive" music in Britain or the shifting rhythmic underpinnings and baffling time signatures of the jazz-rock still popular in the United States. Just as big band jazz had reflected the bustling optimism of the railway age and rock and roll celebrated the erotic individualism of the motor car, this new music, with its emphasis on surrendering to the joy of anonymity, was anticipating a computer age that few people saw coming in 1971.

Between completing the recordings for the Velvet Underground's fourth album, *Loaded*, and its US release in November 1970, Lou Reed left the group. His last performance with them was at Max's Kansas City in late August. It was recorded by the socialite and Warhol sidekick Brigid Polk, who was in the habit of committing her entire day to tape. Polk's recording captures other scene makers such as Jim Carroll calling for a double Pernod and also the halfhearted applause of the small number of people who were there. Even at Max's Kansas City, even among their own people, the Velvet Underground were rarely more than coolly received.

Also in the audience that night, keeping a low profile in case any of the scene makers should wonder if he was that guy they had seen on some TV pop show, was nineteen-year-old Alex Chilton from Memphis, Tennessee. He had just come out of a two-year switchback ride as the voice and face of a hit singles band called the Box Tops. The experience had left Chilton exhausted, old before his time, and looking for a way back into the music business on something like his own terms. It wasn't surprising that he should be another one attracted by the music of Lou Reed, which seemed simultaneously nostalgic, tender, bitter, and just too disturbingly simple for most people.

In February 1971 Chilton returned to Memphis to sort out his divorce. While there he renewed his acquaintance with his old friend Chris Bell and played in a band called Icewater. Chilton went to see Icewater play at the Veterans of Foreign Wars in downtown Memphis and was persuaded to throw in his lot with them. As a base of operations, Memphis had much to recommend it. Bell and Chilton were both from comfortably off Memphis families who didn't mind subsidizing them to spend their days playing music and smoking dope as long as they made some concession to shaping up by signing on to a course at a local college. Chilton and Bell were also fortunate in knowing John Fry, another well-established local who had his own recording studio, Ardent Studios, and was prepared to let them use downtime at no charge to work out their music. Furthermore, Ardent did a lot of work for Stax, and in 1971 Stax was selling so many Isaac Hayes records that it needed to get rid of some of the cash. Stax had to broaden its base and told Fry that it needed a white rock band. Fry said he had one.

In the summer and autumn of 1971, Christopher Bell, Alex Chilton, Andy Hummell, and Jody Stephens worked up their material and began to put it on tape. No unknown band had made a record in quite this way before. The autonomy that most bands had to earn was this group's from the beginning. Fry taught them the rudiments of engineering, supervised the cutting of the basic tracks, and then tossed them the studio keys. In an era when studio time was a precious resource even for established bands, giving a bunch of youths this kind of carte blanche was unheard of. The band took their name, Big Star, from a local supermarket. Some of their Memphis friends considered this a hubristic choice. Others thought it a perfect marker for their ambition. Chris Bell certainly thought their first album was a record that would set the world on its ear. Alex Chilton, having been out there in the self-same world, was unlikely to have been so convinced. Both Bell and Chilton adored the Beatles and modeled their partnership on Lennon and McCartney, crediting everything jointly and strictly alternating lead vocals. Like Lennon and McCartney, each acted as a check on the other's excesses, Bell's sweetness playing against Chilton's edge. It seemed to work.

There is 16 mm film of Big Star in 1971, the year of their first record's creation. It shows them recording in Ardent, rehearsing in the living room of a comfortable parental home, smoking self-consciously, sporting college scarves and neat knitwear, eyeing up the passing schoolgirls in their short skirts, doing art student stunts like walking up to the local draft board and then walking away again, the sort of thing young men have done since time immemorial. Like the music itself, in songs like "Thirteen" and "When My Baby's Beside Me," everything about that first incarnation of Big Star seems like an elegy for lost youth.

They called it #1 Record, which probably didn't do them any favors. When it came out in 1972 it did nothing. This was not helped by Stax's buying itself out of its distribution deal with Columbia and therefore having to promote a white rock record through a black promotion and distribution network. Big Star had never seriously played live and therefore they had never looked the market in the eye. They were not overendowed with ambition. They were stranded in the middle of the country and therefore out of the deal flow. In truth, like many of the groups who revere Big Star's name today, they were probably more comfortable with failure than with success.

They made music that used the same ringing acoustic guitars as the Beatles but there was always something plangent at its heart. Big Star were muscly and rhythmic but you could never actually dance to them. Their songs seemed inspired by the traditional pop preoccupations—finding a girl, going out in the street, getting high—but they were never quite put together in a way that the people who actually did those kinds of things could grasp. When they played around Memphis, audiences didn't warm to them. It wasn't until Bell had left the group, when their label Ardent had the harebrained idea of staging the first international Rock Writers Convention and flew a sampling of scribblers from all over the United States and Europe to Memphis, that they finally played in front of an audience odd, snobby, and ill-coordinated enough to actually like them. Like the Velvet Underground, they had all the attributes of a great pop group apart from the actual popularity. In the future there would be thousands of similar bands.

At the same time as Big Star were in Memphis, sitting on a secret that they confidently expected to delight the world, David Bowie was working in Trident Studios in Soho and preparing to unveil his second coming. Putting yourself in a position to succeed in the music business is very often a confidence trick. The business always aligns itself with those it thinks are about to succeed, and in reaching this conclusion it's influenced largely by what the rest of the business appears to be thinking.

In September 1971 a number of those people appeared to believe that David Bowie was in that fortunate position. His manager, Tony Defries, had persuaded RCA Records in the United States that it should sign him. At the same time he was punting his client as a songwriter. Peter Noone's version of "Oh! You Pretty Things" had been a hit, and he knew that there were other, similarly catchy tunes to come. He even set up a meeting with the horror actor Christopher Lee with a view to providing him with some songs. It may be that Bowie had more confidence in the songs than he had in himself. The first Ziggy Stardust songs had been gifted to Freddie Buretti, his pretty young friend from the gay club, possibly because he thought nobody would accept his playing the rock god himself.

On September 25 Bowie played a show for 250 people at Friar's in Aylesbury. Friar's was a popular place to play, not too far from London but not close enough to be crowded with scene makers. Bowie took the stage with a guitarist whom he introduced as Michael Ronson and started by playing two songs by the Californian songwriter Biff Rose. He then introduced "one of my own we get over as quickly as possible." This was "Space Oddity," which he still seemed to regard as an embarrassing reminder of his time as a one-hit wonder. He then played half a dozen of the songs he had been recording at Trident in Soho with Ken Scott. These included "Changes," "Song for Bob Dylan," "Andy Warhol," and "Queen Bitch," which he introduced as being about a friend called Lou Reed, who was in a group called the Velvet Underground.

Only a few days before this show, he had actually spent time with Reed, the person he had thought he was talking to backstage seven months earlier. On this occasion Bowie was in New York to sign his deal with RCA, who held a party to mark the fact, and invited Reed, who had signed a solo deal with the label. Through somebody else he met at the party, Bowie got an introduction to Iggy Pop, who had recently left the Stooges and, like Reed, seemed to have hit the wall as a member of a group. For both Reed and Pop, the appearance of this interesting guy who was a big admirer and appeared to be poised for success in the UK was a very promising augury indeed. This was the other element of the confidence trick. The Americans thought the Brit was bigger than he was, and he thought they were more legendary than they were. The association with these two names, who were on the radar of tastemakers like John Peel and Richard Williams, helped further legitimize Bowie's claims to fame.

All three were subsequently yoked together in legend and, what was even more unexpected, in the charts. The following year Bowie coproduced Reed's breakthrough album *Transformer*. In 1977 he performed a similar service for Iggy on "The Passenger." At the time they were just three guys who had walked away from a succession of failures. All the leathery rock-and-roll revivalists who had come along in late '60s America had had their shot and failed. The MC5 had never been able to turn their outlaw cachet into a real following. Their 1971 album *High Time* pleased them, but it was a commercial stiff. The same producer, the Englishman Geoffrey Haslam, also assembled *Loaded* from the final sessions of the Lou Reed–led version of the Velvet Underground. Iggy Pop had left the Stooges because they didn't seem to be achieving any traction, and he had a heroin problem. San Francisco's Flamin' Groovies made *Teenage Head* for the Kama Sutra label in January 1971, and then the singer Roy

Loney promptly left. All these American rockers eventually became best known for being unpopular. They were hailed for being passed over, rated for being underrated. Now that even classic outsiders like Neil Young and James Taylor were comfortably in the mainstream, there was little choice but to position themselves as beautiful losers.

These acts all represented a feeling that pop music had gone all soft and responsible and was failing in its duty to excite young people. The irony is that while these groups were all falling apart for lack of support among those very young people, one new act was dramatically growing its popularity on both sides of the Atlantic by delivering tough, teenage-friendly rock and roll and fairly tawdry fairground gimmickry. It was the rock and roll that put Alice Cooper on the charts. It was the tawdry fairground gimmickry that put them on TV. It was TV that made Alice Cooper.

Vincent Furnier, initially the leader of Alice Cooper the group and eventually the character of the same name, had been kicking around the music scene since the midsixties and spent time in Frank Zappa's carnival of oddities alongside the likes of Wild Man Fischer and the GTOs. Convinced that he and his band would never prosper in front of blasé West Coast audiences, he moved them to Detroit, linked up with new producer Bob Ezrin and manager Shep Gordon, and decided to ape the sound of Detroit bands like the MC5, the Stooges, and Detroit, showcasing the music in an act calculated to amuse and enthrall a new generation of fans. It was no coincidence that their first hit record was called "I'm Eighteen." That age, which had previously been the default age of rock fans, was suddenly the mark of a disaffected younger generation. *Melody Maker* sniffily but tellingly described Alice Cooper as being "for the punk and pimply crowd," which is not something it would have said about Led Zeppelin or the Who, both of whom were also beginning to attract a younger and more demonstrative demographic. In a supremely condescending opinion piece for *Life* magazine at the end of July, which is some indication of how many living rooms were suddenly aware of Alice, Albert Goldman wrote, "People project on him, revile him, ridicule him and some would doubtless like to kill him. At the same time he knocks out the young boys with the daring of his act and the rebelliousness of his image. After all, the ultimate rebellion of our time is the simple refusal to be a man."

Alice arrived just as small US radio stations were handing over late-night slots to the house hippie and seeing if they could get an audience of nocturnal dope smokers. Here Alice Cooper were pushing against an open door. No TV producer was going to pass up the opportunity to give airtime to a man who would pretend to electrocute himself, wielding knives and instruments of torture and filling the stage with flags in a way that hadn't previously been seen in rock. TV producers didn't have to like the music. They just had to prefer it to a bunch of blokes standing still and operating heavy machinery, which was pretty much what you got out of a live performance by Pink Floyd and Led Zeppelin. (At the same time, the film director Adrian Maben was planning to circumvent Pink Floyd's lack of animation by filming them in the amphitheater at Pompeii, insisting that at least one song had to climax with somebody banging the large gong at the back of the stage, because that way at least there would be one thing to look at.)

It mattered little that all TV did was expose the vaudeville production values behind Alice's tricks. For the first time, there was the prospect of something that might get genuinely shocking. In Detroit they appeared on *Tube Works*, and in Washington, DC, they did Barry Richards's *Turn-On*. When Alice came to Britain in November, it was just in time to be on one of the first editions of *The Old Grey Whistle Test*. This had been launched by BBC-2, the most minority of the three channels available in Britain at the time, and was intended to do for the burgeoning album market what *Top of the Pops* did for the singles chart. The band were sequestered in a small presentation studio, which was usually reserved for weather forecasts, and mimed to a track because in its early days the program didn't yet have the technology to allow the bands to play live. It didn't matter. It was what they looked like that mattered. The camera lingered on the singer's jumpsuit, which was slit down to his navel, and the glittery stars and fringed sleeves of the band's suits and the mascara, which looked as though it had been applied by a drunken sailor. They looked cheap, but it didn't really matter because where Alice was concerned the thermals of outrage proved so easy to whip up, particularly in Festival of Light Britain, that by the time his next album came out in 1972 he was a bona fide phenomenon.

On November 7, 1971, Alice Cooper headlined at the Rainbow in Finsbury Park. Tony Defries had begged for tickets from the promoter to make sure that David Bowie and his band could get to see the show. Although they were just days away from the release of *Killer*, which would be their second album of 1971, that night they played songs from the earlier *Love It to Death*, including "I'm Eighteen" and "Black Juju," which climaxed with Alice in an electric chair. Bowie's bassist Trevor Bolder, who was worried about Bowie's imminent plans to glamorize his own backing group, was reassured by the band's meat and potatoes hard rock. "They were wearing makeup and were a real heavy band. It was a big jump from being a blues band in T-shirts and jeans, long hair, and beards to wearing makeup and flashy clothes," he remembers. Bolder's defensive "at least they can play their instruments" reaction to these strangely dressed weirdos is the authentic voice of 1971.

By the time David Bowie launched *Ziggy Stardust* in June of the following year and Roxy Music released "Virginia Plain" a month later and Mercury Records got the nerve to sign up the New York Dolls the following summer, Alice Cooper was already playing stadiums, and nobody in the music business was going to bet against his potent combination of glitter and outrage. Alice Cooper had stolen everybody else's clothes and got to the glam rock party before them.

On September 11, 1971, John Lennon and Yoko Ono appeared on Dick Cavett's TV chat show. The US late night talk format had only recently reached the UK with the launch of Michael Parkinson's show in June, but in the United States it was well enough established to have spawned many different varieties. Cavett's reputation was for being hipper and more big city sophisticated than Carson. He regularly hosted music stars such as Jimi Hendrix and Sly Stone, who had a reputation for being difficult to keep on track. (Cavett had recent experience of dealing with very difficult situations. In June 1971 he recorded a program with journalist Pete Hamill and health magazine publisher J. I. Rodale, during which the latter actually died in his chair. Late in 1970 the southern politician Lester Maddox had stalked off Cavett's show, prompting Randy Newman to write the opening couplet of his song "Rednecks.")

On the night of September 11, the entire show was devoted to the couple that Cavett had been instructed to introduce as "John Ono Lennon and Yoko Ono." Lennon entered wearing a military shirt, white bell-bottoms, and polished black boots. Ono was in hot pants, black tights, a beret, and a velour shirt slit to her navel. Lennon carefully placed her between him and the host in order to make sure that he wasn't the main focus of the interview. He did this because, as was evident to all concerned, including himself, he was the main focus of the interview.

Lennon chewed, fidgeted, and smoked throughout the next hour, which unfolded apparently without structure, as most interviews did at the time. There was no sense that a researcher had sat down with the couple and elicited a number of stories that the interviewer would then tee up at prearranged times. It was anything but a collection of polished anecdotes. By modern standards it was rambling, desultory, even dull. The anxiety all three were clearly feeling—Lennon because he was always nervous, Ono because she was the woman who had broken up the Beatles, Cavett because he wanted to look as if he wasn't impressed by having such a star guest—was hidden behind a mask of unconcern. The conversation meandered around various subjects: hair, drugs, politics, Japan, England, other chat shows, and the apparent gulf between the alternative world and the straight one. Much of the agenda had been set by the interview that Lennon had given to *Rolling Stone* earlier in the year.

While nothing was delivered in terms of new information, this appearance might have set the template for the hundreds of subsequent occasions when rock gods have descended from Olympus and entered a TV studio, concealing the nervousness they are clearly feeling behind a display of fake casualness. Most of Lennon's answers trail off into shrugs, non sequiturs, and funny voices. The studio audience laugh nervously as if they don't quite know how this is supposed to work. The main value is in the opportunity it affords to watch these exotic creatures at close quarters. As the playwright Alan Bennett observed, watching people behave is nothing special; watching them trying to behave is always fascinating.

Yoko had been brought there because she was Lennon's consort and also because she could be employed as a human shield to ensure that Lennon didn't have to talk too much about the things that people wanted to know about. This set up a curious dynamic between them. Throughout the interview he set her up to tell stories and then, like so many practiced show-offs, couldn't stop himself telling them himself. He'd been socialized in a group in which nobody deferred to the other members, perfecting a form of choral banter that got them through all interview situations. Nobody could ever compete with that, particularly Yoko, who was curiously uncharismatic and certainly not ready for prime time. After an hour, during which they showed clips from two of Yoko's art films, Cavett said what a shame it was that Lennon couldn't perform a song from the album he had come in to promote, *Imagine*, which was released that day. Lennon apologized that he couldn't find the time to rehearse a band and instead introduced an excerpt from a TV film he promised people would be able to see soon. The excerpt began with the couple walking through the garden of the house in Tittenhurst Park and then Lennon playing the white grand piano in the garden room and singing. The audience, who had not heard the song before, paid close attention to the words. They may have been struck by the contrast between the grandeur of the house and some of the lines, particularly the one that went, "Imagine no possessions, I wonder if you can."

At the very same time Lennon and his wife were on *The Dick Cavett Show* in New York, four men who had little intention of imaging a world without possessions were tunneling their way into a vault beneath Lloyds Bank in London's Baker Street. They had rented an adjacent shop and then locked themselves in for the weekend, methodically drilling their way into a fortune at the bank next door. One of their number was stationed as a lookout on a nearby roof and kept in communication with the men in the vault via walkie-talkie. It so happened that on the same night, a man living in a flat in nearby Wimpole Street retired to his bed with a powerful shortwave radio, intending to pick up the signal from Radio Luxembourg. He found the usual transmissions interrupted by urgent verbal communications between men who were apparently discussing something that was numbered in the hundreds of thousands. Realizing that these transmissions could only be coming from somewhere local, the man contacted the local police, who accused him of an overactive imagination. When he kept hearing the voices, the man called Scotland Yard, who dispatched a couple of detectives to spend the night huddled around his TV set while uniformed men were sent to check every local bank branch for signs of illegal entry. They failed to notice anything was going on at Lloyds, and the following day the robbers escaped with half a million pounds. It was the largest bank haul in British history up to that point.

(The men were subsequently caught and convicted. The Baker Street job remained a favorite source of speculation and myth. In 2008 it was the basis for a film called *The Bank Job*, which suggested that the theft of the money had been a cover for an operation to secure some compromising pictures of Margaret, younger sister of the sovereign, which were being kept in a safe-deposit box by Michael X, a criminal and self-styled black radical who was prominent at the time in London's alternative society and was an associate of Lennon. During the Cavett interview, Lennon talked about how he had cut off his hair and donated it to Michael X to be auctioned to raise money for his headquarters, the Black House.)

On the same Saturday that Lennon was talking to Cavett and the bank job was proceeding in London, Sly & the Family Stone were in the middle of a three-night stand at Madison Square Garden in New York. Sly's record of nonattendance or tardiness at shows had meant that nobody except the Garden's promoter would hire him, and even then his contract was full of penalties that he would incur in the event of his not doing a bang-up job. It didn't appear to make much difference to Sly. On the morning of the concert in New York, he woke up in LA. That day he missed six flights, finally arriving in New York at four thirty in the afternoon and reaching the Garden at eight. At eleven o'clock, the time at which his performance was scheduled to end, he was about ready to go onstage.

His acclaimed album *There's a Riot Goin' On*, which seemed to emanate from a very dark underworld, had just been released, but he hadn't had time to teach the band how to play it, and so the show was dominated by tired performances of golden oldies. The *New York Times* review pointed out that Sly relied too heavily on his party classics. What's more interesting is the review does not make any connection between the music and the very real riot that was taking place only a couple of hours from Manhattan.

Since Thursday of that week, Attica prison in upstate New York had been in the hands of the inmates after one of the most serious riots in American penal history. These riots had been triggered by the worsening conditions in jails, a dramatic shift in the racial balance of the inmates, which had seen Attica go from a majority of whites to a majority of African Americans in less than two years, a rise in black radicalism, and the death two weeks earlier in a California prison of George Jackson, who had been shot by the authorities, reputedly for his left-wing views and all-around uppityness. The rioters were holding thirty-three prison guards as hostages and, in obedience to the recent fashion, even demanding planes to fly key rioters out of the country.

On the day of the concert, the state commissioner of corrections was pictured negotiating with the rioters on the front page of the *New York Times*. By the following Tuesday, the prison had been retaken. The order had been given when the prisoners' leaders, who were mainly Muslim, had allegedly threatened to slit the throats of four guards. There was massive overuse of force in the retaking of the prison, and thirty-eight people died, both prisoners and hostages. The release of Sly's album, with its stars and stripes cover, somnambulant vibe in its music, and sense of anomie hinted at in its lyrics, could not possibly have been more timely. *There's a Riot Goin' On* was the sound of a city falling apart.

It's arguable that Sly's album was the most influential record to come out of 1971. There's a whole world of moody, hypnotic, rhythm-box-based music that would be inconceivable without its example. In fact, the whole category known by the contemporary shorthand "urban" can be traced back to what Sly did in that house in the decidedly suburban surroundings of Bel Air. Celebrated though lots of those records might be, few of them get to number one in the album charts and stay there. *There's a Riot Goin' On* did that.

John Lennon's *Imagine* album went to number one in both the UK and the United States, but its true moment didn't come until 1981, when in the wake of Lennon's death it was embraced as a hymn, as Phil Spector always said it would be. In fact, many of the beginnings made in 1971 didn't reach their public until many years later. "Hospital," from the Intermedia recordings, was not released until the first Modern Lovers album came out in 1976, at which point it was hailed as part of the future of rock and roll rather than the antique it was. The same could be said of the Velvet Underground's *Loaded*, which was their idea of an album full of potential hit singles. That didn't happen, but many years later the songs "Sweet Jane" and "Rock & Roll" became the "Twist and Shout" and "La Bamba" of the alternative set, their initial unpopularity worn as a badge of honor.

Jerry Harrison, the keyboard player of the Modern Lovers, went on to join Talking Heads, who had actual hit records ten years later. Around the same time, the drummer David Robinson was playing with the Cars, a band from Boston who were eventually so big that they bought the studio where they'd done that demo in 1971. In 2015 Loudon Wainwright was approaching his fiftieth year as a performer, still spinning variations on the same comic character, himself. In

2008 he rerecorded many of the songs that he first made at Inter-media for an album called *Recovery*, a recognition that these are still the songs that define him. His song "Motel Blues," which describes the empty but nonetheless quite exciting prospect of anonymous sex with a fan encountered on tour, continues to resound. Bombay Bicycle Club, who weren't born in 1971, did their own version. They were belatedly following in the footsteps of Big Star, who had latched on to it in the '70s. As Bob Dylan wrote, "There's no success like failure." This particular song, with its shrugging acceptance of the tawdriness of the game, was also perfect for Big Star, whose entire legend has, like Nick Drake's, been steadily built up by successive generations of believers on the basis of the fact that, by any earthly measure, they failed. In some respects, indie rock is much like the early church. The whole world of indie, with its bone-deep belief that indie music is too fine, too soulful, too pure to ever appeal to the masses, has been built up around groups such as the Velvet Underground, Big Star, and the Modern Lovers, who signally failed to make it. Alice Cooper and Roxy Music may have had the hits. They have never had quite the same mystique. The mystique ended up being worth almost as much as the hits.

Because the music business hadn't yet become an industry and the music media were relatively underdeveloped, companies hadn't yet got round to copying what appeared to be working for other companies. Bands like the Velvet Underground and Big Star were one-offs, not part of any particular wave. They were interesting and different, and they were all signed by major record companies. They didn't have any problem being drawn to public attention. The problem they had was winning any public approval. Their records, like those of the Stooges, MC5, and Nick Drake, were widely available and widely un-bought. The cliché goes that very few people bought the first Velvet Underground, but every one of them went and formed a band. That may be so, but it took them another five years to do it. When these bands were eventually embraced and had their moment of reverent acclaim, during punk rock, it was as heritage acts. The punk rock moment had flickered in 1971. It didn't catch light, and when it eventually did it was as much nostalgia as anything else.

SEPTEMBER

Sandy Denny: "Blackwaterside"

Bob Dylan: "George Jackson"

Loudon Wainwright III: "Motel Blues"

The Modern Lovers: "Hospital"

Black Sabbath: "Sweet Leaf"

David Bowie: "Andy Warhol"

Can: "Halleluwah"

John Lennon: "Imagine"

The Band: "Life Is a Carnival"

Area Code 615: "Stone Fox Chase"

OCTOBER 10

Will the Circle Be Unbroken

n the autumn of 1971 *Life* magazine, the photo weekly that had celebrated postwar America and the values of the generation responsible for its baby boom, was beginning to feel its age. Facing competition from scores of specialist magazines and finding it difficult to attract young readers, it planned to cut its claimed circulation from 7 million a week to 5.5. It's a measure of the power of print media in the early '70s that this seemed such a precipitous decline. The Jackson 5 were on the cover of the same issue that carried *Life*'s sober coverage of the aftermath of the Attica riots. They were posing amid their many trophies and gold discs with their parents, Joe and Katherine, spearheading a major photo feature titled "Rock Stars and Their Parents." To put together this story, war photographer John Olson traveled all over the world. His brief was to capture these supposed tearaways and reprobates with their proud mothers and fathers. It was clear from the copy where *Life*'s sympathies lay. "What do parents do when a much loved son or daughter stops listening to rock records and leaves home to start making rock records of his own?" said the copy, with the sort of pained concern that would later be reserved for speculating about their sexuality.

Frank Zappa was pictured against the violent purple of his living room with his parents Francis and Rose Marie. Elton John was seen in the Pinner home of his mother, Sheila, who was still working as a government clerical worker. Eric Clapton was pictured with his grandmother Rose Clapp, who had raised him on behalf of her sixteen-year-old daughter. There was no mention of his actual birth mother. The public wasn't yet ready for the degree of complexity that might be involved in a nonnuclear family. Ginger Baker's mother was running a hairdresser. Marjorie Cocker was working as a waitress in a local café. Grace Slick held her new baby, China, upside down while her blue blood mother, Virginia Wing, looked on. Slick was not the only one with a background more privileged than she traditionally let on. Floyd Crosby risked embarrassing his son David by admitting he and his wife were both in the New York Social Register.

Olson reported that all his subjects were uniformly well behaved when their parents were present. It was rare to see rock stars in the context of a family. They preferred to encourage the idea that they had been raised by wolves and had created themselves through the sheer force of their own will. Yet here they were, tamed for once, looking slightly preposterous in their hippie finery amid their parents' lovingly tended ornaments and family photos, wondering if this was still the place they ought to think of as home. The rock stars in these pictures, and scores of others who had risen on the sixties tide and then been beached in the new decade, were having to direct their thoughts to setting up their own versions of home. By 1971 many had accumulated enough funds to establish their newly acquired partners and children in the grand style befitting their nouveau riche status.

The problem was that as a rule they didn't have much talent for domesticity. Years on the road had left them temperamentally unsuited to laying their heads down in the same place they woke up;

it made them at best fidgety nest builders and easily bored. Their situation was made worse by the fact that they were pursued by another family, this one made up of fans. In 1971 Pete Townshend was experiencing the same problems as had driven Dylan out of Woodstock, with fans feeling entitled to turn up at the door of his home in Twickenham as if he were their old mod mate rather than a man with a family. This wasn't conducive to the peace of mind of his pregnant wife. Half the time Townshend was away at work anyway. In 1971 nobody expected men of any kind, particularly high achievers like these, to break their stride to spend time attending the births or getting too involved in the upbringing of their children. In the famous world, just as in the workaday world, nobody contested the idea that work, fame, and status took priority every time.

Paul McCartney was an exception to this rule, raising his children with Linda McCartney in what amounted to a fantasy of rural domesticity on a farm in Scotland, though making sure he was in London close to the best medical care when their daughter Stella was born in September. Anyone who had been a Beatle could be forgiven for not wishing to have any unannounced callers for the rest of their life. In 1970 George Harrison moved into Friar Park, his 120-room Xanadu near Henley-on-Thames. The house was so badly in need of restoration that he and Patti spent the first few months in sleeping bags. His main requirement was that it should be big enough to install a recording studio in, which was indicative of the fact that the priorities were still professional.

Harrison wasn't alone in this. In 1971, at the height of his fame, James Taylor was effectively homeless. The homestead pictured on the back cover of *Mud Slide Slim and the Blue Horizon* was not yet built. When his new girlfriend Carly Simon was first taken to see the property on Martha's Vineyard, she found it had been designed with more thought for recording than food preparation and was horrified that it was used as a crash pad by James's hippie friends. This was a new style of living for those who could afford it. For the first time it was possible to indulge teenage-style whims with a millionaire's bank account. Thus, when Taylor returned from his period in

London, he could pay to have his Ford Cortina GT shipped back to the United States. When he finally returned from tour, he had been away so long that his own dog failed to recognize him.

Graham Nash moved into a house in San Francisco's Haight-Ashbury that had been done up by some hippie friends. His only requirements were a sixteen-track studio, a billiard room in the basement, and a room on the second floor for David Crosby to crash in. Nash's memoir is a good guide to the world as seen by these millionaire princes. He remembers that at Stephen Stills's house there were generally two sisters who were always naked. "These girls were incredible playthings. They were available to whoever they fancied fucking," he mused many years later.

These patchouli plutocrats seemed a new type of human being. They were immensely wealthy but required by their profession to conduct themselves like vagabonds. They had to pretend that they spent most of their time lying on their backs watching the clouds scud across the sky when the reality was that they were consumed by a combination of burning ambition and frantic productivity to which most things around them tended to be sacrificed. The heightened sensitivity everyone applauded in their songs was often achieved at the expense of their own personal relationships, where they moved decisively to dispense with any romantic relationship that was in danger of subtracting more than it was adding.

The work was so all consuming and the act of creation came so easily that they hardly thought of it as work at all. For Neil Young, 1971 was the year he composed and recorded *Harvest*, the album that made him a superstar, and he did it in an almost permanent state of domestic upheaval. At the end of 1970, he had sold the Topanga Canyon home that he had shared with Susan Acevedo, his wife of two years, and bought a 140-acre ranch in northern California. Some say that Susan was expecting to move with him, along with her young daughter. It was made clear to her that this would not happen. Instead, she was compensated with enough to invest in her own restaurant.

Soon after this, Carrie Snodgress caught Young's eye in the

acclaimed film *Diary of a Mad Housewife*. He made contact with her. One of the first intimations of his dawning celebrity status came with the realization that it would not be taken amiss if a rich and famous rock star contacted just about any attractive, prominent young woman merely on the basis of having seen her on a screen or in the pages of a magazine. The actress was amused that Young presented himself as "the man with the single suitcase and two pairs of jeans." She knew he'd been able to pay over three hundred thousand dollars in cash for his new home, so he was clearly no vagabond. Within a very short time, Snodgress's career, which had previously appeared so promising, had been subsumed into the halo of Young's apparent magnificence. She was nominated for an Oscar for Best Actress. When the awards ceremony came that April, they weren't there. Whether this was her decision or his is not clear. What's known is Young complained about having to wear a tuxedo. At the time, Hollywood was way below rock and roll in the prestige stakes and hadn't yet got round to worrying about baubles. Snodgress wasn't there on the big night. Glenda Jackson took the award for *Women in Love*.

Snodgress moved to Young's ranch in 1971, bringing members of her extended family with her. As in the court of a rising baron in medieval times, those who were served at their master's pleasure could be fearsome infighters. In his own book *Waging Heavy Peace*, Young admits that Acevedo, who was credited for patching his famous jeans on the back cover of *After the Gold Rush*, had also made him a waistcoat that she had sewn using some of her own hair as thread. Once she moved in, Carrie Snodgress made sure she unpicked every last stitch.

Harvest had to be made on the fly throughout 1971 because Young spent most of the year on the road as a solo. The songs were pouring out of him in such a stream that they couldn't help but reflect the lives of the characters who found themselves in his orbit. "Old Man" was inspired by a middle-aged man who worked as a caretaker on his ranch. "The Needle and the Damage Done" was about his erstwhile bandmate Danny Whitten, who would kill himself with heroin a year later. Young began recording in Nashville in February. He had gone there to tape his appearance on a TV show in which Johnny Cash sought to restore his rebel values by performing alongside the new generation of singer-songwriters. Young took advantage of the presence of James Taylor and Linda Ronstadt to get them into the studios to sing high harmonies on "Heart of Gold."

When he passed through London in February, he went to Barking Town Hall to record a song with the London Symphony Orchestra. (According to Glyn Johns, who was there as an observer, Young's hipster buddy Jack Nitzsche was relieved of the baton by a member of the orchestra when it became clear that he didn't know how to direct the musicians.) The song was "A Man Needs a Maid." It begins, "My life is changing in so many ways," which was certainly true. The singer doesn't know who to trust anymore. He's thinking that maybe he'd get a maid, just someone to keep his house clean, to cook his meals, and go away. In the years since its composition, it's the song that has most often come in for criticism for its apparent sexist condescension. Neil Young once told me that songs were "just thoughts." In the sense that a lot of the best ones are thoughts that arise from the tumultuous subconscious, "A Man Needs a Maid" is a good deal more honest about his needs and his situation than most rock songs written in that hectic year.

Generation Rock attempted to put down roots in some rum locations. Estate agents on both sides of the Atlantic were beginning to see these long-haired millionaires as the solution to that impractical property that had been sitting on their books too long. In 1971 the impulsive Keith Moon and his wife, Kim, moved into the house in Chertsey that they called Tara in honor of the house in *Gone with the Wind*. It was a futuristic fantasy house that consisted of five pyramids built by an eccentric film producer. In 1970 Jimmy Page bought Boleskine House, Aleister Crowley's old mansion alongside Loch Ness, installing an old school friend to live in it with his family. A university friend of Nick Drake's performed the same role in John Lennon's house at Tittenhurst Park in 1971. One of the apocryphal tales told about Drake has him spending time in the house in summer 1971 when the occupants were away, gazing wistfully at Lennon's collection of Rickenbackers.

Around the same time Elton John had finally moved out of his mother's house in Pinner and used his newfound money to buy an apartment in a development called the Water Garden off Edgware Road. Within a year, his friend John Reid had moved in. Nobody suspected that they might be sleeping as well as cooking together, neither the journalists who turned up there to interview him nor the various members of Elton's family who very much enjoyed the company of the presentable young Scot. As Philip Norman said in his biography of Elton, "There was as yet no general notion of a closet and consequent need of pressure to come out to it. London in 1971 was full of paired young men, unexceptionally living in flats together."

A lot of these new homes, plucked from the property pages of *Country Life*, weren't particularly happy. At the time of life when most of their school contemporaries would have been settling down with a mortgage and watching their children grow up, these apparently lucky people whose knack for hit records had taken them to the stars and distant planets were coming back to earth to find that fitting in wasn't easy. In 1971 the Kinks released *Muswell Hillbillies*. This was a record ostensibly about the dislocation felt by inner London working-class families upon being rehoused in comparative comfort in the suburbs. It could just as well have been about Ray Davies, who had moved from Muswell Hill to a stockbroker house in Borehamwood and was quite unable to relax. For him, like so many others who found themselves unhappy in the mansion on the hill, there was only one thing to do. Go back to work.

In show business, family was a commodity that could always be sold. Family acts were popular in the music business in 1971. The *Billboard* chart for the first week of October has Donny Osmond at number one with "Go Away Little Girl" and his family group at number nine with "Yo Yo." The Osmonds' breakthrough success earlier in the year with "One Bad Apple" had been a fairly shameless pastiche of the leading family act of the year, the Jackson 5. Richard and Karen Carpenter were not far behind at number four with "Superstar." All three of James Taylor's singing siblings made albums in 1971. *Rolling Stone* hailed them as "the first family of the new rock."

On October 28, 1971, *Rolling Stone*'s cover story was all about an outwardly successful but deeply dysfunctional family band from California. The picture featured a group of men in their late twenties, some wearing eccentric headgear, most sporting biblical beards. The cover line read "The Beach Boys: A California Saga."

The story within was destined to become a classic piece from that brief interlude when pop writing collided with New Journalism, in the golden moment before the PRs took control, and press became primarily a matter of disaster avoidance. The style of Tom Nolan's story has since been imitated by scores of writers seeking to get inside those bands who had grown into national institutions. It combined admiration for the group's achievements with distaste for whole areas of their strange, inner world in a way that hadn't been done before, certainly not in the music press. (At the same time, *Rolling Stone* was having a look round Ike and Tina Turner's home for a cover feature. The story quoted a record company executive recoiling from the guitar-shaped table in Turner's living room by musing that he never knew it was possible to spend so much money at Woolworths.)

Very little of the story was about music, which was a significant development. *Rolling Stone* was still the black-and-white double-folded underground magazine with adverts for smoking paraphernalia and *Easy Rider* posters in the back. It had yet to become the *Life* magazine of the denim bourgeoisie. Nolan's story, which abounded in the kind of prurient detail that music fans pretend not to be interested in but clearly are, was the culmination of a yearlong effort by the band's new manager, a former publicist named Jack Rieley, to reposition the group, who seemed to have been left behind by the events of the late sixties and were in danger of being marooned permanently on the wrong side of rock history.

In the first half of the sixties, the Beach Boys could do very little wrong. The second half was a protracted nervous breakdown. Brian Wilson, the leader, songwriter, producer, and oldest of the Wilson brothers, withdrew from touring and buried himself in the studio. Mike Love, the singer and most reliable source of embarrassment, led them into a tour with the Maharishi Mahesh Yogi just as his serene stock was beginning to tank. The band's confidence was so dented that they seriously toyed with changing their name to the Beach. In addition, they were locked in litigation with their record company over unpaid royalties and, most disastrously of all, Murry Wilson, the brothers' overbearing and interfering father, had sold Brian Wilson's catalog of songs, which included the likes of "Good Vibrations," "Don't Worry Baby," "Wouldn't It Be Nice," and "God Only Knows," to the publishing division of A&M. The price was less than a million dollars.

His reasoning at the time was that the value of sixties copyrights were unlikely to hold up in the new decade, and therefore this was a good time to sell. He did it in the same year that the Beatles' publisher, Dick James, looking to retire from the business and realize his assets, sold their even more valuable catalog to ATV Music for what history was to prove a comparable pittance. On top of all that, the drummer Dennis Wilson's unfortunate choice in friends had led to the band being mentioned at the trial of the diabolical family attached to Charles Manson. When the murders committed by Manson's zombies became front-page news, the Beach Boys were forced to admit that Manson had written the B-side of their cheery hit "Bluebirds over the Mountain." What's more, they had neglected to credit him.

Most of Jack Rieley's efforts went into turning around the perception of the group rather than its music. In the late '60s the Beach Boys records had still been popular, but the group itself didn't have a following. They had no aura. They were admired for their singles but had never quite made the shift into the album market, where what mattered most was whether people considered you credible. The Beach Boys didn't feature in any of the big rock festival feature films. They had made a successful attempt to woo the hippies at the Big Sur Festival of 1969 but were too shortsighted to allow themselves to be in the attendant film. Thus, their image was marooned somewhere in the lost land of Pendleton shirts and dads who wouldn't let you borrow the car. In the age of patchouli oil, the Beach Boys still reeked of Pepsodent. Despite all the plaudits directed at *Pet Sounds*, they were still primarily regarded as a singles act. They didn't have the remotest scintilla of hip. When the Grateful Dead invited them onstage at the Fillmore in April 1971, it was as much a shock to the hippies as it would have been to Andy Williams's audience had he brought on Captain Beefheart. The one thing the new conservatives who made up the rock audience couldn't tolerate was the thought of anyone who might be conservative.

Nolan's story in *Rolling Stone*, at the time the only publication in the world that would run long, discursive, almost book-length accounts of rock legends, was the culmination of Rieley's work. Nolan was given access that nobody has had to a rock act since. He was fortunate enough to catch the Beach Boys when they still somehow thought that a lot of what they said to journalists wouldn't make it to the printed page. The piece, which ran in two parts over two issues, started off with a picture of Brian in his bathrobe in his health food store, the Radiant Radish, in the middle of the night. It's a picture that eloquently captures the dislocation from everyday life that is available to people who have too much money and not enough work.

The falloff in the quality and quantity of Brian Wilson's songwriting output following the indifferent reaction to "Heroes and Villains" in 1967 is often explained as the inevitable result of his depressive state, occasioned by the shelving of *Smile*, his intended magnum opus. Another way of looking at it is Wilson was suddenly brought face-to-face with his songwriting mortality and suspected that he couldn't do it any longer. Only Ray Davies, who single-handedly wrote and sang lead on fourteen consecutive brilliant top twenty singles for the Kinks between 1964 and 1968, could possibly understand the pressure that somebody like Wilson was under, to keep coming up with a new tune that everybody could fall in love with. The signs were that he couldn't do the simple stuff anymore. The only way he could follow the ornate "Good Vibrations" was with the grandiloquent "Heroes and Villains." This was a brilliant piece of montage, the kind of thing that attracts admiration rather than love. It wasn't "Don't Worry Baby."

The Tom Nolan piece depicts a twenty-nine-year-old man alternating between long periods of adolescent idleness and bouts of frantic, compulsive behavior. He eats Reddi-Wip from the can. He disappears into his bedroom and won't come out. He has violent mood swings. He has an impractically gigantic dog. When he tells Nolan about his young daughter Carnie playing with the penis of Carl's son, there are glimpses of a world in which hippie fecklessness has conspired with money to seemingly bring about a new strain of opulent neglect. What emerged from Nolan's account was an individual who had been broken by the pressure to maintain his success and feed his extended family; the picture it painted was of an exhausted musician rather than a superman. It ensured that henceforth the Beach Boys music would always exist in the past, suffused with the sadness of a long-gone summer, fated in time to become as distant but every bit as potent as the wartime tunes favored by the old men of the TV comedy hits of 1971, Archie Bunker and Alf Garnett. The article finished with a line from Murry Wilson, the father whose funeral the following year neither Dennis nor Brian could find the time to attend. "Henry Mancini is a God-given talent," he said, "and so is Brian Wilson." We readers of *Rolling Stone* were all meant to snigger at the fatuity of comparing the man who wrote "Good Vibrations" with the guy in the cardigan who hacked out "Moon River." Nobody made the point that they were both just musicians.

The Beach Boys had struck a new record deal with Warner Bros., a deal predicated largely on the company's affection for what the band had been rather than what they were. The new songs, which the other members wrote, varied between adequate and lackluster. This quickly became a problem. If the Beach Boys couldn't provide at least a couple of Brian Wilson songs, Warner Brothers would probably pass. This put the band in a predicament that would be faced by many bands in the future. They had to come up with the songs their record company had paid an advance for. The problem was the one person who had a proven record of composing such songs either couldn't or wouldn't supply them. The Beach Boys had the additional problem that they were a family as well as a group. There were two brothers, a difficult cousin, and two very demanding parents looking to Brian, the older brother, the great white hope, the former genius who was now padding about in a bathrobe, and wondering whether they would ever get their meal ticket back.

Surf's Up, the seventeenth album by the Beach Boys, which emerged in the fall of 1971, started out as a fudge born of desperation but, thanks to good fortune and perfect timing, went on to attract great acclaim. It was probably the first case of a band making a tribute album to itself. It was a celebration of the band's own aura, an attempt to painstakingly re-create as adults what they had once instinctively done as teenagers, a touching bid to prove that the boys of summer could go on and on, singing about their days of wine and roses in much the same way that Sinatra had done for the Korean War generation. It would not be the last album of its kind. If the title wasn't elegiac enough, the cover picture, based on a piece of Western sculpture called *The End of the Trail*, supplied what was missing. Everything about the record harked back to the white-toothed, corn-fed "Disney Girls" of 1957, to the reworking of the Coasters, which was "Student Demonstration Time," to "Don't Go Near the Water," which hankered for the clean ocean of childhood, to the baroque title track that was exhumed from the sessions from *Smile* and restored as agonizingly as a Piero della Francesca.

It was the heritage of the old song, its magical backstory, that made the difference. While the album was being readied for release, Van Dyke Parks, who had cowritten the title song five years earlier, predicted, "If they call it *Surf's Up*, they can pre-sell another 150,000 copies." He was right. The album was the Beach Boys' biggest success since the midsixties, and it resulted in the newly bearded band being embraced by the new rock establishment. As the demographic wheel clicked around and the teenage audience was steadily out-numbered and eclipsed by this burgeoning audience of former teen-agers, the artists of the '60s discovered that their real future was in their past. For the Beach Boys, who had declined the opportunity to play at the Monterey Pop Festival in 1967 because they hadn't pre-pared any new songs, it took a while for this particular penny to drop.

Surf's Up was the beginning of the Beach Boys' second career, a career founded entirely on people's desire to summon up the past, a past that many of them had never lived through. At first, the band were reluctant to include all their old songs about cars and girls, fearing that their new hairy audience wouldn't appreciate them, but eventually, with the success of George Lucas's *American Graffiti* in 1973 and the subsequent release of their multiplatinum greatest hits package *Endless Summer* in the United States, the Beach Boys discovered the great truth, that people were far more interested in the past, theirs as well as the audience's, than they were in the present. It was a realization that the Rolling Stones were yet to make. The past was a market the record business hadn't yet woken up to. At the time, it was impossible to buy a compilation of the greatest hits of the Beatles. The Who were preparing to exploit the same mar-ket in the fall of 1971 with *Meaty Beaty Big and Bouncy*, a collection of their sixties singles, featuring four young fifties urchins on the cover of the album. What the Beach Boys eventually keyed into was a deep need to travel back to a simpler, less hip and edgy world and lyrics that deal with recognizable emotions and situations within the context of tunes you could whistle. In defiance of the sixties wisdom that you're only as good as your last hit, the Beach Boys were the first group to prove that if your last hit was powerful enough, it really didn't matter how long ago it was.

F. Scott Fitzgerald famously wrote that there are no second acts in American lives. The Beach Boys are pop music's contradiction of that idea. In fact, they are a perfect illustration of the characters at the end of *The Great Gatsby*, "boats against the current, borne back ceaselessly into the past." At the time of writing, 2015, they have marked fifty years of fame and prominence. Most of those fifty years have been spent tapping into a legacy that was established in a very short period of time, a period arguably as brief as the three years between 1964 and 1967, when they were producing masterpiece after masterpiece. It's important to bands that they feel they are moving forward, that they can keep coming up with new songs. This is vital for their self-respect. But as one unmemorable album follows another from premature acclaim to the bargain bin of history, each auspicious beginning is followed by the familiar flatness, each round of press interviews and TV appearances gives way to faint embarrassment as the new songs are dropped from the set list never to return, we in the audience increasingly identify with the line that makes a popular T-shirt slogan at festivals—"Play some old." It's now the best part of half a century since *Surf's Up*, almost fifty years during which that elegiac note has been sounded again and again through new albums and untold sun-worshipping compilations. Through deaths, divorces, family fractures, illnesses, breakdowns, court cases, finger-pointing memoirs, and spasms of revisionism, the Beach Boys have continued to hang out the old shingle and, sometimes with the aid of hired hands who have learned them by rote and perform them better than they ever did, to sing those anthems of their youth. The place those songs came from may never have existed. That doesn't stop us all wishing to go there.

On October 12, 1971, broke, busted, betrayed, but still unfailingly polite, the rocker prince of the fifties Gene Vincent died from a perforated ulcer. He had just returned from a discouraging tour of the few English clubs that would still book an act whose main achievements seemed to be so long ago. In his last interview, he confessed that the young people no longer had any interest in what he did, so he ended up playing for the forty-somethings. He was thirty-six, which seemed unconscionably old for a rock star. Sadly, he couldn't stick around long enough to benefit from the revival that would inevitably have come. For artists like Gene Vincent, music was something that went forward in a straight line, and there was no way that those kids would ever be his audience again. What people like the Beach Boys were beginning to see was that music actually followed the motion of a clock, and if you hung around long enough it might eventually be the right time for you all over again.

Gene Vincent may also have worried that his musical style put him firmly in the past. He wouldn't have noticed that there were lots of signs that even the most adventurous musicians were being drawn to the very same past. There were the beginnings of a rapprochement between the most psychedelic bands and the corniest old songs. The Grateful Dead may have wanted to call their 1971 double album *Skullfuck*, but that didn't mean they didn't also want to include their versions of Merle Haggard's "Mama Tried" and Buddy Holly's "Not Fade Away." (When the Dead invited the Beach Boys to join them onstage at the Fillmore in 1971, they played Merle Haggard's "Okie from Muskogee" together. They could all recognize a well-made song when they heard one.)

At the same time, the folk-rock act the Nitty Gritty Dirt Band went into a Nashville studio with traditional musicians Doc Watson, Roy Acuff, and Mother Maybelle Carter in what was billed as an unprecedented meeting of different generations. There was lots of nervousness about whether you could ever bridge the apparent chasm between the traditionalists and the longhairs, between the world of "Wreck on the Highway" and the world of "Both Sides Now," between the old world and the apparently new one. In any event, it wasn't a problem. After all, Doc Watson was only forty-eight at the time, and John McEuen of the Dirt Band was twenty-six. This is an age difference that would scarcely be worth remarking upon now. At the time, it seemed immense. The Nashville sessions brought forth a lavishly packaged triple album of old songs given reverent new treatments. It was the first of three such albums. They all had the same name. *Will the Circle Be Unbroken.*

It was small wonder that the old certainties suddenly seemed an appealing refuge. The modern family seemed under great stress. Between 1970 and 1972, the number of divorces in the UK doubled.

Germaine Greer's *The Female Eunuch*, which had been published in 1970, asserted that "the housewife is an unpaid worker in her husband's house in return for the security of being a permanent employee . . . but the lowest paid employees can be and are laid off, and so are wives. They have no savings, no skills which they can bargain with elsewhere, and they must bear the stigma of having been sacked." In the United States the relaunched *Cosmopolitan* was putting its perky can-do spin on the same issues.

The issue of *Cosmo* that was out when *Surf's Up* was released in the United States published an extract from *Any Woman Can!*, in which "Doctor Reuben told the divorced, single or sexually marooned girl everything she wants to know." The doctor's name was David Rueben, and he was riding high on the success of another book, *Everything You Always Wanted to Know About Sex*. There was a boom in respectable sex manuals such as *The Sensuous Woman* and *The Happy Hooker*, books that could suddenly be openly displayed on the shelves of young marrieds. However, nobody of any prominence would have dreamed of telling the media about any aspect of their sex life, either directly or in fictionalized form. That year, 1971, it was finally considered safe to publish E. M. Forster's novel *Maurice*. The novelist had died the year before.

Very little of these shifts in manners and mores that were taking place in the world seemed to seep into the world of pop music. Since the death of Janis Joplin in late 1970, the music business was down one prominent female voice. Joni Mitchell was still stung by having been described by *Rolling Stone* in its roundup of 1970 as "old lady of the year" because of her affairs with a number of prominent male musicians. Sexual politics were not part of polite conversation, even when popular entertainment seemed to be trying to move them up the agenda. When Sam Peckinpah's film *Straw Dogs*, which featured Dustin Hoffman failing to protect Susan George from a gang intent on rape, was reviewed in the *New York Times*, critic Vincent Canby seemed more bothered about the editing than the content. "Perhaps the toughest—and most erotic—scene in the film is the one in which she is raped by one of the thugs, an old boyfriend, an encounter that begins with the exercise of force and ends with the woman's complete and willing submission." His review of Stanley Kubrick's *A Clockwork Orange*, which came out in December 1971, is less concerned with the morality of the gang rape it depicts than the "tour de force of extraordinary images, music, words and feelings."

On both sides of the Atlantic, the so-called serious press were very serious. In 1971 the *New Yorker* devoted no less than seventy pages to an extract from Charles Reich's best-selling ecology book *The Greening of America*. In October *Ebony*'s cover story promised "Dick Gregory on genocide." Even the arrival of Darine Stern as the first black model on the cover of October's *Playboy* seemed an occasion more for sober congratulation than licentiousness. On October 29, 1971, *Time Out*, the London listings magazine, used a black-and-white picture of a topless female holding a hammer to illustrate nothing in particular. It had been supplied as a still from the Warhol movie *Robert Having His Nipple Pierced*. The female was Patti Smith, then twenty-five and hardly known to anyone except the subject of the film, Robert Mapplethorpe.

The popular press were breezy but seemed to know their place. Because there was no celebrity press, there weren't any celebrities such as we might recognize today. The constellation of sports stars, TV presenters, fashion models, popular authors, disc jockeys, chat show hosts, and pop politicians who keep the bright red ball of public interest in the air today didn't exist nor, obviously, did social media or anything like it. Readers didn't have any expectation that they could look inside the homes and private lives of the stars. Only on continental Europe were there the kind of color magazines that followed every step of the lives of Brigitte Bardot or Johnny Hallyday, that trained long lenses on sun-kissed beaches or published a detailed breakdown of the dresses worn by middling TV actresses. The main celebrity spread in *Life* magazine in October 1971 was its photographic coverage of the party thrown by the shah of Iran for the 2,500th anniversary of the Persian monarchy. Guests included Prince Philip, Madame Tito, Imelda Marcos, and Haile Selassie, who was accompanied by a dog with a diamond collar. Movie stars were glimpsed passing through airports, but their parties, social rites, and body issues were a mystery to most people. It was the high summer of the priapism of Warren Beatty, and yet none of his frantic trouser activity made it into the papers, thanks to the traditional omertà enjoyed by any company town and the parallel convention that no respectable printer would dare to publish the details. Ironically, Jack Nicholson, Beatty's partner in celebrity fornication, starred in the October release *Carnal Knowledge*. Interestingly, he played a man incapable of forming a proper relationship with a woman.

Television exploited traditional stereotypes of the family for entertainment purposes. *The Homecoming*, a major TV movie prepared for Christmas, featured the Walton family and was set in the Blue Ridge Mountains during the Depression. Its promotion of prewar stoicism and family values led to *The Waltons*, one of the biggest franchises in American TV. At the same time, Dolly Parton was releasing her album *Coat of Many Colors*, which celebrated the same kind of poor but honest family she came from in Tennessee. Family stability was celebrated in TV dramas set at both ends of the social scale. On October 10, 1971, ITV unveiled *Upstairs Downstairs*, a costume drama set in the Edwardian era, featuring the Bellamy family of Eaton Square in the carpeted areas and the stock lower-middle-class types downstairs on the linoleum. It was obvious that the English would like it; what was less easy to predict was the appeal it would have for American audiences. It would run for years and provide the template for numerous hit shows, including *Downton Abbey*.

In early 1971 a television producer named Craig Gilbert went looking for an average American family. Gilbert's marriage was unraveling at the time, as were those of some of his friends, and he was interested in what might be happening to that fundamental American institution at the end of the decade of "Do your own thing." Between 1964 and 1975 American divorce rates doubled, from 24 percent to 48 percent. Popular entertainment was still nervous about reflecting this new reality. In 1969 the producers of *The Brady Bunch* had wanted the mother of the family to be a divorcée, but the network vetoed the idea.

Gilbert had persuaded a public interest broadcaster to commission a series of documentaries about the intimate life of an average American family. The expression "fly on the wall" was not in use in TV at the time, nor was "reality television," which explains why he found it so hard to cast his show. He was about to give up on his quest when he was introduced to Pat Loud. Pat was forty-five, a smart and telegenic upper-middle-class housewife, and mother of five from affluent Santa Barbara, California. She and her husband, Bill, agreed to take part in his pioneering project.

There was something of the show-off about both parents. Bill, a permanently tanned alpha male, probably thought it would benefit his business, which was supplying shovel teeth to the mining business. Pat surveyed him and her five teenage children through a plume of smoke and Jackie Kennedy shades, radiating the impression that she was a couple of steps ahead of everyone else. Their children were similarly confident attention hogs. To the amazement of the crew, who were with them twelve hours a day for the best part of nine months, the Louds never once asked for the cameras and sound recording to be turned off.

The crew tracked them through the summer, as they enjoyed a life that would have seemed inconceivable to most average Americans and also probably to Pat and Bill when they were growing up in the 1930s. They and their friends drove fancy cars, smoked long cigarettes, and drank hard liquor by their pools, congratulating themselves on their good fortune, confident that nobody else in the world was having a better time than they were and tacitly assuming that their children would follow in the footsteps they had so energetically hacked out for them. What the camera actually saw was that their children stumbled around in a miasma of unfocused disaffection, assuming that life somewhere else had to be better than the sumptuous idleness in which they were passing their time.

The first day's filming took place in New York in May. This was the filmmakers' first meeting with the eldest Loud son, Lance. Lance, who had spent most of a troubled childhood in his bedroom, venturing out only to see a child psychiatrist, had dropped out of school and college and was living in the Chelsea Hotel on his parents' dime while he sorted out what he wanted to do with his life. Pat traveled out to see him over the Labor Day weekend. There was little about the life Lance had embraced that didn't force her to raise an eyebrow. His roommate at the Chelsea went by the name of Soren Ingenue. On Pat's first night in New York Lance took his mother to see Warhol superstar Jackie Curtis in a transvestite musical. If she did realize that her son was homosexual, she didn't let on to the camera.

In 1971 the word "gay" was not yet common parlance, and the subject of homosexuality was only just beginning to be accepted in polite discourse. In September 1970 Joseph Epstein, a respected man of letters, had written a piece for the cerebral journal *Harper's* called "The Struggle for Sexual Identity," which concluded by saying, "There is much my four sons could do in their lives that might cause me anguish, that might outrage me, that might make me ashamed of them and of myself as their father. But nothing they could ever do would make me sadder than if one of them were to become homosexual. For then I should know them condemned to a state of permanent niggerdom . . . to be lived out as part of the pain of the earth." In April Jill Tweedie had introduced the subject of Gay Lib in the *Guardian*, pointing out the challenge it represented to the status quo. "Gay Lib," she wrote, "does not plead for the right of homosexuals to marry. Gay Lib questions marriage."

By the end of filming, on New Year's Eve 1971, the Loud family had undergone its share of trials. The fractures in the family had climaxed during a vodka-laced lunch to celebrate the Santa Barbara fiesta, when it became clear that Pat was tired of Bill's catting around. "You know that Carole King song 'It's Too Late'?" she says to a friend. "Well, it's too late, baby." She tells her husband, "I think you're a goddamn asshole." One evening when Bill arrives back from another business trip, she tells him, on camera, that she has begun divorce proceedings. Bill takes the news as if it were just another difficult day at work.

The broadcast of *An American Family* in the spring of 1973 was a watershed moment in the history of TV. As Craig Gilbert has said,

"Nobody criticized the film; they just criticized the family." It led to a furious national debate about what the previous five years of prosperity and free love had done to the American family. Viewers dealt with their envy of the Louds' material comfort, the four cars, the foreign trips, the whiskey sours, their unsinkable self-confidence, by tutting over their heedless, unexamined lives. One newspaper called them "affluent zombies."

In subsequent decades, the format would be perfected by people considerably less scrupulous than Craig Gilbert. Scenarios like the one he was unwittingly a party to would be deliberately contrived in pursuit of higher ratings and greater advertising revenue. *An American Family* left a peculiar legacy. Lance Loud went on to become a minor personality on the fringes of punk rock and managed to have a career out of an undefined desire to show off. He was a gay icon before people knew that there were such things. His grandmother, born in a narrower world, described him as "the first of the spoiled." Even *Rolling Stone*, which wasn't traditionally in the habit of looking down on young people, complained, "What Lance knew of life he knew from movies and television shows, from rock records and comic strips." If *Rolling Stone* suddenly sounded like the voice of the older generation, it was because it was. By 1973 those in the sixties generation were starting to settle into the comfortable shoes of domesticity. They couldn't stop themselves disapproving of their younger brothers and sisters, with their tight, glittery T-shirts, their taste for the meretricious temptations of metal and glam, and their lack of interest in the joys of comfort and continuity.

The Beach Boys: "Surf's Up"

The Grateful Dead: "Me and Bobby McGee"

Dolly Parton: "Coat of Many Colors"

Carpenters: "Superstar"

Neil Young: "A Man Needs a Maid"

The Kinks: "Muswell Hillbilly"

Frank Zappa and the Mothers: "Peaches en Regalia"

Laura Lee: "Women's Love Rights"

The Nitty Gritty Dirt Band: "Will the Circle Be Unbroken"

Al Green: "Tired of Being Alone"

NOVEMBER

Hunky Dory

In the autumn of 1971 I spent most of my spare time in a small north London record shop called Harum. It was a friendly place run by a couple of brothers, and it seemed to attract all the would-be cognoscenti in the vicinity. Usually I couldn't afford to buy anything; I was mainly going there to be in the company of records. I would flick through the new releases, hungrily devouring all the details of the personnel listed on the covers. I even got to know the names of the designers and photographers, smirked at the in-jokes in the credits, and noted which musicians' names cropped up most often. When I did buy something, it tended to be from the bargain bin, which generally contained white label review copies of new albums that had been sold to the shop by some lucky music paper journalist who happened to live nearby.

I've still got the copy of Ry Cooder's *Boomer's Story* that I brought back from one of these trips. I've also hung on to the copy of Danny O'Keefe's *Good Time Charlie's Got the Blues*. I don't believe I've ever got past that one song. It's such a great song I didn't really need to. I've also got a record on the Paramount label by a band called Detroit.

Previously, they had been known as Mitch Ryder & the Detroit Wheels. Back in May, the thrusting of Mitch's hips had disturbed some of the feminist activists who had been marching on Washington over the war in Vietnam. This album was Mitch's bid for hip acceptance. It had the first version of Lou Reed's "Rock & Roll" I ever heard. Lou Reed liked the way the guitarist Steve Hunter played and subsequently invited him to play in his band. That's how I really pieced together whatever I knew about rock and roll—from reading the credits on record jackets in Harum. That was the order in which you were introduced to music in 1971. You read about it first and heard it second. It meant you created your own star system in your head.

In building this star system, you learned that certain labels were more likely to be a guarantee of certain qualities than others. There was Island for folk rock like Fairport Convention's *Angel Delight*, Charisma for brow-furrowing greatcoat music like Van Der Graaf Generator's *Pawn Hearts*, Asylum for harmonious music from the West Coast like Judee Sill's "Jesus Was a Cross Maker," Atlantic for crunching house party music like the J. Geils Band's *The Morning After*, Shelter for smart blues-rock hybrids like Freddie King's *Getting Ready*, Elektra for lyrical projects of rare refinement like Mickey Newbury's *Frisco Mabel Joy*, and John Peel's Dandelion label for music like Bridget St. John's *Songs for the Gentle Man*, which was seemingly too delicate for this world.

The vinyl shortage was way off in the future, there was lots of talent around, and no telling what the public might prefer, so a shop like Harum would buy at least one copy of all these records. The actual vinyl would be stored behind the counter in a master bag. The sleeve was put in a plastic dustcover and placed out in the racks under Rock A–Z. It was there where I got my education in what made a record great.

The people who had traditionally worked as "producers" rarely got their names on the covers because they were in the employ of the companies who manufactured and marketed the records. Their job had been to represent the interests of the label's stockholders by ensuring artists signed to that label made the kind of records the label thought it could sell. This usually meant the kind of records that they had been able to sell most recently.

In the latter half of the sixties, this had changed. In the eight years since George Martin, an archetypal example of the producer as company man, had proposed that the Beatles' second single should be Mitch Miller's insufferable "How Do You Do It," the traditional division of labor over which producers would preside had been shattered by the unique genius of those four men. Just as the Beatles had fused the previously discreet disciplines of singing, playing, songwriting, and recording into an entirely new discipline called "making records," so their determination to work both sides of the glass when it came to determining the sound of those records and even the way they should be packaged had inverted the hierarchy between the executive and the factory floor.

The control room of Studio Two at Abbey Road, where the Beatles made most of their records, could only be approached by a steep staircase from the studio's parquet floor, which perfectly illustrated where the power had traditionally resided. All that had changed in the summer of 1967, when the Beatles unveiled *Sgt. Pepper*, a record that seemed to have been made in defiance of all the sacred tenets of the trade. They hadn't entered the EMI studios in that year with songs so much as ideas for records. The first side of *Sgt. Pepper* ended with a song whose lyrics came verbatim from a Victorian circus poster. The second side started with a ponderous piece played on the sitar, an instrument that had previously featured in Western entertainment only as a form of comic relief. The album finished with a sustained orchestral chord that left most listeners unsure whether they should take the record off or not. The finished record came packaged in a cover that didn't make it immediately clear who it was by. The album didn't have a love song on it. It didn't have a dance song on it. It didn't have an old favorite. It had none of the sheet anchors that the old wisdom strongly suggested were important to thrive in the marketplace. None of this prevented it selling in quantity and being celebrated all over the world.

In the wake of the Beatles' unprecedented success, the record business slackened the reins that had given them complete control of the talent. This wasn't because they had been converted to the virtues of creativity unfettered. It was because they had discovered that it appeared to work. A band left to its own devices, working in the studio that the band preferred with the engineer and producer that the band members had chosen themselves, was more likely to come up with a hit than the same act being forced to meekly go along with the company's way of doing things.

This opened the way for a new generation of producers and engineers capable of mediating between the often petulant demands of the musicians and the requirements of the market. Like the filmmakers in F. Scott Fitzgerald's famous phrase, a select few of these producers were the kind of people who could hold the whole equation of making great records in their heads. Because these people worked for themselves and not the record companies, they could negotiate their own royalties on sales and were more concerned than anyone with the quality of what they produced. George Martin left EMI's studio at Abbey Road to start his own studios in the West End of London in order to be able to command the money he never would have earned as the company's salary man. The record companies temporarily abdicated their traditional role in trying to predict public taste and looked to the producers to ensure that the recording was brought in on time and on budget and would sell. With the odd exception, such as Carole King's *Tapestry*, whose producer happened to own the record company, the majority of the big albums of 1971 were made without any involvement from the record company at all.

Sometimes this was a good thing. Sometimes it wasn't. The experience of Pink Floyd in 1971 indicated what happened when nobody was in charge. Pink Floyd had a curious relationship with their record company, EMI. As part of their new deal with EMI, they were given unlimited time in the company's studios. They soon decamped to George Martin's newly established AIR Studios because there they could record on sixteen tracks. This expanding new technology afforded them all manner of new ways of indulging their great weakness, which was not being able to make up their mind. Veterans of the sessions for the record that eventually became *Meddle* recall interminable days taken up with experimentation with the capturing of sounds made by household objects, sessions where each member of the group played without being able to hear the others, Rube Goldberg–style arrangements, where the tape led directly from one tape recorder to another, and eventually a lot of ideas labeled "Nothing One," "Nothing Two," ad infinitum.

Experimentation nonetheless had its place. The 1971 recording that has had the most impact on subsequent generations of music makers is Black Sabbath's *Master of Reality*. Here for the first time guitarist Tony Iommi detuned his instrument by three semitones. He did this in part to slacken the strings and cope with the pain he felt after having injured his fingers as a teenager in an industrial accident in a Midlands engineering works. On tracks like "Into the Void," this had the accidental happy effect of creating the slurry signature sound imitated by scores of young bands over the subsequent twenty years from the age of heavy metal to the era of grunge.

The word "producer," I was learning, could be used to describe a wide range of different skill sets and personalities, from Rodger Bain, the uncelebrated professional who oversaw the genuinely groundbreaking opening trio of Black Sabbath albums, the last of which came out in 1971, through auteurs like Phil Spector, who used musicians to produce the sound they heard in their heads, and craftsmen like George Martin, who knew how to add the dabs of color or extra texture that made the Beatles records so vivid, all the way to impresarios like the lanky, charismatic Richard Perry. In 1971 the Brooklyn-born producer, who had come to notice as the producer of the unexpectedly successful *God Bless Tiny Tim*, produced big albums for Harry Nilsson and Barbra Streisand just as Irving Thalberg produced movies in the golden age of Hollywood. In both cases he took artists worried that they were outside the rock fold and put them in a new frame. In the case of Streisand he nudged her in the direction of songs by writers like Laura Nyro and Randy Newman. Perry was good with people, a cajoler, a ringmaster, a jocular tyrant. His people-handling skills were worthy of Billy Wilder. He knew you had to capture the performance before the artist thought it was perfect, at which point it was actually stale. When the diva was skittish the night before the vocal recording of "Stoney End," Perry made sure she heard him mutter, "I never thought Barbra Streisand would be frightened by a song."

Harry Nilsson was so keen to get him on board he agreed to Perry's stipulation that the producer should call all the shots. "The plan was to make a Beatles quality album. My plan was he would be my Beatles, and I would be his George Martin," Perry recalled. This scenario had been teed up by the band themselves. When the Beatles had been asked to name their favorite group, they nominated Nilsson. They weren't being entirely facetious. They recognized that a lot of what the Beatles had offered was contained within this absurdly talented individual. It was a further part of Perry's plan that Nilsson uproot from Los Angeles and make the record at Trident Studios in London. He considered London the recording capital of the world, an inspiration in itself and home to musicians with a combination of accomplishment and Limey playfulness that might fire Nilsson's imagination.

In 1971 the London studio scene was a crossroads, where somebody like Perry could easily whistle up a leftover jazzer like Herbie Flowers, a rocker like Chris Spedding, tarrying midway between Ian Carr's Nucleus and Andy Fraser's Sharks, former Spooky Tooth man Gary Wright, who was to contribute the opening chords of "Without You," not one but two master American drummers, Jim Gordon and Jim Keltner, who were both waiting, like ancient mariners, at the pleasure of various former Beatles. And because this was Harry, whose reputation for being clubbable went before him and got him into all sorts of trouble, Ringo Starr himself. They all made their way down Wardour Street, where there was never anywhere to park, and down St. Anne's Court, there to load their gear into the ancient iron lift that was the only way to reach the studio on the top floor. The tracks they cut there combined mastery with playfulness in a way that would have been difficult in LA.

You only had to look at the cover of *Nilsson Schmilsson* to realize that slickness wasn't part of the plan. Like so many of the albums of 1971, it was the frayed edges that gave it character. The mistakes were left in. The diamond hadn't been polished. The same vulnerability evident in the title and the cover, featuring a blurred picture of the artist stealing downstairs in the middle of the night in his bathrobe to quell a case of the munchies, came through the music.

There's no better example of this than "Jump into the Fire," which was largely improvised in the studio by drummer Jim Gordon, guitarist Chris Spedding, and bassist Herbie Flowers. As it continued past the five-minute mark with no immediate end in sight, Flowers mischievously slackened his strings hoping he could bring it to a conclusion. His joke remains on the finished version. Martin Scorsese loved "Jump into the Fire" so much that he tried to fit it into every movie he made, until finally finding a place for it in 1990 in *Goodfellas*. When Ray Liotta leaves his house for what will prove to be his last day of freedom, it's to the accompaniment of Herbie Flowers's bass riff. (For his work on this immortal recording, Flowers earned a session fee of twelve pounds, as he did for his even more distinctive bass line in Lou Reed's "Walk on the Wild Side.")

Unsurprisingly, Perry and Nilsson didn't get through the project without butting heads. Perry remembers a summit meeting over tea at the Dorchester where he confronted the artist with his earlier promise that he would let Perry have creative control. "Well, I lied," said Nilsson. They got in a cab, went straight back to St. Anne's Court, and Harry Nilsson immediately delivered the vocal on "Without You."

They spent the month of June making the record. When they were short of material, Perry would march Nilsson around the music publishers of the West End in search of suitable songs. When these were not forthcoming, he would force Harry to eke out whatever fragments he had into songs like "Coconut," "The Moonbeam Song," and "Driving Along." Rarely has an artist gone into the studio with so little and come out with so much. "Without You" was the song that made the difference. Harry had heard Badfinger's comparatively drab version of the song at a party in LA and instantly identified with the sense of utter desolation in the song and intuited how he could use the power in his voice to insert a note that hadn't been there before. In doing so he unwittingly invented the power ballad, a form that has moved a great deal of soda in the years since.

Nilsson Schmilsson came out in November 1971. The ad in *Billboard* said, "Harry's made a rock album." It went on to sell five million copies, picking up many sales from fans who had given up hoping that the Beatles would get back together and were attracted by its combination of passion and whimsy, melody and soul. The following year the same team reconvened in Trident ostensibly to do it all again. RCA had little to do with making the first album; when it asked what it could do to help with the follow-up, Perry got the company to pay for a film to be made of the whole process. By then Harry had tipped too far into drinking and drugging, divorced his wife, abandoned his child in the way that his own father had abandoned him, and succumbed to the feelings of unworthiness that were rarely far away even during his most sublime melodic transports. On *Son of Schmilsson*, the refrain of the catchiest song went "You're breaking my heart . . . so fuck you." Commercially, at least, it was mostly downhill for Harry Nilsson after 1971. Rarely has an artist seemed so determined to undermine his own new success.

Ken Scott was the engineer in charge of the next album to be made at Trident. Like so many of the young men aspiring to the title "producer," Ken Scott had started work as a tea boy in a recording studio in 1964 straight out of school. Since the studio was EMI in Abbey Road, he graduated through the company's civil service–like structure from working in the tape library to eventually becoming a recording engineer. Despite working closely with the Beatles, Jeff Beck, Pink Floyd, and Procol Harum, he was never tempted to dress like the artists. One colleague remembers him turning up for White Album sessions wearing a three-piece suit and carrying a Samsonite attaché case. Where Perry was the bon viveur and orchestrator of mood, Scott was pure nerd.

Like many house engineers, Scott went freelance in 1970, working at Trident Studios in Soho on recordings for Elton John, the Aynsley Dunbar Retaliation, the New Seekers, and everything in between. It was here he met David Bowie, a young man whose direction was sufficiently vague for Scott to be unsure whether he was a session pianist, a producer, or a performer in his own right. The first time Ken Scott engineered a Bowie session, it was in the spring of 1971, and the song was "Hang On to Yourself," but the singer was Freddie Buretti, who was, he remembered, small, campy, and wore silver hot pants to the studio. By the middle of 1971, Bowie was signed to the management company Gem, which could afford to pay to make an album. He wanted a producer which wouldn't boss him around but at the same time would prevent him from making a fool of himself. Linking up with Scott, an engineer seeking to graduate to producing, was a perfect marriage of convenience.

In Scott's memoirs, he remembers the summer of 1971 as a particularly active time. He worked on Van Der Graaf Generator's *Pawn Hearts*, Lindisfarne's *Fog on the Tyne*, and recordings for Apple featuring everyone from Mary Hopkin to the Radha Krishna Temple. On one occasion he was called out to Tittenhurst Park to engineer a John Lennon session for "I Don't Wanna Be a Soldier" and was dismayed to see the working-class hero repeatedly snorting cocaine in the hope that he could get his vocal right. The Bowie sessions, on the other hand, he remembers as being achieved without benefit of either alcohol or drugs. Both Scott and Rick Wakeman, who played piano on the album, remember the first time they heard the songs that would make up *Hunky Dory*. Wakeman called them "the finest selection of songs I have ever heard in one sitting in my life." Scott was less immediately struck, but as soon as they began recording, he realized, "This could be a lot bigger than I expected."

They recorded the new album in two weeks in June as the astronauts of the Apollo 15 mission prepared to use their buggy to go for a drive on the moon, the nineteen-year-old native Australian Evonne Goolagong won Wimbledon, and the situation in Northern Ireland deteriorated further with the killing of more British soldiers. The recording was followed by two weeks of mixing. Bowie, who didn't care for being in the studio, wasn't there for the latter stage. The basic band, guitarist Mick Ronson, drummer Woody Woodmansey, and bassist Trevor Bolder, learned the songs from the demos that Bowie and his publisher Bob Grace had put together in order to get other artists like Peter Noone interested in his songs. Rick Wakeman came in to do the piano parts. They wrote a letter to Dudley Moore to see if he was available. It's not clear if he ever responded.

Most of the vocals were done first take, even the complicated ones. There was no use of "punching in," the technique whereby vocal performances could be assembled line by line, word by word, let alone, as is quite common today, syllable by syllable. Imperfections were turned into features. The phone that can be heard ringing at the end of "Life on Mars?" was from a pay phone in the bathroom the musicians could use to make outgoing calls. Nobody knew the number and consequently it never rung. Until that day.

Although not a hit, *Hunky Dory* perfectly captures the zeitgeist of 1971. From the reference to space travel on its signature song "Life on Mars?" to the "ten new pee to have a go" in "Andy Warhol," from the Ovaltine coziness of the old English saying that provided its title, to the nostalgia for the silver screen that suffuses its cover picture, from the Denmark Street lilt of "Kooks," his song for his first child, to the thin-lipped New York snarl of "Queen Bitch," it is, like so many of the great albums of 1971, neither one thing nor another, and gloriously so. In the summer of 1971 David Bowie enjoyed one perfect, delicious moment when he had nothing to lose, everything to gain, and all the right people behind him. He had no record company giving him advice, he had a bunch of musicians hanging on to his coattails who knew that it was either this or dragging their tails back to Hull to become hairdressers, he had a producer who needed a record to be seen as a success, he had a head full of postcards from his recent travels in America and nights out in the Sombrero club, and no fan following beyond a bunch of people who asked no more than to be pleasantly surprised. What came out was a unique kaleidoscope of previously suppressed feelings, grand gestures, borrowed clothes, gauche versifying, and, more important than all these things combined, great tunes. *Hunky Dory* may have been composed at the piano in Haddon Hall and recorded in a smoky room in Soho. It seemed to have a heart as big as all outdoors.

RCA in New York, which had seen off the competition to sign Bowie, announced the record's release in *Billboard* in the middle of November. The ad used a quote from *Rock Magazine* hailing him as "the most singularly gifted artist creating music today. He has the genius to be to the 70s what Lennon, McCartney, Jagger and Dylan were to the 60s." It was the kind of rhetoric that seemed to match the ambition of the record. The *New York Times* called Bowie "the most intellectually brilliant man yet to choose the long-playing record as his medium of expression." *Hunky Dory* felt like music that was pushing forward into a brave new world, and it was important for the rhetoric to keep pace. The job of a record reviewer, which had previously been to point out that track four was a mid-tempo shuffle in which the lead vocal was shared between John and Paul, suddenly became about finding the words to properly express the new importance of the music.

Hunky Dory didn't come out until the middle of December. By the time it appeared, Bowie had started making the record that would follow it. Again he got Ken Scott involved, although he warned him that he might not like it as much as its predecessor. He took two of the songs he'd been trying with Freddie Buretti earlier in the year, a version of Ron Davies's "It Ain't Easy" that had been supposed to go on *Hunky Dory*, and then wrote a number of new ones that could fit broadly into the idea of a fictional rock in a dystopian future. The record, which was finished by the end of 1971, came to be called *The Rise and Fall of Ziggy Stardust and the Spiders from Mars*, though nobody working on it at the time thought of it as being particularly thematic or conceptual. It certainly had a more clenched and teen-friendly sound. There was no Rick Wakeman. The group sounded like the house band of Kubrick's *Clockwork Orange*, which had just come out, crossed with Marc Bolan's T. Rex. RCA heads were played the finished album by the end of the year and said they didn't hear a single. Bowie, feeling he had proved his point by delivering the album, was happy to go back into the studio the first thing in the New Year to record the radio-friendly "Starman," the song that propelled him into a whole new kind of pop stardom in the UK when it came out in spring 1972.

By then he could look back on twelve months during which he had made his first life-changing visit to America, made contact with Lou Reed and Iggy Pop, fathered his first child, released two albums, recorded a third, and come up with "Changes," "Oh! You Pretty Things," "Life on Mars?," "The Bewlay Brothers," "Hang On to Yourself," "Five Years," "Ziggy Stardust," "Suffragette City," and "Starman." If all we knew of David Bowie was what he did in 1971, it would be more than enough.

Solo artists could be difficult for a producer. They were nothing like as demanding as a band. Every band, no matter how placid they may appear on the surface, is a combination of a family, dissatisfied business unit, and warring political party. The producer that the bands increasingly asked for by name in 1971 was Glyn Johns. In 1971 Johns was twenty-nine. He came from the same Home Counties background as the Rolling Stones. He also had played in bands, but at the age of seventeen he got a job as a junior in an independent recording studio, and it was his ability to get a good sound from a rock group that made his name. A good proportion of the great quicksilver 45s of the sixties came from faders manipulated by Glyn Johns: the Who's "My Generation," the Small Faces' "Tin Soldier," the Rolling Stones' "Honky Tonk Women," and the Kinks' "All Day and All of the Night" being just four of them. His reputation was equally high when it came to the longer form. He engineered the Rolling Stones' *Beggars Banquet* and the first albums by the Steve Miller Band.

Johns's great quality was his willingness to tell star musicians things they might not have wished to hear. He only took on jobs that he felt were right for him. Late in 1971 David Geffen summoned him to the United States twice to see what he thought of an exciting new band signed to Geffen's management and to his label. The members of the band, particularly the handsome, confident lead guitarist, were under the impression that their forte was rocking. Johns didn't agree. He was on the point of passing on them altogether when he heard them amusing themselves at rehearsal one day by singing in close harmony. Then he realized that this group could be a latter-day Everly Brothers rather than just another Rolling Stones. He went on to produce their first two albums. They were called the Eagles.

In February 1971 Glyn Johns was called by Kit Lambert, manager of the Who, to ask if he would get involved with their new album. The band were already engaged in a Pete Townshend brainchild called "Lifehouse," which was supposed to be a film, a multimedia epic, a unique collaboration between performer and audience, and, on some level, a "crowd-sourced" piece of art in which the band would facilitate the audience in reaching a new level of consciousness. The Who's weekly concerts at the Young Vic, which had begun in January, had been part of this project, which was so complex and yet so nebulous that none of the band or indeed their management understood the idea sufficiently to get behind it. Johns was very keen to work with the Who again, but he was direct enough to tell Townshend the truth when nobody else would. Pete, he said, nobody understands your film idea. Let's drop that and just make a brilliant record.

Townshend didn't put up a fight. Kit Lambert, whose background was in classical music and who was even more given to grand schemes than Townshend, really wanted another rock opera in the mold of *Tommy. Jesus Chris Superstar* was then enjoying a mainstream success that rock bands could only dream about, and the common view among members of the Who was that *Tommy*, which came out in 1968, had been their peak. Just as Elvis had believed that musical success was just a step toward movies, in the late sixties, many believed that the increasing sophistication of rock would inevitably lead it into long form. Lambert wanted to believe this for reasons of scale and prestige. Townshend wanted to believe it because it seemed the only proper vehicle for his seriousness. By being prepared to say that he didn't understand the idea, Glyn Johns delivered us all from that.

The Who moved the recording to New York. The story goes that Lambert was so excited by the way they were sounding and so at a loss to know what to do about it that he just wrote out a note saying, "Keep going!" and pressed it to the control room glass. When Johns came on board, he listened to what they had and suggested that they should start again. So they came back to London, working initially with the Rolling Stones mobile truck at Stargroves, Mick Jagger's country home, and then at Olympic studios in Barnes, which was always Johns's location of choice. Like Stax in Memphis, Olympic had started life as a cinema. It was originally intended for use as a soundtrack studio and therefore had a big room that could accommodate an orchestra. When the future proved to be in rock bands, the acreage of floor space and high ceilings made it ideal for recording loud rock bands in a way that preserved their drama and dynamics.

While they were making the album, the Who were still setting off to play gigs, sometimes as far north as Dundee. There was nothing they had played and recorded that they couldn't perform onstage. Their set list changed all the time, scribbled out by Roger just minutes before shows at the Top Rank Suite in Sunderland, the Mayfair Suite in Birmingham, the Assembly Hall, Worthing, or the Pavilion in Bath. They had a full diary. That was how they knew they were a band. "Between 1965 and 1972," recalled Roger Daltrey later, "we lived out of a suitcase."

The work paid dividends. No rock-and-roll band before or since has been more accomplished live than the Who in the years from 1968 to 1972. They had proven it the year before when they had recorded shows at the universities of Leeds and Hull for the album that became *Live at Leeds*. Nik Cohn, the chronicler of '50s and '60s rock, called it "the best live rock album of all time," a title it still holds. The fact that they managed to reach the kind of cohesion they show on *Live at Leeds* without the usual overdubs with which live albums are usually made ready for public consumption is remarkable enough. That they made such a gigantic sound with just the four of them continues to boggle the mind. When they appear onstage in the twenty-first century, they need a handful of extra musicians in order to make the sound they could once make as a four-piece within minutes of tumbling out of the van. It is as if, as Chris Charlesworth said in *Melody Maker* at the time, they grew a fifth musician in the process of playing live.

In 1971 they were as volatile as ever, but Moon had not yet entirely succumbed to alcohol. Daltrey said they were "never nearer to breaking up" than at the time, just as the Beatles had done and the Stones had almost done. Townshend's anxiety attacks were made worse by the fact that he was nearing thirty and his wife had just had their first child. In his case the standard songwriter's fear of the next single was compounded by the expectation that he would produce another entire opera. Everybody was looking to him to take them forward into the new decade, and his problem at the time was that he had too many ideas rather than not enough.

Although Johns is listed only as "associate producer," he was the one we have to thank for what may be the best album of 1971. He was the one who persuaded Townshend to salvage some big ambitious songs from the big ambitious project, where they would only be weighted down with tiresome exposition, and put them on one single long-playing record. Although the overarching idea of "Lifehouse" didn't survive, it's in the nature of pop that its essence is best distilled into small, powerful units, that it communicates in glimmers and slivers rather than in the sustained narratives and slowly unfolding themes of the grown-up arts, that in fact *Who's Next* is way better than "Lifehouse" could ever have hoped to be and that it continues to be played, enjoyed, and pilfered from long after the likes of *Tommy* and *Quadrophenia* have grown tiresome. This is largely because of one tune, which may well be the best recording of the best year in the history of recording, the five-minute opening cut, "Baba O'Riley."

One of the things that made Glyn Johns a production genius was his lack of interest in how things were supposed to work and his readiness to understand what actually did work. Townshend's opening figure was played on a Lowrey organ and then put through a synthesizer. Only a handful of musicians at the time could be bothered to try to work this new instrument, and it was the first time one had been used to provide not washes of color but a propulsive rhythm track. In the cases of both "Baba O'Riley" and "Won't Get Fooled Again," Keith Moon played in time to a rhythm dictated by a machine. In years to come all records would be made like this. Similar experiments elsewhere in the spring of 1971 may have been leading other bands to the same conclusions—though since a synthesizer was so expensive only people who had made a lot of money could afford one—but when "Baba O'Riley" hit FM radio in August of that year, it was, as far as most people who were listening were concerned, the first time. Because "Baba O'Riley" is poised perfectly between what had been and what was about to be, it's a unique pop record.

The singer might not have known what was in Townshend's head when he wrote the lines "Out here in the fields I fight for my meals," but nobody in the world was better suited than Roger Daltrey to the act of singing it as though the thought had just entered his head. "Baba O'Riley" is an intoxicating salmagundi of whims and profundities, of grand schemes and shortcuts, of the future as represented by the apparently unmanned keyboard figure at the beginning and the past as embodied in the devil's elbow fiddle at the end, of the religious impulse represented in the name of Townshend's guru Meher Baba, and the technical nod implicit in the name of Terry Riley, whose music had inspired it, of the earnest desire to lift the audience meeting the pressing need to give it something to get down to, of the psychedelic colors of the sixties meeting this brown new decade, of the AM sensibilities of the group who gave us 45s like "Substitute" piercing the Marshall stacks of what was yet to become arena rock. "Baba O'Riley" sits at the center of *Who's Next*, providing a tent pole so reliable that they could even afford to reserve their other big gun, "Won't Get Fooled Again," for the very end. *Who's Next* sits at the center of 1971's claim to be the most perfect moment in the short history of rock and roll, and with each passing year that claim grows stronger.

"Baba O'Riley" enjoys a rich afterlife. It's used to ramp up the drama when the Los Angeles Lakers come on the court. It's been covered by countless young bands who dearly wish they could come up with anything with quite the same surge. It had a new lease on life in 2003 when it was used as the theme for *CSI: NY*. It closed out the London Olympics of 2012, the two surviving members of the band joined by what seemed like an orchestra of accompanying musicians, the lyrics bowdlerized in deference to the event so that Daltrey now sang, "There's more than Teenage Wasteland."

At the beginning of November 1971, the Who headlined three nights at the newly opened Rainbow in Finsbury Park, north London. This venue was previously the Finsbury Park Astoria, the starting point for the package tours that used to take live music around the country. An unprecedented nine thousand tickets were sold in nine hours. It didn't appear that live rock could possibly get any bigger.

While the cover of *Who's Next*, which shows the members of the group retreating down a slag heap having evidently just urinated on a concrete monolith, did at least feature the performers, the fourth album by Led Zeppelin, which was in the window of Harum just a week after the Who had begun their opening stand at the Rainbow, was a complete departure from all the accepted tenets of product packaging.

On the front was a hand-tinted picture from the Edwardian era of an elderly rustic presumably returning home after a day's collecting branches of wood from the forest owned by his master. He is so bowed down by the weight of this firewood that he has to lean on his stick. The photograph is framed and hangs on the wall of an old house, possibly occupied by his forebears, who may have moved to the city to find work in industry. Pull back again and we see the house is presumably an old row house in the city, and as we fold out the full cover, we realize that we are meant to conclude that this house has been knocked down and the occupants rehoused in the charmless high-rise on the back cover.

Designer Aubrey Powell's work here has been subject to many interpretations over the years. Some Led Zeppelin scholars even think they recognize the man on the cover and can trace a link from him to Page via the work of his favored occultist, Aleister Crowley. What's known is that the picture was found by Robert Plant, and its use as one of the two key motifs on the record was an important statement about what Led Zeppelin thought of themselves.

What it said most immediately was, we are not Grand Funk Railroad. Led Zeppelin had seen enough of the new generation of hard rock bands coming up in their slipstream—many of them pandering to the same cheap wine and cheaper drugs crowd as they did— to strongly suspect that there was a danger of the finer points of what they did being lost to sight. Their music may have taken them into amphitheaters in the midst of vast parking lots, but it was still composed in a folksy style around the fireplace of one of England's many stately ruins. The performers may have been sleeping in silken sheets in air-conditioned aeries at the top of luxury hotel blocks and conveyed to performances in their own monogrammed planes, but they had all grown up in the narrow chill of bomb site Britain and knew the thousand indignities and inconveniences that this life was heir to. Their music in performance may have been amplified at a level that burst or beggared any form of measurement placed before it, but it was initially composed on acoustic guitars, mandolins, and recorders. The fifteen-year-old in Sam Goody who was trying to decide between Led Zeppelin and the latest by Bloodrock or Black Oak Arkansas would never have dreamed that the new one from the Limeys had been composed under the influence of Fairport Convention's *Full House* or the Incredible String Band's *The Hangman's Beautiful Daughter*.

The choice of that man with his bundle of sticks for the cover rather than an expensive shot of Robert's glistening chest was a way of reemphasizing the great little band that was getting lost inside a band who increasingly seemed to have been put on this earth to redefine the term "big." In 1971 Led Zeppelin made the old math look silly. It was as though they had discovered an entirely new wing in what had previously been thought to be a compact family house. In Barney Hoskyns's book *Trampled Under Foot*, Chris Dreja, formerly the bass player in the Yardbirds, recalls that when Peter Grant got in touch to say Led Zeppelin were playing Madison Square Garden, Dreja assumed that he'd got the name of the venue wrong. He simply didn't believe bands could play venues that big.

The design of the album was also an expression of the band's sheer commercial heft and the extent to which they now held the power in the relationship with the traditional star-making machinery. Not only did the cover not have the traditional picture of the musicians who made the record; it didn't even feature the name of the band or the record. This monument to inscrutability was something not even the Beatles in their pomp had dared do. Atlantic was provided with the finished artwork and told that was the way it would be. Atlantic argued but without any great force. Led Zeppelin and Peter Grant got their way.

At no stage did Led Zeppelin seem to accommodate the things that the market expected. They did few interviews, they didn't appear on television, they didn't go in for much in the way of advertising—none of which seemed to harm their commercial prospects. What it did mean is that they didn't have many allies, and other bands were deeply resentful of their success. Critics who knew there was very little chance of being called upon to interview them felt no compunction in dismissing them, particularly in some of their more excessive flights of fantasy. Their musical peers felt that they were never invited in. Led Zeppelin weren't in the family. They didn't participate in all-star jams, they didn't schmooze the industry, and the industry didn't schmooze them, through a combination of arrogance, timidity, and fear of Peter Grant and Jimmy Page. Led Zeppelin had a reputation for being unpleasant and getting their way, a reputation they were quite happy to see grow.

While Keith Richards was being exalted as the good, even the virtuous spirit of rock and roll, Jimmy Page was the one people talked about behind their hands. They muttered about his worrying interest in the occult, the age of his girlfriends, the extent to which he might have leaned on the songs of Willie Dixon or the licks of Randy California. You couldn't argue about the power of the music. What nobody could contest was the buckle-kneed heft of the music that Led Zeppelin had made in the early part of 1971. *Led Zeppelin IV* was truly music that sold itself.

The November 6 issue of *Billboard* came with a quarter strip ad across the bottom of its front page. The ad bore four symbols that would have meant nothing to any of its readers. The only thing it was possible to read was the logo of the record company—Atlantic. *Shaft* was at number one, and in Amsterdam Rod Stewart was being presented with five gold discs to recognize the success he had seen since the release of *Every Picture Tells a Story* in July. There was a four-page ad for *E Pluribus Funk*, the new album by Grand Funk Railroad, an ad that featured color portraits of all three members of the band. Next to *Led Zeppelin IV* this looked gauche and needy.

In the second week of release, the record went from number 36 to 8, the following week to 5, then to 2, where it remained over Christmas, looking up at Sly & the Family Stone, holding off Carole King's *Music*, which overtook it over Christmas. But while in time those other records slipped away, *Led Zeppelin IV* never did. Along with Carole King's *Tapestry*, it pioneered a new dimension of the music business, which could only be expressed via the compound adjective "multiplatinum." To sell in these kinds of quantities, you are no longer reliant on the normal levels of marketing. To sell week in, week out for months, even years, you need a product that is its own most powerful advocate.

Making music louder is not difficult. Making music sound louder is a lot harder. The year 1971 was the age of the Marshall stack, of mutually assured tinnitus, the time when Pete Townshend was telling the inventor of the Marshall amp that he needed "bigger weapons," when impressionable young men sat on their bony backsides on the cold floors of venues and passed the time waiting for the headliners by calculating the amplification equipment arrayed against them, like cavalry counting the mouths of the cannon they were about to face.

The Zeppelin record starts with the slurring of a tape being run back to a cue point, followed by a brief moment of silence. Then the snorting of a wakened beast, the first cough of a semitruck on a cold morning, a noise that announces something is about to occur. What matters is the microsecond of silence between it finishing and Robert Plant's echo-soused "Hey, hey, mama, said the way you move / gonna make you sweat, gonna make you groove." Then a drum tattoo that sounds like somebody's pushed a wardrobe full of bricks from the top of a stone staircase announces what seems like a cross between Link Wray's "Rumble" and Samson pulling down the pillars of the temple. It's the most bravura opening to what may be the most bravura rock-and-roll album of the era.

Led Zeppelin IV was a glorious grab bag of the polished and the gimcrack, the rootsy and the brilliantined, of hop-infused Midlands folk and the cheap whiskey of the Delta lands, of ancient and modern, of quiet and loud, of hippie philosophy and apprentice-boy aggression, such as had never been done before and probably never was to be done again, of rock and roll and progressive rock, of mock profundity and the odd genuinely bleak insight. It sounds like the actual caverns depicted on its artwork. It feels like the very water coming through the levee. It has the sublime daftitude of the Dave Clark Five married to the sexual threat of Muddy Waters. Some called it "progressive," which was the word applied to anything longer than five minutes around that time. In fact, it was anything but. Whereas some of their contemporaries seemed to be trying to make sounds that belonged in classical music, Led Zeppelin seemed in fact to be trying to tunnel back to the crudest basics.

Andy Johns, younger brother of Glyn, was the twenty-year-old engineer whose idea it was to suspend a microphone from two floors above the entrance hall of Headley Grange and set up John Bonham's drum kit facing the door like a gift for a small boy on Christmas morning. This allowed him to record it in such a way that the groove at the beginning of "When the Levee Breaks" bounced off the stone walls in a unique simulacrum of coiled power so compelling that fifty years later kids in bedrooms who have never even heard of John Bonham borrow it for their mixes. Andy remembered that even back then it struck him that this combination of talents and this moment might not come around again. "I used to get up in the morning, thinking, 'Today I have another chance to do something that's never been done before.'"

To which you could add, and also something that won't be done again. There are reasons why you couldn't do this all again now. A surprising number of them are to do with technology. Since all records are now made and mixed digitally, a certain snap-to-grid slickness has arrived at the expense of something with which *Led Zeppelin IV* abounds: a sense of air. Since the world went Pro Tools, people mix as much by sight as by ear, seeking to pack the spectrum with detail and reduce the amount of space in which the imagination can roam. Page's riffs, which had a catchiness that promised further layers of catchiness, were great smudges of sound cutting shapes in an atmosphere that seemed gravid with foreboding. They were like the first footprints in the snow. Today, the click track would make sure "Rock & Roll" didn't speed up in the way it does. The insistence on a single would mean that one track would be dulled by familiarity by the time you got the album home. The increased visibility due to a more ubiquitous video presence would have meant that the people going to see the band would have some idea of what to expect. It wouldn't be Sandy Denny dueting with Robert Plant on "The Battle of Evermore." It would be somebody who'd already had a number of hits in their own right whose presence could open the door to another market. Finally and most importantly, social media, the element within which we all swim today, splashes daylight all over the twilight world of disreputable behavior, the very world in which Led Zeppelin's mystique took root. Mobile phone technology alone would certainly have cramped the style of their on-tour for-nication, with fatal consequences for the unapologetic swagger with which they carried themselves in the fall of 1971.

Ken Scott is in no doubt that the record contracts of 1971, which in many cases required the acts to come up with two albums a year, made for better records. "You made decisions quickly because you had to. There was no second-guessing yourself." It is a truth almost universally acknowledged in the record business that the longer somebody takes making a record, the thinner its commercial pros-pects are likely to be. The first thought is usually the best thought, and the more time an artist has, the more that thought is likely to be overridden by further thoughts that are not quite so good.

Great producers usually have a highly developed sense of when something is finished. Glyn Johns helped make *Who's Next* into a great record by persuading Pete Townshend to row back on some of his ambitions for "Lifehouse." Like many of the best long-playing records that came out of 1971, it was made immeasurably stronger by the fact that somebody knew when it was finished. In fact, some of the biggest records of the year, records such as *Tapestry*, *Every Pic-ture Tells a Story*, and *What's Going On*, were by modern standards rushed out before they were apparently ready. The next record Johns produced after *Who's Next* was the first one by the Eagles, and here he came up against a very different way of doing things, a way that indicated how the record business was likely to go in the future.

It was customary in 1971, as it had been in 1968 or 1957, to release an album as soon as humanly possible—the moment the lacquers could be supplied to the pressing plant and the jackets manufac-tured. There was no machine to prime, no marketing scheme to be perfected, no budget to be hammered out, no accompanying image to be developed, no complex network of media deals to be synchro-nized, no *Vanity Fair* profile to be timed to make way for the antici-pated street date, no complex hullabaloo to be orchestrated.

David Geffen was in a unique position of power with the first Eagles album. Since he managed the band, was their agent, and ran their record company, he was in a position to put his foot on the ball.

He was happy with most of what the band had done at Olympic with Glyn Johns, but he felt it needed another Don Henley vocal. Even though Johns had moved on to other projects, Geffen called him up and asked him to have another go at producing the band's version of the Jackson Browne song "Nightingale." They argued about the usefulness of doing such a thing, and eventually Johns relented and flew to the States to try again. It didn't make any difference, but the significant thing was that Geffen thought it was worth trying no matter what the expense in terms of man-hours and studio time and sitting around agonizing.

The first album by the Eagles indicated the way the world was going to go. As the rewards of apparently getting it right became greater throughout the seventies, as it became clear that the big hit albums of 1971 were still hanging about the charts years later, it became even more important to do anything you could to minimize the slightest chance of failure. Once people learned how much money could be made by rolling a double six, they mistakenly thought that their chances would improve if they spent months blowing on the dice. Time and again, the market has told them this isn't true.

It was different looking through the new releases rack in Harum in 1971. The rules of the game hadn't yet been written. There were a handful of opportunities and a handful of remarkably talented people in position to take advantage of them. Terry Manning is a recording engineer from Memphis who worked with Led Zeppelin in the early seventies. He remembers Jimmy Page saying to him back in the days when they were peeling off this music like there was no tomorrow, "Our time is different, and I don't think the general public or other musicians will ever get what we do or catch up to it."

As Manning admits, that sounds egotistical. It also sounds true.

War: "Slippin' into Darkness"

Tony Christie: "(Is This the Way to) Amarillo"

Led Zeppelin: "Stairway to Heaven"

Boz Scaggs: "Runnin' Blue"

Bridget St. John: "City-Crazy"

The Who: "Baba O'Riley"

Stevie Wonder: "If You Really Love Me"

Mickey Newbury: "An American Trilogy"

The Staple Singers: "Respect Yourself"

Joe Simon: "Help Me Make It Through the Night"

DECEMBER 12

American Pie

Looking back on the movies of the year in the *New York Times*, critic Vincent Canby reflected on what he called their "blank gaze." In *A Clockwork Orange*, *The French Connection*, and *Carnal Knowledge*, he remarked, the audience is not invited to root for or against the main characters. Around the time he was writing this, Eddie Egan, the New York cop on whom Gene Hackman's character, Popeye Doyle, had been based in *The French Connection*, was dismissed from the police department without benefits just before his retirement for acting in real life the way Hackman's character behaved on the screen, and movie audiences had applauded the character.

There was even less ambivalence in *Dirty Harry*, the Don Siegel thriller, which was released just before Christmas. Clint Eastwood played corner-cutting enforcer Harry Callahan. "He doesn't play any favorites," says a colleague. "Harry hates everybody." When Harry strolled through the mayhem in midtown San Francisco, doggedly chewing the last of his breakfast as he pointed his Magnum at a wounded bank robber and asked him to guess whether he had

263

a bullet left in the chamber, the audience was clearly being asked to identify with Eastwood as the put-upon defender of law and order. While he enjoyed the film, critic Roger Ebert said that its "moral position is fascist." That didn't prevent it being such a success that it spawned four sequels, each containing a twist on the same scene.

In his roundup, Canby remarked that it seemed possible for a film to perform well on America's coasts and yet die in its heartland, pointing out that most of the stylish alternative pictures made in the wake of *Easy Rider*, such as the James Taylor film *Two-Lane Blacktop* and *Drive, He Said*, had actually flopped. The movie industry had looked at the grosses, written off its flirtation with the hippies, and gone back to making movies that reflected the concerns of middle-aged Americans. It would be the Christmas of *Fiddler on the Roof*, *Diamonds Are Forever*, and *Willie Wonka & the Chocolate Factory*.

In 1971 cinema attendance was at an all-time low. From $78 million a week in 1946, admissions had slumped to less than $16 million in 1971. The studios were hemorrhaging cash. A movie like *Dirty Harry* wasn't as big a story as *Music*, the second new album by Carole King released in 1971. The movies seemed to be over. Pictures weren't events. More people saw a TV movie that was broadcast in late November than saw Clint Eastwood's tale of fear and loathing. This TV film, *Duel*, was about a man who, while driving through the desert, found himself pursued by a malevolent truck with an invisible driver. *Duel* struck the same chord as *Dirty Harry*. The outside world, whether that meant the potholed streets of Brooklyn or the desert roads of California, was full of monsters and was best kept at bay with a gun. The director making his debut was a young man named Steven Spielberg.

As Christmas 1971 approached, Frank Zappa could have been forgiven for looking forward to a rest. He was about to turn thirty-one, he had a young family at home in California, and he had spent most of the year on tour at the head of his latest version of the Mothers of Invention. This one featured singers/lampoonists Mark

Volman and Howard Kaylan, otherwise known as Flo & Eddie. Zappa's career relied on his ability to stir up outrage. It required a certain amount of energy to deal with the consequences. Back in February, the management of London's Royal Albert Hall had canceled Zappa's plans to have the Royal Philharmonic Orchestra perform his original compositions, such as "Penis Dimension," for the soundtrack of his film *200 Motels*. This led to a legal case that didn't come to court until 1975. Members of the orchestra, including the distinguished trumpeter John Wilbraham, had pronounced themselves disturbed by the idea of being expected to play songs inspired by the sex lives of rock musicians.

Zappa played both sides of the street. While his declared heroes were Stravinsky and Varèse, he made sure his act was never too far removed from the lewd humor of the Fabulous Furry Freak Brothers. In June he had recorded a live album at the Fillmore East, the climax of which had been a topical opera inspired by the incident at Seattle's Edgewater Inn where members of Vanilla Fudge, abetted by Led Zeppelin tour manager Richard Cole, were said to have sexually assaulted a groupie with a fish they had reeled in from the balcony adjoining their room. This was widely regarded as hilarious, as was the Dutch documentary made about Zappa in the same year. In this, he didn't need much encouragement to turn the conversation to the casual sex available to even a group as lacking in handsomeness as the Mothers of Invention. The documentary is a reminder of the blasé manners of the time. Partly filmed at the Zappa home, it features members of Zappa protégées, the GTOs, reminiscing about their own sexual adventures with rock stars while looking after the Zappa infants Dweezil and Moon. Smoking a cigarette within inches of the head of a naked baby did not strike anyone as particularly unusual at the time. In the same film, Zappa shruggingly outlines his code of the road: "I like to get laid. How does my wife feel about that? She grumbles every once in a while, but she gets used to it. I come home with the clap, and she goes and gets us some penicillin."

In the winter of 1971 Zappa and his band were testing their

immunity on a long tour of Europe. December 4 found them playing at the Montreux Casino near Geneva in Switzerland. Just as Don Preston embarked on the synthesizer solo in "King Kong" somebody in the audience thought it would increase the gaiety of the evening if they launched a firework into the rattan covering of the ceiling. Unsurprisingly, the place burst into flames. There were three thousand fans in that room—which was significantly over capacity—and they miraculously managed to escape. Because there were fans outside who were still trying to get in, somebody had chained the fire doors shut. The members of Deep Purple, in town to make their new album using the Rolling Stones mobile recording truck, witnessed the conflagration from across the water, a vision that inspired Roger Glover to compose "Smoke on the Water" about their temporary inconvenience. Montreux could very easily have been one of those tragedies too serious to write an up-tempo rocker about. It was a miracle it wasn't.

Back at their hotel, their equipment destroyed, Zappa's band were all for going directly home. However, their existence at the time was so hand to mouth that it would have meant returning penniless at Christmas. Hence it was decided to borrow some equipment and go to London, where they were booked to play four relatively lucrative shows in three days at the Rainbow. This proved to be an unfortunate decision. At the end of the first of those shows, on Friday, December 10, just six days after they had escaped incineration, Zappa led the band back onstage for an encore and announced that they would play the Beatles' "I Want to Hold Your Hand." This was a surprise choice, possibly inspired by the fact that in its previous incarnation the Rainbow had been the venue for the Beatles' Christmas shows. Before the band could begin the song, a twenty-one-year-old laborer named Trevor Howell had materialized from the side of the stage and launched Zappa off its edge. The iconoclast fell twelve feet onto the concrete floor of the orchestra pit below, his guitar still around his neck. He didn't move. From the way he landed, his neck appeared to be broken. The band thought he was dead.

Zappa was in hospital in London for weeks making his recovery. During that time, he worked up a grudge about the country that had brought him ill fortune in so many different forms and pondered the unpredictable consequences of fame. The first explanation of the incident offered was that Howell had assaulted Zappa because he was jealous of the effect the guitarist was having on his girlfriend. A later report suggested he was cross because he didn't feel he was getting value for money. Certainly, stalls tickets were £1.50, which was a significant increase on prices at the beginning of the year. The courts took the matter seriously. When the case came to trial the following year, Howell got twelve months in prison.

The incident, though widely taken as a joke at the time, was the beginning of an emphasis on artist security, which was long overdue. Howell's attack, like the stage invasions that had wrecked the Newport Festival in the United States and the Pink Floyd fans who had spoiled the band's planned spectacle at their Crystal Palace show in the summer by wading into the water and letting the air out of the Floyd's inflatable octopus, suggested that as rock got bigger and the venues grew to accommodate the demand, the audience could no longer be relied upon to "be cool."

On the night of Zappa's misadventure, the fledgling Roxy Music played a show at Slough Community Centre. Included in their set were many of the songs that would be on their first album the following year: they began with "2HB" and finished with "Virginia Plain," which would be their first single. Bryan Ferry's group had had an excellent week. Their plan to make their name without submitting to the rigors of the clubbing circuit appeared to be paying off. That week they had signed a management deal with the same people who looked after Emerson, Lake & Palmer and King Crimson, and Richard Williams had written the first feature about them in the *Melody Maker*, saying they "had a freshness and flexibility about them which made the majority of their contemporaries sound tired and tawdry" and applauding their "welcome awareness of the roots and history of pop." Also on the same night the Who were playing Long Beach Arena in California. They were nearing the end of a year that had seen them play seventy-five shows, appear in movies, cause the standard amount of mayhem, move house, have children, and make the best record of their career. In the United States, they were moving into bigger and bigger venues to cater to the exploding demand. The dangers of this escalation were more apparent to those on the stage than those looking up at it. At the Long Beach show, Roger Daltrey, seriously concerned that people down at the front of the stage were getting crushed, tried to get the crowd to take a step back. When they didn't comply, Pete Townshend took over and demonstrated his knack for being quotable and opaque in the same sentence. "That's how much power rock and roll stars have got. Fuck all. Now either sit down, lay down, but shut up. This is a rock and roll concert, not a fucking tea party!"

As Zappa was being rushed to hospital, his ambulance went past London's Inn on the Park, where Lou Reed was now living in unaccustomed splendor. RCA was paying the bills for him and his producer, New York scenester Richard Robinson, and his wife, Lisa, while he made his first solo album at Morgan Studios in Willesden. The musicians playing on the record included two members of Yes: guitarist Steve Howe and keyboard player Rick Wakeman, who had joined the progressive five-piece in time to play on *Fragile*, their second hit album of the year. The majority of the songs on *Lou Reed*, which came out in the middle of 1972, had previously been performed with the Velvet Underground, the group Reed had left in 1970. He appeared to be the beneficiary of that rarest of things in pop music—a second chance.

On the night a year earlier when Reed had left the group, his parents had picked him up and taken him home to their big house in the suburbs, for all the world like a college boy who'd found the big wide world too much to cope with. Reed had retired from the music business at that point, apparently abandoning any hope that his songs might ever find a place in the world, and going to work as a typist at his father's accountancy firm. Glenn O'Brien, then editing Andy Warhol's *Interview* magazine, remembers Reed settling down with an attractive former cocktail waitress named Bettye Kronstad. "Lou, who had no choice about being hip, was fascinated with squaredom. That was part of the appeal of Bettye. She was a nice square chick. They got married. Then I remember seeing her with a black eye that never seemed to heal." O'Brien saw Reed as salving his bitterness at his own lack of success with the belated acclaim he was getting from younger performers like David Bowie and Jonathan Richman. His erstwhile bandmate John Cale mused that his return was the making of Lou because he seemed to find suburbia more inspiring than bohemia. By May 1971 he was recording demos of new songs, including "Walk on the Wild Side" and "Berlin," in the Robinsons' apartment. When he got the deal with RCA and the chance to go and record what he liked in London in December 1971, it was both debut and comeback.

While London bohemians like David Bowie were taking inspiration from American acts like the Velvet Underground and the Stooges, New York's bohemians were exalting the English end of the Special Relationship. When Keith Richards appeared on the cover of *Rolling Stone* in August 1971 (a watershed moment in the establishment of the cult of Keef), two young New Yorkers took particular notice. It wasn't the music that inspired them so much as their desire to emulate the way Keith looked. They liked the way he carried himself, the sweet smell of danger that entered the room before he did. Both started with the hairstyle. One was Patti Smith, who was previously mainly known for her striking appearance and her keenness to glom on to anyone famous. In 1971 Smith was the girlfriend of Todd Rundgren, which didn't stop her giving his new album a glowing review in *Rolling Stone*.

The other disciple of Keith Richards was John Genzale from Queens. John played guitar and had recently joined a band called Actress. In late 1971 Actress found a singer named David. David wasn't the world's greatest singer, but he had more front than Macy's, had done some roles as a child actor, and most importantly looked like a younger version of Mick Jagger. On Christmas Eve the new lineup played their first gig under their new name at a welfare hotel on Columbus called the Endicott. There was no money, but it was a gig. The only audience were the residents. The band played under-rehearsed versions of songs by Archie Bell & the Drells and Otis Redding. The look was more important than their sound. John Genzale was by now known as Johnny Thunders, and he was playing the Keith Richards to David Johansen's Mick Jagger. The band were introduced as the New York Dolls. It would be another two years before they got their chance to be the next big thing with the release of their first album and after that another four years before the arrival of punk rock made them quite well known, by which time they would be no more.

The big hit single of December 1971 was such a big hit that the man who wrote it never needed to work again. Don McLean came from New Rochelle in Westchester County, New York, in the heart of postwar prosperity. Like Lou Reed, he had a comfortable background that he preferred to play down. He wasn't as rich as some—"I knew a lot of kids who were born on third base and thought they hit a triple"—but he was very comfortable and knew that he, like his neighbors, could probably look forward to an even more comfortable future.

McLean was keen on the guitar and, like so many successful musicians, thanks to childhood illnesses keeping him away from school, he managed to get good at it. At the same time, he was also having opera lessons paid for by his sister and swimming underwater to improve his breath control. When he was only fifteen, his father died. From that point Don felt able to pursue his dream with the guitar. He was confident enough to venture to the city and seek out the help and advice of established names on the folk circuit such as Erik Darling and manager Harold Leventhal. He dropped out of college in 1963 and spent six years playing every folk club that would have him. He was also pursuing a master's degree in business administration at night school.

In 1970 he released his first album, which was called *Tapestry*. This was on a small label that was subsequently bought by United Artists. On March 14, 1971, while opening for Laura Nyro at a college show in Philadelphia, he unveiled a new song called "American Pie," which was notable for riddling words, a hooky chorus, and taking almost ten minutes to play. Its appeal wasn't immediately obvious to everyone. When he played the songs for his proposed second album to his producer, the latter asked why he hadn't got a single. McLean said that not only was "American Pie" the single; it was also the title track. He was so confident that he'd already taken the cover photographs in which a star and stripes was painted on his outstretched thumb.

The producer, Ed Freeman, put McLean and his band to work on the song in a rehearsal studio for the best part of two weeks. Then, on the day of the session, he introduced Paul Griffin, the piano player who had made distinguished contributions to everything from Dionne Warwick's "Walk On By" to Bob Dylan's "Like a Rolling Stone." It's Griffin's rippling, almost facile piano that prevents "American Pie" collapsing under the weight of its determination to be the Great American Song and makes it one of the first great pop records that is about great pop records.

There was a gentle ache at the center of it, like there was in so much music that year. McLean wasn't just a Buddy Holly fan. He felt Holly was the alpha and omega of pop songwriting, and when he died the music had died with him. Not everyone tried to decipher all the song's metaphors, to work out who was the jester who sang in a voice he'd borrowed from James Dean or the quartet who practiced in the park, but everyone from America's most learned critic to the teenagers dancing along to the chorus recognized that "American Pie" was about the loss of innocence, in pop music as well as in the grown-up world.

"American Pie" came out as a single in November. It was eight minutes long, which necessitated it being mastered at half-speed and spread over both sides of a seven-inch 45. This didn't prevent it being one of the biggest hits of the year, dominating the airwaves during December and spending five weeks at number one in the early part of 1972. It also played a part in the national conversation, turning it to the time twelve years earlier when the plane carrying Buddy

Holly, Ritchie Valens, and the Big Bopper had gone down in Clear Lake, Iowa, back to the vanished world of pink carnations and pickup trucks, back to Chevys driven to the levee, back to the blithe, dreamlike stability of the fifties, back to the distant land of lost content.

Its most ringing phrase, "the day the music died," became one of the few lines from a pop song to put its brand on not only a date but also a subtle feeling of regret that was the first intimation of a generation reluctantly growing up. Its title was subsequently borrowed for a series of winningly vulgar teenage comedies. Its revival provided Madonna with a new start as her career entered its third decade. It has been called one of the five key American songs of the twentieth century, just below "Over the Rainbow" and "White Christmas." Like them, it's certainly one of those tunes that enjoys almost 100 percent familiarity, even among people who aren't aware of liking it. It taught the young Mike Mills, later of REM, "This is how you can write a song." For McLean, it's the gift that goes on giving. In April 2015 he auctioned the song's original manuscript for over a million dollars.

"American Pie" was a straw in the wind that December. In the same month, the *Village Voice* announced that the mood of nostalgia had "reached epidemic proportions." This came in many forms. Laura Nyro teamed up with Labelle, formerly known as Patti LaBelle and the Bluebelles, to release a record of reverent covers of '50s and '60s soul tunes called *Gonna Take a Miracle*, following which she retired to get married. At the time, a loose family of musicians around Fairport Convention were enjoying a boozy holiday at the Manor, the Oxfordshire studio recently opened by Richard Branson, in order to record *Rock On*, their own tribute to the songs of Buddy Holly, the Everly Brothers, and Carole King. The first album by Paul McCartney's group Wings contained their version of Mickey & Sylvia's "Love Is Strange." Paul held the launch party at the Empire Ballroom. He turned up with his hair molded into a quiff, as if it were 1959 all over again.

* * *

In December Stanley Gortikov, the Capitol Records executive who was head of the American record industry's trade association, gave an interview to *Billboard*. He was asked whether he thought the record business would ever be able to aim its products at adults or whether it would remain, like the toy industry, primarily focused on "the kids."

"Adults over 30 or 35 have largely been written off as potential record buyers," he said. "They don't buy; they're over the hill. . . . Nobody seems to be trying to tap that vast market, despite the basic universality of music. . . . A marketing breakthrough is needed."

Gortikov may have been slow to notice what was already occurring. In the same edition, a spokesman for an East Coast chain of shops named Schwartz Brothers Harmony Huts said, "This Christmas looks exceedingly good" and added that for the first five days of December they could report sales that were 78 percent ahead of the previous year. This was clearly not being caused by an exceptionally affluent set of teenagers. The signs were already there that lots of the established bands were selling records to people over the age of twenty-one. Columbia announced it expected to sell more than a million copies of the four-record set recorded by Chicago at Carnegie Hall. Procol Harum had just finished recording their best-known songs with the Edmonton Symphony Orchestra for a live album to be launched early in 1972. This was not aimed at teenagers.

The Rolling Stones' back catalog was suddenly available on the compilation album *Hot Rocks 1964–1971*, allowing access to a generation who'd been too young to appreciate "Satisfaction" the first time around. Suddenly, rock heritage was marketable. The distant past—the records of five, even six years earlier—was now something to aspire to. The retail industry was waiting with bated breath for the release of the souvenir of George Harrison's Concert for Bangladesh in August. This would eventually come out in the United States in Christmas week, having proved to be far more complicated an endeavor than Harrison ever thought possible. It was almost thirteen dollars in the United States and nearly six pounds in the UK, in both cases unprecedented prices, and it had a starving child on the cover. Not much teen appeal there.

Its reviews were rather better than they deserved to be, tending to focus on the purity of the artists' motives rather than the quality of their performances. "This is rock reaching for its manhood," said Jon Landau in *Rolling Stone*, perhaps unconsciously reflecting that the only women credited in the entire undertaking were three of the backing singers.

When the Band played at the Royal Albert Hall in London in the summer of 1971, Richard Williams, writing in the *Melody Maker*, described it as the greatest rock show he had ever seen. Sadly, the Band's moment as a vital creative force had passed. In September they had released *Cahoots*, their fourth studio album, which indicated that the things that used to come easily now sounded forced. Many of their songs seemed to be trying to measure up to the expectations produced by all that critical adulation. At the same time, the fissure between Robbie Robertson, who wrote their big songs, and Levon Helm, who sang them, had widened to a canyon. When they finished the year by playing four nights at New York's Academy of Music, they were accompanied by a horn section directed and arranged by the great Allen Toussaint, whose production of Lee Dorsey's brilliant *Yes We Can* had caused Robertson to call him up, but they played only two songs from the album. The rest were oldies. On the last night of the year, 1971, as the clock struck midnight, they brought on their old employer Bob Dylan. Announcing his last song, he said, "We haven't played this in years." Then, as he would do for the rest of his life, he launched into "Like a Rolling Stone." Heritage rock was born.

The twelve months just passed had been an averagely strange one in the life of Elvis Presley. The original rock-and-roll star had turned thirty-six in January 1971. A few days before Christmas of the previous year, stung by a conversation with his father, Vernon, and wife, Priscilla, who had both suggested that his spending on gifts for his cronies was getting out of hand, he took a plane to Washington, DC, accompanied by just two of the dozen courtiers who normally made up his entourage.

On the flight he fell into conversation with a Republican senator and sought to impress upon the legislator his steadfast belief in traditional American values and his growing concern that these were being threatened by the apparently opposing values of the Woodstock generation. Encouraged by the exchange, he wrote a note to President Richard Nixon, in which he offered his services as a warrior for stability and abstinence from drugs and an agent working within the music business. What only his intimates knew was that his dependency on prescription drugs was so great that he almost rattled when he walked.

Elvis and his friends dropped this note off at the White House at six thirty in the morning. Thanks to the security guard having recognized him, later that morning he received an invitation to drop by the Oval Office and say hello to the president. After being told, to his evident disappointment, that it would not be OK for him to take a revolver into the president's office and present it to him, he was ushered in, wearing what looked to the puzzled Nixon rather like his performing regalia. His face was swollen by an allergic reaction to the chocolate he had insisted on eating during the flight.

Between the nervous pleasantries, he sought to assure the president that he was determined to resist the erosion of the moral fabric of the young, for which he blamed the Beatles, use his power with them to put them on the right road, and secure for himself a badge advertising him as a deputy of the Bureau of Narcotics and Dangerous Drugs. Nixon got his snap with the King. The King got his badge, which was the thing that really mattered to him. It wasn't the only bauble he picked up in those few weeks. In January 1971 Elvis was presented with an award from America's Junior Chamber of Commerce for being one of the most notable examples of the benefits of free enterprise. This token of his standing in society meant more to Elvis than any gold records. Touchingly, he subsequently took this award with him everywhere he went, much like the orb and scepter of a medieval sovereign.

In late January he began a season at the International Hotel in Las Vegas. His manager, Colonel Tom Parker, continued to reject the stream of offers that came in for him to tour Europe, citing "personal security" as the main reason. Others speculated that as someone who had come to the United States as an illegal immigrant, Parker had no passport. It wasn't an issue within the Presley court. His client didn't appear to have much interest in going abroad, which was one of the most American things about him. The Vegas arrangement suited all concerned. It allowed Parker to indulge his vice, which was gambling, and it brought the audience to the King rather than expecting him to go to them. The many millions that the Presley machine turned over that year were spent before they could be banked. Most of it never left Vegas. The artist's share went on guns and toys. The manager's percentage went straight back to the house in the shape of his losses.

In March Presley went into the studios in Nashville to record an album for the Christmas market and to have a shot at some of the folksy material both he and the contemporary market appeared to favor. He did "Amazing Grace," the old devotional tune that had been turned into a huge hit by Judy Collins, Gordon Lightfoot's "Early Morning Rain," and Kris Kristofferson's "Sunday Morning Coming Down." He was only intermittently engaged with the material. So many members of the salaried posse who laughed at his jokes and applauded his displays of machismo crowded into the control room to listen to the playbacks that there was no room for the musicians. While his wife, Priscilla, and their three-year-old daughter, Lisa Marie, were away supervising the decoration of a new home in California, he was accompanied by one of his rotating cast of mistresses. Joyce Bova was such a regular at the sessions in June that some members of the band assumed she was his wife. Priscilla, meanwhile, realizing that her husband was lost in showbiz and to her as well, was spending her considerable energies in improving her martial arts and seeking her own romantic solace.

The producer Felton Jarvis tried everything to trick Elvis into the mood in which he might deliver. He dressed the studio with a Christmas tree and presents in the middle of summer. He tried to make sure the band was actually playing as he walked in the studio. Nothing worked. The Colonel made sure the dollars kept coming in by securing more advances from RCA for new and repackaged albums. The records slid out piecemeal. They didn't seem to matter to anyone apart from the faithful.

Only onstage could Elvis count for something. In the fall he undertook a tour of large indoor venues. This time, he was in front of his heartland fans, rather than the blasé high rollers of Vegas. Sensing the difference, Elvis put more effort into the presentation side of his act. The wife of his musical director Joe Guercio heard the Richard Strauss fanfare *Also Sprach Zarathustra*, newly popularized through its use in Stanley Kubrick's *2001: A Space Odyssey*, and suggested, tongue in cheek, that it would work for Elvis. The King was bucked up by the idea of beginning the show with a climax and then building from there. "He didn't want to be a guy just walking out there," said Guercio. "He wanted to be a god."

Although the band contained the finest session players and singers that money could buy, it was a piece of theater rather than a musical show. The most memorable moments were visual: the guitar he used as a prop but never played, the daunting displays of karate through which he advertised his maleness, the moment at the end when he held his arms outstretched to reluctantly receive the acclaim of the multitude—some of it was rock and roll, lots of it was show business, all of it was spectacle.

On December 30, 1971, after a Christmas subdued by Presley standards, Elvis confided to his inner circle that Priscilla wasn't coming back. His baby had finally left him. In the last issue of *Rolling Stone* of the year, Jon Landau wrote a long review of his experience seeing Elvis on that tour in Boston. It was a full page. At the top was

Elvis in his cape, arms outstretched. The headline read "In Praise of Elvis Presley." This was a key moment in the reconciliation between the self-styled rock intelligentsia and the person without whom their whole world would not have existed and was now widely regarded by hip opinion as a busted flush. Landau's entire review was about forgiving Elvis his Hollywood trespasses and at the same time forgiving *Rolling Stone* for having doubted him. It concluded: "He remains an artist; in fact, an American artist, and one we should be proud to claim as our own."

This review, written by the magazine's most senior rock journalist, who was all of twenty-four at the time, about a performer who seemed almost biblically ancient at thirty-six, was a glimpse of something entirely new: a performer whose best work was behind him still managing to command vast crowds and the highest ticket prices; an idol inviting people to come unto him to give thanks for his past and their past and to bask in a precious moment of shared proximity.

At the time, Presley was the only one offering this kind of experience. Chuck Berry and Little Richard and the rest were low rent, playing lashed-together oldies shows and not attracting any of the same veneration. Sinatra had slipped away. The Beatles had gone somewhere to fight. The Rolling Stones were preparing to come back. Bob Dylan was putting his toe in the water. Led Zeppelin and Pink Floyd and the rest of the comers weren't yet superstars.

But Elvis was something else. Elvis was the essence of a star. The kind of experience that Landau described was clearly an unusual one for him. He was accustomed to seeing bands who performed with the urgency of people who had just had their best idea. Presley's complacency was a new thing. "Elvis wants his people to have fun and he wants to have fun with them. But it's all middle-aged now and he wants them to have a middle-aged kind of fun." He pointed out that at the end, the audience members screamed and shouted and applauded, and as soon as the house lights were on they trooped out. "They never once move to get out of their seats."

At the time, this seemed strange. Rock hadn't quite settled into its role as a branch of the entertainment industry.

What Landau saw the thirty-six-year-old Elvis Presley do onstage in Boston was what almost all the rock class of 1971 would end up doing as their careers matured. He was playing the old hits because the audience couldn't summon more than a polite interest in the new ones. He was tapping into the pressing need of an audience of adults to be made to feel young again. He was celebrating his own legend, surrounding himself with a supporting cast whose role was to reflect his own majesty and to help justify charging top dollar for admission to his presence. This was a special once-in-a-lifetime night out. It wasn't something you did every day.

What Elvis was doing in what turned out to be quite a short time in Vegas was pioneering the way popular music would be presented and perceived in the twenty-first century. All the acts who have endured from that time and beyond have ended up doing what Elvis was already doing in 1971: taking the stage in front of ranks of musicians, dancers, special effects artists, and assorted supernumeraries, fronting a show in which nothing has been left to chance, a show designed above all to reflect the performer's magnitude and make the money required to keep putting on another show. And like Elvis, they are relying on the one commodity that endures after the voice is no longer quite the same, the moves have grown rusty, and the inspiration no longer flows quite as readily. That is the audience's deep, surprising love for the music they made in the past.

Jon Landau would go on to manage, mold, and some would say project himself through Bruce Springsteen, the American artist most closely attached to the mission of Elvis Presley. He would see his charge playing in front of crowds far more numerous than Elvis ever played to, in countries that weren't even countries in 1971, in a world where thirty-six would no longer qualify as even middle-aged, a world, in fact, where middle-aged superstars would become the rule rather than the exception. Like Cortez on his peak in Darien, when Landau looked at Elvis, what he was seeing was a great blue ocean of possibility, a future of unimaginable scale and spectacle, of riches and ritual, of endless repetition of what had gone before for the benefit of those who weren't even born when it all went down, a future of whizbangs and worship, of dancers and dazzle, of special effects and souvenirs, of vast crowds comprising all age groups and nationalities paying huge sums of money for the privilege of being able to say they were there, of appearances that weren't so much musical performances as visitations from Planet Fame. When he looked at Presley with his arms outstretched, his superhero's cape ajar, accepting all the adoration the fans had to give, Landau could have been forgiven for thinking he was seeing rock's past. In fact, he was looking at its future.

DECEMBER

Elvis Presley: "Funny How Time Slips Away"

Bob Dylan and the Band: "Like a Rolling Stone"

Don McLean: "American Pie"

Title music from A Clockwork Orange

Roxy Music: "Virginia Plain"

King Curtis: "A Whiter Shade of Pale"

James Brown: "Hot Pants (She Got to Use What She Got to Get What She Wants)"

Mountain: "Nantucket Sleighride"

Carly Simon: "Anticipation"

John & Yoko/Plastic Ono Band: "Happy Xmas (War Is Over)"

EPILOGUE

As I said at the beginning of this book, anyone can make a case for the popular music of their youth. It's something we all feel fiercely protective about. Our youth was unique. Our feelings were deeper. Our rebellion was more justified. We lived through such a moment as will never be lived through by anyone in quite the same way again.

There's plenty of that feeling in these pages. A lot of it is rooted in how I remember feeling at the time. But I've also got a certain amount of time on my side, and I can base my argument in the number of records and musicians from the year 1971 that have proved to have lasting appeal.

Every year in the UK, rock critics gather and hand out the Mercury Music Prize for the most distinguished UK album of the year. Lots of the records on the short lists and even some of the winners are, within a few years, entirely forgotten.

Had there been a Mercury Music Prize in 1971, the short list would have included: *Hunky Dory, Every Picture Tells a Story, Who's Next, Led Zeppelin IV, Imagine, Ram, Meddle, Madman Across the Water, Sticky*

Fingers, and *Aqualung.* There's nothing there that's been forgotten, almost fifty years later.

These days in the United States, the records that win Grammy Awards tend to be the ones that have sold the most copies. The ones that win critics' awards tend to be records most people have never heard of. In 1971 America's most acclaimed albums—*Tapestry, There's a Riot Goin' On, What's Going On, Nilsson Schmilsson, Blue, Pearl, American Pie, L.A. Woman,* and *Mud Slide Slim*—were also its biggest sellers.

But it's not just the big hits of 1971 that seem to have achieved a kind of immortality. The new traditionalists, who weren't born at the time, revere 1971 releases like Nick Drake's *Bryter Layter,* John Martyn's *Bless the Weather,* Sandy Denny's *North Star Grassman and the Ravens,* Gene Clark's *White Light,* and the early records by John Prine, Bonnie Raitt, Judee Sill, and Loudon Wainwright, none of which meant a thing at the time.

The spoor of 1971 is transmitted in many ways. Although it was long before the next really big change in pop music, the hip-hop revolution, there are trace elements in the 1971 records of Sly Stone, Curtis Mayfield, Norman Whitfield, and Gil Scott-Heron without which it's pretty much inconceivable. Ever since hip-hop, all records have been made to some extent the magpie's way, and some of the most discriminating borrowings have been from the textures, rhythms, and musical idiosyncrasies of 1971 recordings by Led Zeppelin, the Who, Black Sabbath, Can, and even Little Feat. By 1971 the basic building blocks had been put in place. Obviously, no single year marks the end of anything, but it's fair to say, as Churchill said after El Alamein, this was the end of the beginning. The outlines of the rich tapestry were clearly marked.

Pop is as much about technology as it is about music. Any student of recorded sound will tell you that 1971 was the golden moment when technology became a help and wasn't yet a hindrance. There's something about the recordings of 1971 that makes them sound more right almost fifty years later than they sounded at the time. Particularly in their original vinyl forms, they have a warmth, crispness, sensuality, and presence that generations of recording software engineers have been trying to bottle and market ever since. You can now buy invisible plug-ins for your desktop recording setup that promise to make your record sound like "the big room" at Olympic studios, where many of the biggest-sounding rock records of 1971 were recorded. To all intents and purposes they're selling the very air of 1971.

The sound of 1971 is the sound many acts are still trying to make today. You can hear Rod Stewart and Lindisfarne in Mumford & Sons; Sly & the Family Stone all over hip-hop; the spirit of Joni Mitchell's *Blue* in Laura Marling and a thousand other acoustic bluestockings; Pink Floyd's *Meddle* in the tunes to which office workers chill out in Ibiza; and Led Zeppelin in numberless generations of young men who take up electric guitars to slay dragons and attract girls. The sound of 1971 is all around us today, in ads for sports shoes, in the soundtracks of movies, at moments when TV producers and similar mood mongerers feel the need to reach for something reliably hip and soulful. When musical directors were looking for a note on which to close out the 2012 Olympic Games, they reached not for Muse or Coldplay but for the Who's "Baba O'Riley." They knew that no contemporary sound would hit the spot that this 1971 album track hit. It crackles in a way that records simply don't crackle anymore for the simple reason that they're made in a different way.

David Bowie's *Hunky Dory* isn't an archetype of anything. However, only in 1971 could a still unproven artist make such an album while out of contract, starting it with a Tin Pan Alley song like "Oh! You Pretty Things," which was first put before the public in a recording by the lead singer of Herman's Hermits, then finishing it with the Freudian maze that is "The Bewlay Brothers," wrapping it in a picture of Bowie dragged up as Veronica Lake, then getting a major record company to put it out. In 1971 there wasn't a little indie niche you could insert a record like that into. The middle of the road was the only place to be. Underground was over ground; anything could be a hit. It was into this moment of panic and opportunity that all these 1971 masterpieces were hurled.

There were background factors behind this pop renaissance. The fact that the Beatles had broken up meant there was a prize to play for. The record business was expanding at such a rate that the companies signed up anyone they thought might have an outside shot. Music was king: TV was nowhere, movies were in retreat, radio was growing, record stores were sprouting up like coffee shops, and the only material goods that anyone who counted was remotely interested in were black, vinyl, and twelve inches across.

The glories of the sixties had been on seven-inch black vinyl singles. The seventies were all about albums, which in the previous decade had been strictly for middle-aged swingers and fans of Ray Conniff. The numbers that were sold in the sixties would be dwarfed by seventies numbers, which were driven by the mania for stereo, the hi-fi setups that could reproduce it, and the new mass audience made up of baby boomers for whom a hi-fi would be the first piece of furniture they would install in the damp bedsits they would provisionally call home.

If any of my children were to be cast away in the year 1971, they would be lost. They wouldn't be able to calculate in pounds, shillings, and pence, would be frightened by the fact there were no seat belts in cars and you could smoke on the London Underground, surprised that the only people who could afford to travel between continents were millionaires, taken aback by the fact there were just three channels on the TV, no such thing as a personal computer, and no openly gay public figures. However, they would feel entirely at home with the records that were made that year.

If my twenty-one-year-old self could have been transported from 1971 to 2016, he would be struck dumb by the laptops, the phones, the affluence, the foreign tongues on the street, the idea that music could be accessed as if from a tap, the fact that three out of five stories in the news were about the sex lives of famous people, and the puzzling realization that I couldn't just go out on Saturday evening and buy a ticket on the door for any show in town.

If my twenty-one-year-old self wasn't paying close attention, he might at first think that the alternative society that had been sketched out in the pages of the underground papers of 1971 had actually come to pass. In some respects the subculture appeared to have conquered the mainstream. A black man in the White House, openly gay people in public life, women leading political parties, hot entertainment stories leading the news, and rock festivals taking place all over the world. Everything that was once alternative is now mainstream.

The rock-and-roll subculture started with the release of "Rock Around the Clock" in 1954. That's the first collision between exciting sound and personal charisma that defined the rock-and-roll age. That's when the hysteria began. If we take the starting point of the rock-and-roll era as 1954, then 1971 is a mere seventeen years into that era, close enough to the beginning of the race for people to still remember the noise of the starting pistol. There were direct quotes from that revolution still in some of the big records of 1971, in Elvis's "That's All Right" on Rod Stewart's *Every Picture Tells a Story*; in Led Zeppelin's "Rock and Roll," which was modeled on Little Richard's "Keep A-Knockin'," and even, sentimentally, in Don McLean's "American Pie." In 1971 rock and roll was still just seventeen. This feels about right. Maybe rock and roll should always be just seventeen.

Most of the musicians who became superstars in 1971 and are still revered today were war babies. A large proportion of them were between twenty-five and thirty, which may prove to be the most significant age for creativity in musicians. They were slightly older than rock and roll itself, and therefore they could remember a world before it existed. This stayed with them as a reminder of a black-and-white world, a life less congenial, like the weight of Brylcreem on the back of their neck or the discomfort of a girdle. When Lou Reed wrote "Rock & Roll," he wasn't dialing up a familiar cliché from the lifestyle pages. He was describing the moment when he heard the sound that convinced him for the first time that, as he put it, "There was life on this planet."

What these people in their midtwenties were doing, although none of them were aware of it at the time, was building the rock canon. In this they were more successful than they could have dared hope. Many of the musicians who made those 1971 records are still playing today, in bigger venues than ever, in front of huge, multi-generational crowds made up of the children and even the grand-children of their original fans. The songs those crowds most want them to play are the songs from 1971: "Stairway to Heaven," "Brown Sugar," "Baba O'Riley," "Tiny Dancer," "American Pie," "Heart of Gold," "Mandolin Wind," "The Last Time I Saw Richard," and "Oh! You Pretty Things." Thanks to the radio, the movies, the commer-cials, and the new ubiquity of all manner of music via YouTube and Spotify, to name just a few sources, these songs are as heavily imprinted on the minds of many twenty-somethings as they are on the people who first heard them forty years ago. These records are not just remarkably good and uniquely fresh; they have also enjoyed the benefit of being listened to more times than any recorded music in human history. It's not surprising the music of 1971 is in every-one's bloodstream. It no longer belongs to the people who made it or just to those of us who were lucky enough to be there when they did so. Now it belongs to everybody.

APPENDIX

1971 IN 100 ALBUMS

The germ of this book was a column I wrote for the British magazine the *Word*. The headline was "1971 was the annus mirabilis of the rock album." These are just some of the albums that support that argument.

Alice Cooper: *Killer*

Allman Brothers Band: *At Fillmore East*

America: *America*

Badfinger: *Straight Up*

Barbra Streisand: *Stoney End*

Beach Boys: *Surf's Up*

Bill Withers: *Just As I Am*

Black Sabbath: *Master of Reality*

Can: *Tago Mago*

Carly Simon: *Anticipation*

Carole King: *Tapestry*

Carpenters: *Carpenters*

Cat Stevens: *Teaser and the Firecat*

Colin Blunstone: *One Year*

Crazy Horse: *Crazy Horse*

Creedence Clearwater Revival: *Pendulum*

Curtis Mayfield: *Roots*

Dan Hicks & His Hot Licks: *Where's the Money?*

David Bowie: *Hunky Dory*

David Crosby: *If I Could Only Remember My Name*

Deep Purple: *Fireball*

Dolly Parton: *Coat of Many Colors*

Don McLean: *American Pie*

Donny Hathaway: *Donny Hathaway*

Doors: *L.A. Woman*

Dory Previn: *Mythical Kings and Iguanas*

Electric Light Orchestra: *The Electric Light Orchestra*

Elton John: *Madman Across the Water*

Emerson, Lake & Palmer: *Tarkus*

Faces: *A Nod's as Good as a Wink to a Blind Horse*

Flamin' Groovies: *Teenage Head*

Frank Zappa and the Mothers: *Fillmore East–June 71*

Freddie King: *Getting Ready*

Funkadelic: *Maggot Brain*

Gene Clark: *White Light*

Genesis: *Nursery Cryme*

Gil Scott-Heron: *Pieces of a Man*

Gilbert O'Sullivan: *Himself*

Gordon Lightfoot: *Summer Side of Life*

Graham Nash: *Songs for Beginners*

Grateful Dead: *Grateful Dead (Skull and Roses)*

Grin: *Grin*

Groundhogs: *Split*

Harry Nilsson: *Nilsson Schmilsson*

Humble Pie: *Performance: Rockin' the Fillmore*

Isaac Hayes: *Shaft*

Isley Brothers: *Givin' It Back*

J. Geils Band: *The Morning After*

James Taylor: *Mud Slide Slim and the Blue Horizon*

Janis Joplin: *Pearl*

Jethro Tull: *Aqualung*

Jimi Hendrix: *The Cry of Love*

Jimmy Webb: *And So: On*

John Lennon: *Imagine*

John Martyn: *Bless the Weather*

John Prine: *John Prine*

John Stewart: *The Lonesome Picker Rides Again*

Johnny Cash: *The Man in Black*

Joni Mitchell: *Blue*

Judee Sill: *Judee Sill*

Judy Collins: *Songs for Judith*

King Curtis: *Live at the Fillmore West*

Kinks: *Muswell Hillbillies*

Kris Kristofferson: *The Silver Tongued Devil and I*

Laura Nyro and Labelle: *Gonna Take a Miracle*

Led Zeppelin: *Led Zeppelin IV*

Leon Russell: *Leon Russell and the Shelter People*

Leonard Cohen: *Songs of Love and Hate*

Linda Ronstadt: *Linda Ronstadt*

Little Feat: *Little Feat*

Loudon Wainwright III: *Album II*

Mahavishnu Orchestra: *The Inner Mounting Flame*

Marvin Gaye: *What's Going On*

Merry Clayton: *Merry Clayton*

Michael Hurley: *Armchair Boogie*

Michael Nesmith: *Nevada Fighter*

Mickey Newbury: *Frisco Mabel Joy*

Moody Blues: *Every Good Boy Deserves Favour*

Mountain: *Nantucket Sleighride*

Move: *Message from the Country*

New Riders of the Purple Sage: *New Riders of the Purple Sage*

Nick Drake: *Bryter Layter*

Paul McCartney: *Ram*

Pink Floyd: *Meddle*

Randy Newman: *Randy Newman Live*

Roberta Flack: *Quiet Fire*

Rod Stewart: *Every Picture Tells a Story*

Rolling Stones: *Sticky Fingers*

Sandy Denny: *The North Star Grassman and the Ravens*

Santana: *Santana III*

Serge Gainsbourg and Jane Birkin: *Histoire de Melody Nelson*

Shuggie Otis: *Freedom Flight*

Sly & the Family Stone: *There's a Riot Goin' On*

Staple Singers: *The Staple Swingers*

T. Rex: *Electric Warrior*

Van Morrison: *Tupelo Honey*

Who: *Who's Next*

Wings: *Wild Life*

Yes: *The Yes Album* and *Fragile*

SELECTED BIBLIOGRAPHY

Aubrey, Crispin, and John Shearlaw. *Glastonbury: Festival Tales.* Ebury, 2005.

Beckett, Andy. *When the Lights Went Out: Britain in the Seventies.* Faber and Faber, 2009.

Biskind, Peter. *Easy Riders, Raging Bulls.* Bloomsbury, 1998.

———. *Star: The Life and Wild Times of Warren Beatty.* Simon & Schuster, 2010.

Blake, Mark. *Pigs Might Fly: The Inside Story of Pink Floyd.* Aurum, 2008.

Boyd, Pattie. *Wonderful Tonight: The Autobiography.* Headline Review, 2007.

Bracewell, Michael. *Roxy: The Band That Invented an Era.* Faber and Faber, 2007.

Bruck, Connie. *Master of the Game: Steve Ross and the Creation of Time Warner.* Simon & Schuster, 1994.

Cann, Kevin. *Any Day Now: David Bowie, the London Years 1947–74.* Adelita, 2010.

Carlin, Peter Ames. *Bruce.* Simon & Schuster, 2012.

———. *Catch a Wave: The Rise, Fall and Redemption of the Beach Boys' Brian Wilson.* Rodale, 2007.

Clapton, Eric. *The Autobiography.* Arrow, 2007.

Cohn, Nik. *Ball the Wall.* Picador, 1989.

Davies, Hunter. *The Glory Game.* Mainstream, 1972.

Davies, Ray. *Americana: The Kinks, the Road and the Perfect Riff.* Ebury, 2013.

Davis, Clive. *Inside the Record Business.* Morrow, 1975.

Davis, Erik. *Led Zeppelin IV.* Continuum, 2005.

Doggett, Peter. *You Never Give Me Your Money.* The Bodley Head, 2009.

Edmonds, Ben. *Marvin Gaye: What's Going On and the Last Days of the Motown Sound.* Canongate, 2002.

Faithfull, Marianne. *Faithfull*. Michael Joseph, 1994.

Farren, Mick. *Give the Anarchist a Cigarette*. Pimlico, 2001.

Fisher, Marc. *Something in the Air: Radio, Rock, and the Revolution That Shaped a Generation*. Random House, 2007.

Fong-Torres, Ben. *Willin': The Story of Little Feat*. Da Capo Press, 2013.

George, Nelson. *Where Did Our Love Go?: The Rise and Fall of the Motown Sound*. Omnibus, 2003.

George-Warren, Holly. *A Man Called Destruction: The Life and Music of Alex Chilton*. Viking, 2014.

Gladwell, Malcolm. *The Tipping Point: How Little Things Can Make a Big Difference*. Abacus, 2002.

Goodman, Fred. *Allen Klein*. Houghton Mifflin Harcourt, 2015.

———. *The Mansion on the Hill*. Pimlico, 2003.

Gordon, Robert. *Respect Yourself: Stax Records and the Soul Explosion*. Bloomsbury, 2013.

Graham, Bill. *Bill Graham Presents*. Doubleday, 1992.

Green, Jonathon. *Days in the Life: Voices from the English Underground 1961–71*. Heinemann, 1988.

Greenfield, Robert. *Exile on Main Street: A Season in Hell with the Rolling Stones*. Da Capo Press, 2006.

Holder, Noddy. *Who's Crazee Now?* Ebury, 1999.

Hoskyns, Barney. *Trampled Under Foot: The Power and Excess of Led Zeppelin*. Faber and Faber, 2012.

———. *Waiting for the Sun: The Story of the Los Angeles Music Scene*. Viking, 1996.

Houghton, Mick. *I've Always Kept a Unicorn: The Biography of Sandy Denny*. Faber and Faber, 2015.

Iommi, Tony. *Iron Man*. Simon & Schuster, 2012.

Johns, Glyn. *Sound Man: A Life Recording Hits with the Rolling Stones, the Who, Led Zeppelin, the Eagles, Eric Clapton, the Faces . . .* Blue Rider, 2014.

King, Carole. *A Natural Woman*. Little, Brown, 2012.

Lewis, Miles Marshall. *There's a Riot Goin' On*. Continuum, 2006.

Loewenstein, Prince Rupert. *A Prince Among Stones*. Bloomsbury, 2014.

McDonough, Jimmy. *Shakey: Neil Young's Autobiography*. Vintage, 2003.

McNeil, Legs, and Gillian McCain. *Please Kill Me: The Uncensored Oral History of Punk*. Little, Brown, 1996.

Mason, Nick. *Inside Out: A Personal History of Pink Floyd*. Phoenix, 2004.

Milner, Greg. *Perfecting Sound Forever: The Story of Recorded Music*. Granta, 2009.

Nash, Graham. *Wild Tales*. Penguin, 2014.

Neill, Andy, and Matt Kent. *The Complete Chronicle of the Who 1958–78*. Virgin, 2005.

Neville, Richard. *Hippie Hippie Shake*. Bloomsbury, 1995.

Norman, Philip. *Elton*. Hutchinson, 1991.

———. *The Stones*. Harper, 1993.

Palin, Michael. *Diaries 1969–1979*. Weidenfeld & Nicolson, 2006.

Paytress, Mark. *Bolan: The Rise and Fall of a 20th Century Superstar*. Omnibus, 2002.

Richards, Keith. *Life*. Weidenfeld & Nicolson, 2010.

Ritz, David. *Divided Soul: The Life of Marvin Gaye*. Grafton, 1986.

Ronstadt, Linda. *Simple Dreams: A Musical Memoir*. Simon & Schuster, 2013.

Sampson, Anthony. *The New Anatomy of Britain*. Hodder & Stoughton, 1971.

Sanchez, Tony. *Up and Down with the Rolling Stones*. John Blake, 2010.

Sandbrook, Dominic. *State of Emergency: The Way We Were—Britain 1970–74*. Penguin, 2010.

Schmidt, Randy L. *Little Girl Blue: The Life of Karen Carpenter*. Omnibus, 2010.

Scott, Ken. *Abbey Road to Ziggy Stardust*. Alfred, 2012.

Shipton, Alyn. *Nilsson: The Life of a Singer Songwriter*. Oxford University Press, 2013.

Sounes, Howard. *Down the Highway: The Life of Bob Dylan*. Doubleday, 2001.

Stewart, Rod. *The Autobiography*. Century, 2012.

Thomson, Graeme. *George Harrison: Behind the Locked Door*. Omnibus, 2013.

Townshend, Pete. *Who I Am*. HarperCollins, 2012.

Turner, Alwyn W. *Crisis? What Crisis?: Britain in the 1970s*. Aurum Press, 2013.

Turner, Steve. *Trouble Man: The Life and Death of Marvin Gaye*. Michael Joseph, 1998.

Wall, Mick. *When Giants Walked the Earth: A Biography of Led Zeppelin*. Orion, 2008.

Weller, Sheila. *Girls Like Us: Carole King, Joni Mitchell, Carly Simon and the Journey of a Generation*. Ebury, 2008.

White, Timothy. *Long Ago and Far Away: James Taylor—His Life and Music*. Omnibus, 2001.

Willets, Paul. *The Look of Love: The Life and Times of Paul Raymond*. Serpent's Tail, 2013.

Young, Robert. *Electric Eden: Unearthing Britain's Visionary Music*. Faber and Faber, 2010.

ACKNOWLEDGMENTS

This book started life as a column in the *Word* magazine. Some of its ideas emerged from conversations with Mark Ellen, Kate Mossman, Fraser Lewry, Alex Gold, and Mike "Seventies" Johnson. What larks.

Whether they realized it or not, talking to Rob Dickins, Andy Murray, Terry Reid, Chris Johnson, Paul Henderson, Jonathan Morrish, and Danny Baker helped.

Thanks to Bill Scott-Kerr, Darcy Nicholson, Richard Shailer, and Sally Wray at Transworld; Gillian Blake at Holt; and my agent Charlie Viney.

ILLUSTRATION CREDITS

Insert I

1. © Popperfoto/Getty Images
2. David Hepworth, courtesy of Rolling Stone LLC
3. © Jack Kay/Daily Express/Hulton Archive/Getty Images
4. © Ron Burton/Mirrorpix
5. © Earl Leaf/Michael Ochs Archives/Getty Images
6. © Jim McCrary/Redferns/Getty Images
7. © Estate of Keith Morris/Redferns/Getty Images
8. Courtesy of David Hepworth
9. © Popperfoto/Getty Images
10. © Mirrorpix
11. © Popperfoto/Getty Images
12. © Michael Ochs Archives/Getty Images
13. © Michael Ochs Archives/Getty Images
14. © Michael Ochs Archives /Stringer/Getty Images
15. Anthony Pescatore/NY Daily News/Getty Images
16. Ray Brigden/ANL/REX/Shutterstock
17. © Express/Getty Images
18. © Lichfield/Getty Images
19. © Lichfield/Getty Images
20. David Hepworth, courtesy of Rolling Stone LLC
21. © Frank Fischbeck/The LIFE Images Collection/Getty Images
22. © David Fenton/Getty Images

23. © Ian Tyas/Keystone Features/Getty Images
24. © The LIFE Picture Collection/Getty Images
25. © MacDonald Alisdair/Daily Mirror/Mirrorpix
26. Courtesy of David Hepworth
27. © Pictorial Parade/Archive Photos/Getty Images

Insert 2

1. David Hepworth, courtesy of Rolling Stone LLC
2. Courtesy of David Hepworth
3. © Michael Putland/Getty Images
4. © Peter Simon Photograph
5. © LFI/Photoshot
6. © LFI/Photoshot
7. © Leonard Detrick/NY Daily News Archive/Getty Images
8. © Bill Ray/The LIFE Picture Collection/Getty Images
9. © Charlie Gillett/Redferns/Getty Images
10. © Henry Diltz/Cache Agency
11. © Michael Ochs/Corbis
12. © Henry Diltz/Corbis
13. © Henry Diltz/Corbis
14. David Hepworth, courtesy of *Melody Maker*
15. Courtesy of David Hepworth
16. © Richard Creamer/Michael Ochs Archives/Getty Images
17. © Dan Farrell/NY Daily News Archive/Getty Images
18. © WNET
19. David Hepworth, courtesy of Rolling Stone LLC
20. © John Olson/The LIFE Picture Collection/Getty Images
21. © John Olsen/The LIFE Picture Collection/Getty Images
22. © Michael Putland/Getty Images
23. David Hepworth, courtesy of *Melody Maker*
24. Courtesy of David Hepworth
25. © Michael Ochs Archives/Getty Images
26. © ANL/REX/Shutterstock
27. © ullstein bild/ullstein bild/Getty Images

INDEX

A&M Records, 20–22, 36, 37, 49, 224
Abbey Road, 15, 17, 240–41, 245
Abbey Road, 161, 174
Abrams, Lee, 32–34
Adler, Lou, 22–27
advances, 56, 99, 174, 227
After the Gold Rush, 144, 193, 220
agents, 58–59, 63, 179, 260
"Ain't No Sunshine," 190
AIR Studios, 241
air travel, 40–41, 141
Alpert, Herb, 20, 37
albums, 4, 18–19, 224, 281–84
  black music, 78–90
  compilation, 173, 273
  greatest hits, 228
  Hunky Dory, 134, 246–49, 283
  Led Zeppelin IV, 254–59
  live, 61–66, 251–52, 273–74
  multiplatinum, 257
  Sticky Fingers, 107–13, 118, 121
  stores, 38–40, 125, 238, 284
  Surf's Up, 227–29

Tapestry, 21–32, 39, 43, 144, 149, 189, 241, 257, 260
Who's Next, 252–54
  see also covers, album; *specific albums and artists*
Aldon Music, 22
Aletti, Vince, 76
Ali, Muhammad, 51
Allen, Woody, 108
All in the Family, 7, 226
Allman Brothers Band, 8, 63–67, 136, 138
  At Fillmore East, 64–66
  "Whipping Post," 66
All Things Must Pass, 6, 18, 168–69, 172, 173, 181
alternative society, 122–40
"Amazing Grace," 67, 152, 276
"America," 14, 19
America, 194, 196
American Family, An, 233–36
American Graffiti, 228
"American Pie," 271–72, 280, 285, 286
amps, 257–58
Anderson, Jim, 128–30

androgyny, 113–16
"Andy Warhol," 205, 215, 247
Anka, Paul, 191
Anthony, Dee, 60–61, 63
"Anticipation," 121, 147, 280
Apple Records, 18, 172, 182, 246
Aqualung, 108
Ardent Studios, 202–4
Argent, 11
Armstrong, Louis, 143, 166
art school, 198–200
Asylum Records, 188–90, 193, 239
At Fillmore East, 64–66
Atlantic Records, 13–14, 63, 98, 109, 191,
    239, 256, 257
Atomic Rooster, 11, 196
Attica prison riots, 212–13, 216
Ayres, Tom, 43–44

"Baba O'Riley," 253–54, 262, 283, 286
"Baby Blue," 183
Bacharach, Burt, 36
Badfinger, 19, 171–72, 182–83, 245
Baez, Joan, 73
Baker, Ginger, 174, 217
Baldry, Long John, 162
Band, 186, 215, 274, 280
Bardot, Brigitte, 106, 232
Barsalona, Frank, 58–59
BBC, 13, 15, 57, 95, 134, 136, 148–49, 207
Beach Boys, 33, 94, 115, 136, 223–30
    Surf's Up, 227–29, 231, 237
Beatles, 1, 2, 12, 27, 28, 52, 55, 60, 86,
    114, 123, 125, 136, 152, 158, 163, 165,
    169, 171–75, 184, 203, 218, 224,
    240–45, 252, 266, 275, 278
    breakup, 1, 17–19, 144, 173–75, 209, 284
    reunion rumors, 169, 173–74
    Sgt. Pepper, 109, 240
Beatty, Warren, 31, 115, 144, 233
Beck, Jeff, 55, 159, 245
Bee Gees, 185
Beggars Banquet, 109, 249
Bell, Chris, 202, 203
Berry, Chuck, 113, 154, 278
Big Star, 202–4, 214
Billboard, 24, 86, 189, 222, 245, 248,
    257, 273

black music, 68–90, 184–85, 190
Black Sabbath, 215, 242, 282
Blanco, Ronnie, 78, 79
Blind Faith, 174
Blue, 21, 139, 141, 144, 283
blues, 59, 258
Bob Dylan's Greatest Hits Vol II, 178
Bolan, Marc, 150–58, 163, 165, 249
Bolder, Trevor, 134, 208, 247
Bonham, John, 56, 57, 258–59
Boston, Mass., 195–97
Bowie, David, 1, 41–45, 134–35, 165,
    204–5, 208, 215, 246–49, 269, 286
    Hunky Dory, 134, 246–49, 283
    *Rise and Fall of Ziggy Stardust and the
    Spiders from Mars, The,* 44, 208,
    248–49
    "Space Oddity," 41, 204–5
Boyd, Joe, 47–48, 52
Boyd, Pattie, 170, 218
brand, 98–99, 117–21, 178–79
Bridge over Troubled Water, 25
Bright Tunes Music, 180–81
Brown, James, 114, 184–85, 280
Browne, Jackson, 189–90, 261
"Brown Sugar," 95, 98, 99, 107–13, 121,
    286
Bryter Layter, 47–52
Byrne, David, 200

Cahoots, 274
Caine, Michael, 51, 102
Cale, John, 196, 197, 269
Can, 200–201, 215, 282
Canned Heat, 33, 100
Capitol Records, 23, 273
Captain Beefheart (Don Van Vliet),
    186, 225
Carnal Knowledge, 233, 263
Carpenter, Karen, 20–22, 35–38, 223
Carpenter, Richard, 20–22, 35–38, 223
Carpenters, 25, 35–38, 223, 237
Carpenters, 22
Cars, 213
Carson, Johnny, 34–35, 108, 209
car stereo, 40
Cash, Johnny, 221
cassettes, 40

"Cat Stevens Sings Cat Stevens,"
148–49
Cavett, Dick, 208–12
Cecil, Malcolm, 78–82
Celebration of Life Festival, 136–38
celebrity and fame, 94–121, 127, 142–43,
146–50, 155, 164–66, 176–79, 219–22,
232–33. *See also specific artists*
"Changes," 134, 205, 249
Charles, Ray, 98, 154
"Chelsea Hotel #2," 148
Chicago, 273
Chicago, Ill., 191
Chiffons, "He's So Fine," 179–81
Chilton, Alex, 201–4
China, 91–94, 120–21
Christie, Julie, 106, 135, 144
Churchill, Randolph, 131, 132
Cicalo, Hank, 23
"City of New Orleans," 191, 193
Clapton, Eric, 63, 100, 103, 128, 167,
170–72, 175, 192, 217
Clark, Dick, 82
Clark, Gene, 193, 194
Clockwork Orange, A, 232, 249, 263, 280
Cocker, Joe, 9, 20, 35, 170
Cohen, Joe, 177–78
Cohen, Leonard, 37, 50, 144, 148, 166
Cohn, Nik, 251–52
Collins, Judy, 67, 152, 276
Columbia Records, 98, 189, 203
Concert for Bangladesh, 163, 167–84,
273–74
concerts, 9–17, 53–66, 174, 204, 208, 212,
219–20, 254, 264–68
Allman Brothers, 63–66
Concert for Bangladesh, 167–84,
273–74
Elvis, 276–80
festivals, 132–40, 156–57, 163,
224–25
Led Zeppelin, 53–60
Rolling Stones, 94–95, 113, 120–21
Who, 251–52, 267–68
Zappa, 265–66
see also security; *specific artists and
venues*
Cooder, Ry, 111, 185, 186, 238

Cooke, Sam, 22, 159
Cooper, Alice, 166, 206–8, 214
Cornelius, Don, 82–84
Cosmopolitan, 231
Costello, Elvis, 49
country music, 192, 193, 230
covers, album, 21, 49, 109, 114–15, 128,
150, 239, 254–56
Led Zeppelin IV, 254–56
Sticky Fingers, 109
Tapestry, 20–21
Cowan, Glenn, 91–92, 119
Crazy Horse, 193, 194
Cream, 13, 56, 128
Crosby, David, 66, 121, 217, 219
Crosby, Stills, Nash & Young, 13, 17,
25, 174, 189
4 Way Street, 62–63, 108
Crumb, Robert, 126, 128

Daltrey, Roger, 139, 251–54, 268
"Dance to the Music," 85
Dark Side of the Moon, 31
Davies, Ray, 222, 225
Davis, Clive, 85, 86, 98, 189
Davis, Miles, 87, 136
Decca, 109, 110
Deep Purple, 266
Defries, Tony, 41, 135, 204, 208
Delaney & Bonnie, 35, 65, 175, 179
Dennis, Felix, 128–30
Denny, Sandy, 9, 215, 259
Derek and the Dominos, 170–71
Detroit, 206, 238–39
Detroit, Mich., 34, 42, 68–75, 78,
206–7
Diamond, Neil, 22, 152, 194
Diary of a Mad Housewife, 220
Dirty Harry, 263–64
divorce, 230–31, 233–36
"Domino," 8, 19, 187, 188
Doobie Brothers, 188
Doors, 115, 141–44, 166
Dorfman, Stanley, 148–49
Dowd, Tom, 63–65
Drake, Nick, 47–52, 67, 214, 221
Bryter Layter, 47–52
Dreja, Chris, 256

drugs and alcohol, 4, 16, 55, 72, 84–87, 100–101, 117, 134, 136, 139, 142, 155, 170–71, 176, 190, 220–21, 245, 255, 275

Dylan, Bob, 2, 51, 52, 81, 122, 123, 155, 158, 167, 170, 175–79, 187, 191, 194, 214, 215, 218, 271, 274, 278, 280
  Concert for Bangladesh, 175–84

Eagles, 31, 34, 189, 190, 250, 260–61
Earth, Wind & Fire, 88
Eavis, Michael, 131, 132
Edmunds, Dave, 19
Electric Lady Studios, 81
Electric Warrior, 154, 156
Elektra Records, 114–15, 142, 239
Ellington, Duke, 76
Emerson, Lake & Palmer, 62, 267
EMI, 75, 240, 245
engineers, 23, 47, 63–65, 75, 78–81, 182, 241, 245–61. *See also specific engineers*
Eno, Brian, 199
Ephron, Nora, 29, 30
Epstein, Brian, 12, 18
Ertegun, Ahmet, 13–14, 98–99, 105, 154, 189
"Everyday People," 85
Every Picture Tells a Story, 158–64, 166, 257, 260, 285
Excello, 99
Exile on Main Street, 110, 117–18

Faces, 24, 158–66, 249
Fairport Convention, 11–12, 140, 239, 255, 272
Faithfull, Marianne, 102–3, 106, 110, 111, 142
family, 216–37
  acts, 35–38, 222–30
  television, 232–36
"Family Affair," 86, 90
fashion, 4, 7, 100, 101, 105, 113–14, 118, 124, 135, 164, 199, 208, 209, 232
Ferry, Bryan, 198–200, 267
festivals, 15, 61, 132–40, 156–57, 163, 224–25. *See also specific festivals*
Fillmore East, 58, 61, 64–66, 105, 265

Fillmore West, 53, 58, 225
Fitzgerald, F. Scott, 228, 241
Flamin' Groovies, 108, 140, 205–6
Fleetwood Mac, 31, 34
Flo & Eddie, 154, 265
Flowers, Herbie, 243, 244
Flying Burrito Brothers, 20, 110, 191, 193
Fonda, Jane, 7, 101
football, 163
"For All We Know," 36
Four Tops, 71, 73
4 Way Street, 62–63, 108
Fragile, 268
Frampton, Peter, 59, 61, 100, 171
Frampton Comes Alive!, 61
France, 94–107, 116–19, 141–42
Franklin, Aretha, 25–27, 53, 90
Free, 62
French Connection, The, 6, 171, 263
Frey, Glenn, 136, 189, 190, 250
Fulfillingness' First Finale, 81, 82
funk, 82

Gaye, Marvin, 23, 68–69, 72–78
  "What's Going On," 73–75, 90
  What's Going On, 73–78, 84
Geffen, David, 188–90, 250, 260–61
Geldof, Bob, 168
gender, 4, 28–31, 111–16, 231–32, 274
Genesis, 140
Genzale, John, (Johnny Thunders), 269–70
George, Lowell, 185, 186
Germany, 200–201
Get Carter, 45, 51
"Get Down and Get With It," 11, 12, 19
"Get It On," 154–55, 156, 185
Gilbert, Craig, 233–36
"Gimme Some Lovin'," 135, 140
Ginger Baker's Air Force, 174
glam rock, 208, 236
Glastonbury Fayre, 132–36
Godfather, The, 87–88
Goffin, Gerry, 22, 26
Goodman, Steve, 191
"Good Vibrations," 224, 226
Gordon, Jim, 135, 243, 244
Gordy, Berry, 68–78, 81

Gortikov, Stanley, 273
Graham, Bill, 58, 63, 65
Grammy Awards, 282
Grand Funk Railroad, 59–60, 141, 257
Grant, Peter, 18, 54–60, 63, 256
Grateful Dead, 132, 133, 225, 230, 237
Great Britain, 9–10, 24, 30, 50–56, 62,
    75, 122–40, 207–8, 221, 233, 255, 281
  London boys of 1971, 141–66
Green, Al, 90, 237
Greer, Germaine, 126, 131
Griffin, Paul, 271
Grin, 193
Grossman, Albert, 81
"Groupie (Superstar)," 35, 37
Guardian, 183, 235

Haggard, Merle, 230
Ham, Pete, 183
Hamlisch, Marvin, 89
Hardin, Tim, 162
Harold and Maude, 147
Harris, Emmylou, 191
Harrison, George, 6, 18, 152, 167–84,
    192, 194, 218
  All Things Must Pass, 6, 18, 168–69,
    172, 173, 181
  Concert for Bangladesh, 167–84,
    273–74
  "My Sweet Lord," 168, 173, 174,
    179–82
Harrison, Jerry, 195, 213
Harvest, 17, 149, 219–21
Haslam, Geoffrey, 205
Havens, Richie, 137
Hayes, Isaac, 89–90, 202
  "Theme from Shaft," 89–90
"Heart Like a Wheel," 191–93
"Heart of Gold," 221, 286
Helm, Levon, 274
Hendrix, Jimi, 56, 100, 142, 145, 209
Henley, Don, 136, 189, 261
"He's So Fine," 179–81
Hillman, Chris, 191
Hoffman, Abbie, 139
Holder, Noddy, 9–12
Holly, Buddy, 230, 271–72
Holzman, Jac, 114

homosexuality, 35, 44, 129, 222, 235, 236
"Honky Tonk Women," 249
Hope, Bob, 108
Hopkins, Telma, 90
Hotel California, 31
"Hot Love," 152–53, 156
"Hot Pants," 184–85, 280
Hot Rocks 1964–1971, 273
Hot Tuna, 192–93
Howe, Steve, 268
Humble Pie, 59–61, 67, 153, 171
Hunky Dory, 134, 246–49

"I Don't Need No Doctor," 61, 67
"I Don't Want to Talk About It," 193,
    194
"If You Really Love Me," 80, 262
"I Heard It Through the Grapevine," 72
"Imagine," 138, 174, 210, 215
Imagine, 130, 210, 213
"I'm Eighteen," 206, 208
In Concert, 134, 135
Incredible String Band, 255
"Inner City Blues," 76–77
Intermedia Studios, 195, 213, 214
Iron Butterfly, 8, 13, 14
Island Records, 48–50, 199, 239
Isle of Wight Festival, 15, 131, 133
"It's Too Late," 25, 45, 235

Jackson, Ray, 162
Jackson 5, 72, 216, 223
Jagger, Bianca, 99–107, 115–21
Jagger, Mick, 12, 94–121, 130, 142, 251
jazz, 15, 24, 74, 77, 138, 143, 144, 201
"Jeepster," 154, 156, 166
Jefferson Airplane, 174, 192
Jesus Christ Superstar, 45, 250
Jethro Tull, 25, 67, 108, 131
Jewell, Derek, 183
J. Geils Band, 59, 60, 67, 239
John, Elton, 1, 17, 19, 149, 162, 163, 170,
    217, 222, 246
  "Tiny Dancer," 121, 193, 286
  Tumbleweed Connection, 24, 170
John Barleycorn Must Die, 135
John Lennon/Plastic Ono Band, 17, 173
Johns, Andy, 62, 258–59

Johns, Glyn, 249–53, 258, 260–61
Jones, Brian, 96, 97, 110
Jones, John Paul, 54, 58
Joplin, Janis, 24, 45, 98, 100, 142, 148
   "Me and Bobby McGee," 27
   Pearl, 24, 27
"Jump into the Fire," 244

Kapelow, Stephen, 136–37
"Keep A-Knockin'," 57, 285
Keltner, Jim, 172, 243
Kent State massacre, 8
Kerr, Andrew, 131–36
Keys, Bobby, 107, 111
King, Carole, 19, 20–32, 66, 150, 257,
   264, 272
   Tapestry, 21–32, 39, 43, 144, 149, 189,
     241, 257, 260
   "You've Got a Friend," 23, 25
King, Freddie, 67, 239
King Crimson, 50, 267, 280
Kinks, 222, 225, 237, 249
Klein, Allen, 18, 96–97, 173–74, 181
Klute, 7, 101, 171
Knight, Terry, 59–60
"Kooks," 134, 247
Kraftwerk, 200–201
Kristofferson, Kris, 27, 115, 147, 191, 276
Kubrick, Stanley, 232, 249, 277

Lambert, Kit, 250–51
Landau, Jon, 27, 274, 277–80
Lane, Brian, 14, 15
Lane, Ronnie, 99–100, 162, 164
Larkey, Charles, 23, 24
"Layla," 63, 170
Layla and Other Assorted Love Songs,
   170–71
Lea, Jim, 10–12
Led Zeppelin, 1, 16, 18, 27, 52–60, 65–67,
   135, 207, 254–62, 265, 268, 282–86
   Led Zeppelin IV, 31, 254–59
   "Stairway to Heaven," 54–55, 262
Led Zeppelin IV, 31, 254–59
Leeds, 16, 62, 251–52
Lennon, John, 6, 12, 17–19, 66, 101, 119,
   130, 152, 169, 173–76, 181, 203,
   208–12, 221–22, 246, 280

   Cavett interview, 208–12
   "Imagine," 138, 174, 210, 215
   Imagine, 130, 210, 213
   "Power to the People," 123, 140
Let It Be, 123
Let It Bleed, 96, 111
Life magazine, 6, 7, 29, 51, 206, 216–17,
   232
"Life on Mars?," 193, 247, 249
"Like a Rolling Stone," 2, 271, 274, 280
Lindley, David, 135
Little Feat, 185–86, 194, 196, 282
Little Richard, 11, 57, 278, 285
Live at Leeds, 62, 251–52
Lloyds Bank robbery, 211
Loaded, 42, 66, 201, 205, 213
Loewenstein, Rupert, 97, 98, 106, 119, 121
Lofgren, Nils, 193
London, 11, 16–18, 41, 44, 71, 95, 102,
   103, 122–30, 144, 158, 198, 211,
   221–22, 238, 243, 265–68, 284
   boys of 1971, 141–66
Los Angeles, 7, 20–24, 38–44, 71, 72, 83,
   185–93, 220
Loud, Lance, 234–36
Lou Reed, 268
Love, Stuart, 195, 197
Love Story, 24, 25, 88, 106

Mad Dogs and Englishmen, 9, 20, 35, 170
Madison Square Garden, 51, 66,
   167–84, 212, 256
Madman Across the Water, 170
"Maggie May," 161–63, 166
Mamas and Papas, 22
managers, 12, 14, 18, 41, 54–61, 81, 85,
   96–97, 110, 142, 154, 155, 161,
   173–74, 181, 183, 187–90, 199, 223,
   250. *See also specific managers*
"Mandolin Wind," 159, 161, 162, 164,
   286
"A Man Needs a Maid," 221, 237
Manning, Terry, 261
Manson, Charles, 224
Man Who Sold the World, The, 41
Marcus, Greil, 87
Margouleff, Robert, 78–82, 154
Marley, Bob, 140

Martin, George, 240–43
Martyn, John, 51, 140
Master of Reality, 242
Max's Kansas City, 201
Mayall, John, 110, 174
Mayfield, Curtis, 83, 87, 90, 282
McCartney, Paul, 1, 12, 17–18, 25, 74, 81,
    100, 102, 121, 152, 169, 173–75, 182,
    203, 218, 272
    Ram, 108
McCrary, Jim, 20–21, 24
MC5, 205, 206, 214
McGarrigle, Kate and Anna, 191
McLean, Don, 270–72
    "American Pie," 271–72, 280, 285, 286
"Me and Bobby McGee," 27, 147, 236
Meaty Beaty Big and Bouncy, 228
Media Sound, 78–81, 154
Melody Maker, 15, 50, 54, 123, 142, 198,
    206, 252, 267, 274
Mendelsohn, John, 43, 160
Mercury Music Prize, 281
Mercury Records, 41, 43, 158, 208
Midler, Bette, 35, 37, 38, 192
Miller, Jimmy, 113, 117, 119
Mitchell, Joni, 1, 21, 23, 26, 27, 45, 51,
    139, 148, 149, 189, 231, 286
    Blue, 21, 139, 141, 144, 283
Modern Lovers, 195–98, 213, 214–15
"Money (That's What I Want)," 70
Monkees, 23
Monterey Pop Festival, 22, 228
Montrose, Ronnie, 188
Moody Blues, 11, 103
Moog synthesizer, 79–80
Moon, Keith, 107, 139, 176, 221, 252, 253
Morrison, Jim, 141–43
Morrison, Van, 8, 9, 187–88, 192
    "Domino," 8, 19, 187, 188
    Tupelo Honey, 187–88
"Motel Blues," 191, 214, 215
Mothers of Invention, 186, 237, 264–68
Motown, 49, 68–75, 81
Mountain, 153, 280
movies, 5–7, 24, 30, 51, 61, 78, 87–90,
    108, 123, 144, 147, 171, 185, 211, 220,
    228, 231–32, 263–64, 277, 283–86.
    See also specific movies

Mud Slide Slim and the Blue Horizon, 25,
    39, 108, 218
Muswell Hillbillies, 222, 237
"My Generation," 249
"My Sweet Lord," 158, 173, 174, 179–82

Nash, Graham, 62, 139, 144, 166, 219
National Lampoon, 6, 92
Nelson, Paul, 158
Neville, Richard, 128–30
Newman, Randy, 121, 185, 186, 209, 243
Newport Festival, 138, 267
Newsweek, 29, 108
New York, 5–7, 17–19, 58, 64–66, 71, 78,
    87, 115, 154, 176–78, 212, 251
    Concert for Bangladesh, 167–84
New York Dolls, 113, 208, 270
New Yorker, 232
New York magazine, 29, 30
New York Times, 5, 108, 115, 141, 143,
    178, 183, 184, 212, 231, 248, 263
Nilsson, Harry, 24, 166, 183, 242–45
Nilsson Schmilsson, 244–45
Nitty Gritty Dirt Band, 230, 237
Nixon, Richard, 7, 93–94, 119, 136, 275
Nolan, Tom, 223–26
Noone, Peter, 134, 204, 246, 283
Northern Ireland, 51, 53, 54, 247
"Not Fade Away," 230
Nyro, Laura, 189, 192, 243, 270, 272

O'Brien, Glenn, 268–69
"Oh! You Pretty Things," 134, 204, 249,
    283, 286
Old Grey Whistle Test, The, 207–8
Oldham, Andrew Loog, 12, 97
Olson, John, 216–17
Ono, Yoko, 17, 173, 208–12, 280
Orlando, Tony, 90
Osmonds, 222–23
Oz magazine, 121, 126–30

Pacino, Al, 6, 171
Page, Jimmy, 53–60, 221, 255–61
Pallenberg, Anita, 106, 111, 117
Parker, Colonel Tom, 276, 277
Parks, Van Dyke, 185–86, 227
Parsons, Gram, 110–13, 119, 190–91, 197

Parton, Dolly, 233, 237
Pearl, 24, 27
Peel, John, 57, 127, 151, 155, 160, 201, 205, 239
Perrin, Les, 104, 105, 106
Perry, Richard, 242–45
Pet Sounds, 225
photography, 20–21, 104–6, 109, 114, 116, 118, 178, 216–17
Pickett, Wilson, 64, 89, 193
Pieces of a Man, 88–89
pill, 30
Pink Floyd, 1, 15–17, 132, 133, 137, 140, 207, 241–42, 245, 267, 278, 283
    Dark Side of the Moon, 31
plagiarism, 179–81
Plant, Robert, 54, 56, 163, 255–59
Plastic Ono Band, 17, 173–75, 280
Playboy, 108, 232
Play Misty for Me, 30, 34
politics, 6–7, 51, 91–94, 108, 122–24, 231, 232
Pop, Iggy, 43, 45, 205–6, 249
Povich, Lynn, *The Good Girls Revolt*, 29–30
"Power to the People," 123, 140
Premier Talent, 58–60
Presley, Elvis, 44, 187, 250, 274–80, 285
press, 6, 15–17, 27, 29, 54, 104–8, 116, 121, 142–43, 156, 159, 160, 169, 174, 176, 183–84, 192, 209, 216, 223–26, 231–36, 274, 277–78
    alternative, 125–30
    see also specific publications
Preston, Billy, 86, 111, 172
Primal Scream, 113
Prine, John, 191, 194
Procol Harum, 186, 245, 273
producers, 22, 62, 113, 148–49, 154, 161, 187–90, 239–61. *See also specific producers*
promoters, 58–59, 63, 65, 138, 161, 192. *See also specific promoters*
publishing, 18, 22, 110, 224, 244
punk rock, 4, 197, 214–15, 236

Quittenton, Martin, 162

race, 4, 6–7, 68–90, 212–13, 232
radio, 8–9, 32–34, 42, 44, 75, 108, 134–35, 139, 156, 160, 207, 253, 284, 286
Raitt, Bonnie, 185
Ram, 108
RCA, 43–44, 88, 204, 205, 245, 248, 249, 268, 269, 277
Ready Steady Go!, 145, 149
"Reason to Believe," 162
record companies, 13, 18, 20, 40–44, 49, 68–75, 98–99, 109–10, 114, 185–93, 214, 226–27, 239–41, 260, 273. *See also specific record companies*
Record Mirror, 160
Record Plant, 81
Reed, Lou, 42–44, 196, 201–2, 205, 239, 244, 249, 268–69, 285
Reid, Terry, 135, 140
Richards, Keith, 12, 94–121, 190–91, 257, 269
Richman, Jonathan, 195–98, 213, 269
Rieley, Jack, 223–25
"Roadrunner," 197
Robertson, Robbie, 274
Robinson, David, 196, 213
Robinson, Smokey, 71, 72
"Rock & Roll," 42, 213, 239, 285
"Rock Around the Clock," 285
Rock Writers Convention, 204
Rolling Stone, 4, 17, 27, 43, 60, 72, 76, 92, 106, 118, 143, 159–61, 209, 231, 236, 269, 274, 277–78
    Beach Boys cover story, 223–26
Rolling Stones, 16, 25, 52–53, 55, 62, 66, 94–121, 136, 164, 200, 228, 249, 252, 266, 273, 278
    brand, 98–99, 117–21
    "Brown Sugar," 95, 98, 99, 107–13, 121
    Exile on Main Street, 110, 117–18
    Sticky Fingers, 107–13, 118, 121
Ronson, Mick, 134, 204, 247
Ronstadt, Linda, 34, 94, 136, 192, 221
Ross, Diana, 69, 72
Ross, Steve, 186–87
Roxy Music, 198–200, 208, 214, 267, 280
Royal Albert Hall, 54, 265, 274

royalties, 17, 18, 96–99, 174, 224, 241
Ruddy, Albert, 87–88
Rumours, 31
Rundgren, Todd, 45, 80–81, 182, 269
Runt, 80–81
Russell, Leon, 35, 167, 169–70, 172, 184, 192, 194
Ryder, Mitch, 239

Sager, Carole Bayer, 26, 27
San Francisco, 33, 38, 42, 53, 58, 219
Santana, 28, 65, 90, 98, 111
"Satisfaction," 156, 273
Scaggs, Boz, 115, 192, 262
Scorsese, Martin, 61, 244
Scott, Ken, 245–49
Scott-Heron, Gil, 88–90, 282
Secunda, Tony, 155
security, 16, 104–5, 137, 157, 176–79, 267–68, 276
Sedaka, Neil, 22
sel-sync technology, 23–24
Selwood, Clive, 142
sex, 4, 30–33, 72, 102–4, 111–16, 124, 128–29, 147–48, 161, 184–85, 219, 222, 231–35, 258, 260, 265, 284
Sgt. Pepper's Lonely Hearts Club Band, 109, 240
Shaft, 89–90
Shankar, Ravi, 33, 136, 151, 168, 169
Sharp, Martin, 128
Shelter Records, 239
Siddons, Bill, 142, 143
Sill, Judee, 193, 194, 239
Simon, Carly, 114–16, 147–48, 218
"Anticipation," 121, 147, 280
"You're So Vain," 115–16, 120
Simon & Garfunkel, 19, 25, 27, 28
Sinatra, Frank, 23, 51, 136, 159, 185, 187, 227, 228
singles, 4, 18, 74, 75, 77, 107–8, 112–13, 125, 152, 213, 224, 240, 271, 284. *See also specific singles*
"Sister Morphine," 110, 111
Slade, 9–13, 19
Slick, Grace, 217
Sly & the Family Stone, 84–87, 136, 212–13, 257, 283

"Family Affair," 86, 90
There's a Riot Goin' On, 86–87, 212–13
Smith, Patti, 232, 269
Snodgress, Carrie, 219–20
Solomon, Russ, 38–39
"Something," 180
"Something in the Way She Moves," 180
soul music, 68–90, 184–85
Soul Train, 82–84
Sounds, 50, 150
"Space Oddity," 41, 204–5
Spector, Phil, 57, 180, 213, 242
Spedding, Chris, 243, 244
Spirit, 54
Springsteen, Bruce, 2, 8–9, 148, 188, 279
"Stairway to Heaven," 54–55, 262, 286
"Starman," 249
Starr, Ringo, 100, 167–74, 183, 243
Status Quo, 19, 157, 195
Stax, 88, 89, 202, 203, 251
Steel Mill, 8–9
Steppenwolf, 11
stereo, 27–28
Stevens, Cat, 115, 145–55, 158, 165–66
Stewart, Rod, 1, 158–66, 193, 283, 286
Every Picture Tells a Story, 158–64, 16, 257, 260, 285
"Maggie May," 161–63, 166
Sticky Fingers, 107–13, 118, 121
Stills, Stephen, 106, 121, 219
Stone, Sly, 84–87, 209, 212–13, 282
Stooges, 43, 205, 206, 214, 269
Straw Dogs, 231
Streisand, Barbra, 26, 242–43
Sullivan, Ed, 6
supergroups, 174
superstar (term), 162
Supertramp, 196
Supremes, 71, 72, 90
Surf's Up, 227–29, 231, 237
Sweet Baby James, 23
"Sweet Jane," 42, 45, 213
Sweet Sweetback, 88

T. Rex, 19, 131, 150–58, 249
"Get It On," 154–55, 156, 185
"Jeepster," 154, 156, 166

table tennis, 91–94
Taj Mahal, 192
"Take It Easy," 189–90
Talking Heads, 200, 213
Tapestry, 21–32, 39, 43, 144, 149, 189, 241, 257, 260
taxes, 4, 72, 95–99, 179
Taylor, James, 23, 26, 31–32, 66, 115, 121, 144–50, 180, 189, 206, 218–19, 221, 223, 264
  Mud Slide Slim and the Blue Horizon, 25, 39, 108, 218
  "You've Got a Friend," 26, 45
Taylor, Mick, 95, 101, 110–11, 117
Teaser and the Firecat, 146, 148
technology, 4, 14, 23–24, 27–28, 40, 79–81, 149, 207, 241–42, 253, 257–60, 282
television, 6, 7, 28, 34–35, 42, 108, 136, 148–49, 165, 169, 172, 206–12, 221, 233–36, 264, 283, 284
  An American Family, 233–36
  soul music, 82–84
  see also specific programs
Templeman, Ted, 187, 188
Temptations, 45, 71, 72, 87
Ten Years After, 11
"Theme from *Shaft,*" 89–90
There's a Riot Goin' On, 86–87, 212–13
Time magazine, 29, 92, 131
"Tiny Dancer," 121, 193, 286
Tommy, 17, 35, 250–52
Tonight Show, The, 6, 34–35, 108
TONTO (The Original New Timbral Orchestra), 79–80
Tonto's Expanding Head Band, 79
Top of the Pops, 15, 73, 83, 95, 134, 148–49, 153, 157, 164, 165, 207
Toussaint, Allen, 274
Tower stores, 38–40
Townshend, Pete, 35, 139, 176, 218, 250–54, 257, 268
Traffic, 130, 135, 140
Transformer, 205
Trident Studios, 243–46
Troubadour, 28, 39, 147
Tumbleweed Connection, 24, 170
Tupelo Honey, 187–88

Turner, Ike and Tina, 114, 150, 223
2001: A Space Odyssey, 277

United Artists, 270
Universal Music, 49
universities, 16, 29–30, 56, 251

Vadim, Roger, 105, 107
Vanilla Fudge, 265
Van Peebles, Melvin, 88
Velvet Underground, 42, 43, 196–99, 201, 204–5, 214, 268–69
  Loaded, 42, 66, 201, 205, 213
  "Sweet Jane," 45, 213
Verve, 113
Vietnam War, 7, 51, 75, 93, 94, 125, 239
Vigoda, Johanan, 81
Village Voice, 272
Vincent, Gene, 229–30
Visconti, Tony, 154
Voorman, Klaus, 169, 174

Wainwright, Loudon III, 191–92, 195, 213–15
Waits, Tom, 39
Wakeman, Rick, 154, 246–49, 268
Walker, Jerry Jeff, 192
"Walk on the Wild Side," 244, 269
War, 38, 87, 262
Warhol, Andy, 43, 109, 146, 201, 232, 268
Warner Bros., 98, 109, 162, 185–91, 195, 197, 226–27
Warwick, Dionne, 138, 271
"Watching the River Flow," 170, 194
Watson, Doc, 230
Watts, Charlie, 95, 113, 117
Weberman, A. J., 177
Weeley Festival, 156–57, 163
Weil, Cynthia, 22, 26, 31
Wein, George, 138
Welch, Chris, 54
Wenner, Jann, 17
"We've Only Just Begun," 36, 37
Wexler, Jerry, 26
"What Is Life," 168, 194
"What's Going On," 73–75, 90
What's Going On, 73–78, 84

Where I'm Coming From, 80
"Whipping Post," 66
Whisky a Go Go, 38
Who, 16, 58, 107, 139–40, 163, 176, 228,
    249–54, 282
    "Baba O'Riley," 253–54, 262, 283, 286
    Live at Leeds, 62, 251–52
    Tommy, 17, 35, 250–52
    Who's Next, 139, 252–54, 260
Who's Next, 139, 252–54, 260
"Wild Horses," 110–13, 121
Williams, Richard, 198, 205, 267, 274
"Will You Still Love Me Tomorrow?,"
    22, 25–26
Wilson, Brian, 185, 224–30
Wings, 272
Winter, Johnny, 64, 67, 131, 153
Winwood, Stevie, 135
Withers, Bill, 190
"Without You," 166, 183, 244–45
Wolf, Peter, 60
women's movement, 30
Wonder, Stevie, 72, 78–82, 154, 262
"Won't Get Fooled Again," 139, 176,
    253–54
Wood, Ronnie, 100

Woodstock, 11, 15, 61, 86, 132, 133, 137,
    139, 192
Woodstock, 61, 85, 187
Wright, Gary, 243
Wyman, Bill, 95, 97, 113, 117

Yardbirds, 56, 256
Yes, 11, 13–15, 19, 268
Yes Album, The, 13–15, 24
"Yesterday," 173
"(You Make Me Feel Like) a Natural
    Woman," 22, 23, 26
Young, Neil, 17, 37, 62–63, 149, 194, 206,
    219–21, 237, 286
    After the Gold Rush, 144, 193, 220
    Harvest, 17, 149, 219–21
"Young Blood," 184
Young Vic, 17, 250
"You're So Vain," 115–16, 120
"Your Song," 19
"You've Got a Friend," 23, 25, 45

Zappa, Frank, 66, 206, 217, 237, 264–68
Zero Time, 79
Ziggy Stardust, 43, 44, 204, 208, 248–49
ZigZag, 174

ABOUT THE AUTHOR

DAVID HEPWORTH is a music journalist, writer, and publishing industry analyst who has launched several legendary British magazines, including *Q*, *Mojo*, and *The Word*, among many others. He was a presenter of the BBC's rock music program *Whistle Test* and anchored the BBC's coverage of Live Aid in 1985. He has won the Editor of the Year and Writer of the Year awards from the Professional Publishers Association and the Mark Boxer Award from the British Society of Magazine Editors. He writes about radio for *The Guardian*, comments on cultural and media issues for many magazines and newspapers, and blogs at whatsheonaboutnow.blogspot.com.

Hepworth, David, 8/16
1950-

Never a dull moment.